ESSAYS IN METAPHYSICS

BY MEMBERS OF THE

PHILOSOPHY DEPARTMENT

THE PENNSYLVANIA

STATE UNIVERSITY

ESSAYS IN METAPHYSICS

edited by Carl G. Vaught

THE PENNSYLVANIA

STATE UNIVERSITY PRESS

University Park and London

To the Memory of Our Colleague

Henry Albert Finch

Who
Devoted
His Life
to
Philosophy

Library of Congress Catalogue Card Number 71–121785
Standard Book Number 271–00123–2
Copyright © 1970 by The Pennsylvania State University
All Rights Reserved
Printed in the United States of America
by Heritage Printers, Inc.
Designed by Marilyn Shobaken
The Pennsylvania State University Press
University Park, Pennsylvania 16802
The Pennsylvania State University Press, Ltd.
London W. 1

CONTENTS

[v]

INTRODUCTION

In 1962 this department first published a volume of papers entitled *Essays in Philosophy*.* Its purpose was to exhibit a philosophical orientation which stands in contrast to the dominant thrust of Anglo-American philosophy. Accordingly, the papers were intended to reaffirm the value of the Western tradition and to make responsible contact with contemporary European thought. It was believed that only in this way could the richest dimensions of philosophy be preserved in the face of technical and atomistic tendencies which are inimical to traditional philosophical inquiry.

In large measure, the present undertaking accords with the aims of the earlier one. They must simply be rearticulated. However, it is necessary to pursue them again, both to clarify the aims themselves, and in order to indicate their relevance to the current situation.

In the past eight years, it has become increasingly evident that ontology stands once again at the center of philosophy. This situation is illustrated, not only in European thought, but also in some of the more important strands of the analytic movement. In addition, philosophers of all persuasions seem to be increasingly concerned with the history of philosophy. The tradition has come to serve more explicitly as at least a preliminary ground for philosophical reflection. Finally, since the translation of *Sein und Zeit* and other later writings of Heidegger, the impact of Continental

[1]

thought upon American philosophy has become even more strikingly evident. Direct acquaintance with it has reminded us of the need for careful reflection upon the meaning of human existence. It might thus be said that the shifting scenes of philosophical fashion accord more closely with our present aims than was the case nearly a decade ago.

On the other hand, we might wonder whether the current shift of scene is merely a fashion, and thus subject to continued change. We must not forget that fashion has no permanent form. What then is permanently valuable in the contemporary interest in ontology, the history of philosophy, and the themes which form the subject-matter of phenomenological and existential reflection?

As the following papers suggest, philosophy at its best is achieved on those occasions when there is a merging of the eternal, the historical, and the immediately encounterable dimensions of man's experience and reflection. The function of the first of these dimensions is to provide a standard, however vague, in terms of which inquiry may be guided and sustained. The recent rebirth of ontology represents an attempt to refocus this standard, even if the attempt sometimes degenerates into an empty reconsideration of traditional metaphysical problems.

The second, historical dimension of philosophical reflection introduces a remedy for the potential defects of the first. The vagueness of the Truth Itself and the difficulties which prevent its direct apprehension are mediated, in part, by reflective consideration of the philosophical tradition. There we find a series of attempts to apprehend what is ultimate, fundamental, and final. These attempts provide us with a set of indispensable clues which enable us to sustain the pursuit of philosophy itself.

Finally, the immediately encounterable aspects of direct experience and reflection remind us of the existence of a concrete context with which philosophy begins and to which it must periodically return. This context is brought clearly to focus in the phenomenological and existential traditions. Philosophizing out of concern for human existence has been the *raison d'être* of the existentialist; examination of things in their objective and concrete appearance for the inquirer has characterized the phenomenological movement. Such concerns make it ultimately impossible to escape to the merely speculative and exclusively historical dimensions of philosophy.

It is not to be expected that the papers which follow should speak with a common voice. Nor would I expect my colleagues to accept without reservation the foregoing account of our aims and purposes. However, despite inevitable differences in stress and emphasis, the papers taken as a whole indicate our common concern with those very aspects of philosophical activity which I have attempted to adumbrate. Thus, among the papers to follow, some stress the eternal. Others begin in explicitly historical fashion. Still others attempt to exhibit the concrete richness of human experience.

Nevertheless, all of these papers belong to the tradition which has concerned itself explicitly with metaphysics. As essays in metaphysics, they all pertain to the concepts of Being and Existence. Although in some of the papers these notions are focused explicitly, while in others they appear indirectly, the two concepts in question do provide us with a common theme. The volume begins with those papers which are more evidently grounded in history. Most of the remaining papers appear in pairs in the attempt to provide contrasting views of common problems.

I wish to express my appreciation to Carl R. Hausman, Henry W. Johnstone, Jr., and Robert G. Price, who served with me on the department editorial committee. We also wish to acknowledge the generous support of the Central Fund for Research and the Institute for the Arts and Humanistic Studies in the preparation and publication of the manuscript.

CARL G. VAUGHT

University Park, Pennsylvania
February, 1970

* The Pennsylvania State University Press, University Park and London, 1962.

JOHN M. ANDERSON

ON THE PLATONIC DIALOGUE

I

It was Socrates' suggestion that the pervasive effects of man's determining influence on language be taken into account not by striving to eliminate them in the construction of a completely objective language; but by developing language as a discussion in which man's agency is explicitly incorporated. His bold approach was to take into language its originators and users, treating their agency and, in turn, their expressed beliefs and opinions as essential ingredients of linguistic structure. In the course of Socratic discussion, then, the originators and users of language are introduced—in terms of the responses of protagonists and their expression of beliefs and opinions—into the contexts in which they find themselves. This introduction enables Socrates to interrelate the originative contributions of human agency to language so that they constitute a discussion; thus he guides the discussion toward a Whole.

One of the entrancements of a Socratic discussion is its reference to the Whole as a standard of its development. It weaves statements and themes into beliefs and opinions in ever more intricate ways, so that a protagonist (or a reader) is caught up in a developing linguistic structure in which nothing occurs by chance; in which all originative expression comes to have significance in relation to something else; and in which every speech, indeed every sentence of every speech, is required if the significances implicit in the way things are expressed by men are to be caught and held in the developing pattern of the language of discussion. A Socratic discussion is a carefully woven pattern constructed of a weft of rhetorical points and counterpoints, of themes and their restatements; and a warp of circumstances taken as man responds to and expresses them. Within the discussion human expressions are never left isolated, but are always connected in many ways by the developing interrelation afforded by language. The magic of Socratic discussion seems powerful enough to transform the relativity and contingency of the beliefs and opinions expressed by protagonists (and readers) who participate in it into a significant vision. In the course of Socratic discussion, whatever beliefs and opinions seem to originate through the agency of men come to be understood as necessary since they fall under the aegis of the Whole.

The discussion of justice in the *Republic* (one of the most Socratic of Plato's dialogues) begins with originative acts of the participants, as the desire of Socrates to pray to a strange goddess and to observe a strange festival, and the desire of Polemarchus and Glaucon to discuss politics which leads them to force Socrates to do so. The expression of such originative agency is caught up in the developing discussion, interconnected by the structure of the language, and so comes to signify not merely as human expression, but through the interrelations developed in the language of the discussion. Desire comes to suggest justice, for instance, through the *discussion* of the healthy city, and in the variety of views formulated on the nature of eros. Force comes to suggest justice by the emergence of Thrasymachus as a protagonist in the discussion, and the mode of his verbal participation; by the elaboration through discussion of the activities of the class of warriors; and by the implicit knowledge of the writer (and presumably of the reader) that some of the participants are to suffer from a misguided effort to establish a just city in the Piraeus in the later course of Greek history. Indeed, as implicit in the developing discussion, the sense of this future failure suggests that justice is to be found beyond human agency in that Whole toward which man's expressions may be seen to project when they are caught and transformed, not into fixed meanings, but into the patterns of language as these are constituted by Socratic discussion.

Certainly one of the functions of Socratic irony is to de-

[6]

velop the discussion of expressions of human agency to carry a reference to the Whole. Socratic irony suggests that each human response expresses significance as each participant is involved in discussion in such a way as to formulate his opinions and beliefs in relation to the beliefs and opinions of other protagonists. It is this interrelation which presupposes that orientation to the Whole which guides the development of the discussion. Thus Socratic irony constitutes a reference to the Whole as the standard guiding the use of language, and ensures that the discussion does not terminate in any one belief, opinion, or view; the determinate configuration of which could be only the expression of human agency. In this way Socratic irony transforms the movement of human origination by means of linguistic usage into a movement toward the Whole; and the expressions attributable to human agency, as parts to be interpreted in the terms of the Whole. It defines Socratic discussion as a special language deriving its power from this reference beyond the scope of the expressive contributions of human agency, and as constituting this reference on the basis of a deeper understanding of human nature.

II

The beginning of what appears to be a Socratic discussion, the opening conversation in the *Timaeus*, is concerned with the question of the possible existence of that perfect city whose nature was sketched in the *Republic*. One implication of the Socratic discussion which is such an important part of the *Republic* is that a perfect, a just city could hardly come to exist through the originative powers of human agency alone. The recapitulation, in the opening discussion of the *Timaeus*, of exactly those changes in human society which would need to be made by man to actualize the perfection attributed to the *Republic*—the community of goods, wives and children, and the deceit necessary in the nuptial lots, for example—emphasizes the paradoxical nature of the ingression of perfection into the human world. The Socratic discussion in the *Republic* formulates the conditions of the existence of perfection in such a way as to suggest that no society organized by humans can be utopian. Yet the explicitness of this formulation suggests something more than Socrates himself would have liked to say; it implies that the language of Socratic discussion cannot formulate the nature of those creative movements which do carry the ingression of perfection. It is this inadequacy of language, not only a language dependent upon human powers but the language of Socrates with its reference to the Whole beyond man, which raises the problem underlying the development and use of language in the *Timaeus* and the *Critias* fragment; the problem of the nature of a language adequate to take account of creation.

Socrates indicates the fundamental character of this problem by his modest refusal to lead the discussion in the *Timaeus*, thus implying that *he* does not know how to speak of the ingression of perfection; that such a language has not been given to him. Usually Socrates' modesty reflects his irony, and so is the humility of one who loves the Whole. But in the opening speeches of the *Timaeus*, Socrates' humility is deeper than this irony, for his speech and action admit that the movement toward the Whole originating in Socratic discussion does not participate in the ingression of perfection. Indeed, Socrates indicates that only those different from himself, as for example, Critias and Timaeus who are practicing politicians, can be expected to originate discussion which can reflect the becoming of such a perfect state as the Republic, and so the ingression of perfection as such. Socrates' suggestion implies that the magic of his own guidance of discussion is not adequate to disclose the deepest mysteries, that is, the perfection implicit in creation.

To ask one practiced in the art of politics to speak about the coming into being of a perfect state seems natural; for the practice of an art is a kind of originating, and the language appropriate to an art seems especially apt for speaking of such a movement. Yet when Critias speaks initially to this point in the *Timaeus* he does not use the language of a craft. As he recalls that most ancient and almost wholly forgotten time when, having been founded by Athena, Athens saved the Mediterranean world from Atlantis, he repeats an account of Solon. Critias tells us he heard this story from that eminent politician, who, in turn, had heard it in Egypt and who had the talent to make it into the best poetry, but did not—being far too preoccupied with the problems of practical politics. In this way Critias informs us that the language he uses is, in virtue of its repetition of ancient lore, *myth*, and as myth, especially appropriate to reflect the ingression of perfection, creation itself.

There is evident justification for Critias' suggestion that the language of myth is better adapted to reflect the mysteries of creation than is the language of a craft. If a perfect city comes to be, as myth suggests it did, in some Golden Age, as

[8]

when Athens was created very like the ideal Republic, the language giving an account of this origin must be a language capable of reflecting the ingression of perfection. A myth speaks of coming into being in the terms of a source, as the account of the founding of Athens by Athena illustrates; and, in myth, this source, as Athena, is presented as ultimate—or at least related directly to what is ultimate, as Athena is herself not a result of sexual reproduction, having sprung from the head of Zeus. The relatively high degree of perfection attributed by myth to very old things, as for example, ancient cities, and the fact, connected with this, that the sources of these more perfect created things may be presented as the gods, and so as the perfect ground of created perfection, comprises an especial merit of myth as the language of creation. In the Golden Age, in the very beginning, what came to be was complete of its kind, so that what needs to be spoken seems to be the connection of the completed creature with its source; a connection which can be suggested in the languages of myth. A myth portrays, in its attribution of the ingression of perfection to the remote past, a primordial moment when a perfect source is the ground of the creation of concrete completeness.

It seems to be a part of Plato's intention at the beginning of the *Timaeus* to suggest that the language of myth and Socratic discussion must be combined. In the *Timaeus* the language of myth is introduced initially to take account of the ingression of perfection in the primordial moment of creation; and its use suggests that the sources of perfection, the gods, are related to the Whole which, as a Whole, is revealed in Socratic discussion to be the ground of the intelligibility of human beliefs and opinions, of those human expressions which are the results of human originative powers. Socrates' refusal to lead the discussion of the creation of a perfect city, and of creation as such, reflects his awareness (in a Platonic dialogue at least) that there is more to be said than the language of Socratic discussion can say; but his continued presence indicates that any discussion he initiates is in harmony with the insights conveyed by myth.

The language of the participants at the beginning of the *Timaeus* might be called discussion—myth. The mythical elements in the language of discussion—myth refer to the sources of perfection in the movement of creation; and the Socratic elements refer to the Whole which completes the partialities found in human expressions. Plato puts this language into the mouths of compound men like Critias and Timaeus, who are philosophers

[9]

and men of practical competence. Even if as philosophers inspired by Socratic discussion these men are oriented toward the Whole, as human artificers they cannot have the capacity to originate a language which can reflect the ingression of perfection. As *their* speech this language could be but an artifact, and thus inadequate to this task. Because their natures are compounded of an orientation toward the Whole and of technical competence, their speech is compound as well. They may be able to suggest that an adequate language must take account of both the ingression of perfection and the Whole; but they are not able to provide such a language. The problem of an adequate language is deeper than this modification of Socratic discussion would imply.

III

If the *Republic* is dominated by a Socratic discussion, and the *Timaeus* by a myth, they are both, still, dialogues. This is evident in their explicit structure, and, more fundamentally, in the way they carry significance. What happens and what is said in these dialogues does not simply take place; it takes place as told by Plato, whose mode of formulation is an integral aspect of the telling. Thus it is in virtue of Plato's telling that we are aware that the element of myth is relatively less central to the *Republic* than to the *Timaeus*; and that the *Timaeus* (and the *Critias* fragment) supplement the more Socratic discussion of the *Republic* by introducing an account of the creation of a perfect polity. It is Plato who writes dialogues.

The *Timaeus* may begin with an explicit juxtaposition and contrast of Socratic discussion and myth; but its claim that an adequate language must involve both of these structures cannot be supported in this way. For this, these structures must be fused. A dialogue, that is, must be that language, and the writer of a dialogue must have that nature, which replaces the compound language of discussion—myth, and the compound nature of such men as Timaeus and Critias. A dialogue does not only suggest that a reader accept the ingression of perfection in creation; it exemplifies this acceptance.

Specific persons and concrete contexts emerge in a dialogue and take on meaning and significance. Thrasymachus appears in the *Republic* to become a violent man, Glaucon to become a rash one; their entry into the dialogue begins a movement developing their expression of responses, beliefs, and opinions. A dialogue presents its own beginnings as the originative movement of language. Thus its protagonists emerge as expressing their beliefs and opinions in terms which reflect the origination of human discourse and its development in context. Moreover, in the course of the *Republic*, Thrasymachus is tamed and Glaucon's rashness modified. Whoever and whatever enters a dialogue and so contributes to the beginnings of speech risks transmutation in its course. Because the movement in a dialogue is the movement of the origination of language itself, it reveals these origins and continues to evoke them in its course. Dialogue discloses beginnings.

The disclosure of these beginnings in the course of a dialogue incorporates man's originative powers as participative in an originative movement. In dialogue the structure of this participation is formulated in the artistic focus of Plato's own originative powers. His handling of words and materials and his development of movement in a dialogue as a dramatic structure establish such participation. In a dialogue dramatic structure opens language to beginnings, freeing it from the dominance of its human origins, and so providing the artistic matrix necessary for their acceptance. The focus of artistic effort does not dissolve into the exercise of technical mastery and control in a dialogue. Rather, it enables the author (and the reader) to transcend the human drive for mastery which ordinarily clouds man's concern for origins and to participate in a movement of creation which man does not dominate. Such participation accepts the beginnings disclosed in this movement as a standard of its development.

Yet a Platonic dialogue is not only an art-work for it includes, as the central point of the Socratic discussions so often a part of the drama, a reference to the Whole as a standard of its development. This standard also exacts of man an acceptance of what is not human. In dialogue, however, the Socratic orientation toward the Whole is relaxed and then renewed. In dialogue human orientation toward the Whole takes the form of a repeated focus, since it is always qualified by an openness to beginnings. Dialogue presupposes that man's nature is not defended as Socratic eros which is too cold to be human, but as a daimonic balance of such eros and of possession by the powers of creation. In a dialogue man's acceptance of the Whole as a standard is interwoven by the movement of the dialogue with an acceptance of creation as a standard in the terms of the beginnings of speech which are given there and developed, but never controlled.

If a dialogue is that language which does fuse the structures of Socratic discussion and myth, what is the nature of its author—and of those readers who come to understand it? To speak a language which is at once adequate to formulate a movement toward the Whole and the movement of creation requires an integral nature of its speaker; that is, a nature in which the gift of orientation toward the Whole is balanced by the gift of participation in the movement of creation. If men are able to use a language reflecting the ingression of perfection, they can do so only when their originative powers are qualified and their natures characterized by the acceptance of these gifts.

IV

Plato's belief that human nature is the key to the development of a language adequate to reflect creation repeats and develops an insight characteristic of the tradition of Greek thought. Greek thinkers rarely lose a sense of the central importance of creative movement. They have this in view, for example, in their accounts of the authority of law, the founding of the state, and the sequence of events in history and their augury. The nature of their accounts may differ, but the focus of their view does not. And in the course of the tradition of Greek thought there is a growing awareness that the language used to formulate any account of creation is inevitably marked by major human contributions to its character and powers. Thus Greek thinkers are at once aware of their intent to accord centrality and ultimacy to creation and the inescapable qualification of any account by the language used in formulating it. Their characteristic belief that human nature is a key to the development of an adequate language derives from their awareness of the special place of man as himself originative and contributive to the language of any account of ultimate things.

Certainly by the time of Socrates and Plato the Sophists had shown that any language, the structure of which is determined by an unrecognized and, in turn, uncontrolled influence of the originative powers of man is unable to take adequate account of ultimate things. They noted explicitly the many ways in which man's contributions to language result in ambiguity of statement and relativity of meaning which traduces any intent to speak in ultimate terms. But the achievement of the Sophists was not only to show this; they also were aware—as were their Greek predecessors—that the character of man's contributions could be changed. Certainly men like Protagoras and Theatetus analyzed the modes of dependence of language on man in order to formulate a radically different language. They developed this new language to change those human originative contributions coming to *implicit* expression in responses, and beliefs and opinions by interpreting these explicitly in the terms of man's nature as egoist, that is, as defined by his needs and interests. They formulated the structure of this new language as the technique and craft of persuasion which could carry through such an interpretation, which could reorient by this means the members of an audience. The key to their language is its technique for bringing to a focus on human needs and interests those originative powers of man which are ordinarily variously and diffusely expressed.

The Sophists clearly recognized that the craft of persuasion is itself not an expression of human originative powers. They understood it as a means for interpreting these powers in the terms of man's true nature, and so changing the nature of his contributions to language, making it more adequate to take account of ultimate things. Thus Thrasymachus sees his craft of persuasion as focusing the energies of his audience to release them as the powers of collective action. He sees a Sophist in the exercise of his craft as confirmed in his insight by the accolade of his audience, and constituted as a tyrant by his evocation of the collective powers of this audience. But even the best Sophists, who intend to teach wisdom, teach this same lesson in some form. Their exercise of the craft of persuasion has its significance in the way it transmutes human originative contributions to language from expressions as presented in responses, and beliefs and opinions to the collective actions of men, thereby overcoming some of the limitations of language in taking account of creation.

The change in the character of man's contributions to language effected by the Sophists and formulated in the terms of a language of persuasion enables them to reflect a deeper level of creation than that of human originative expression. The Sophists can speak of collective action, and be understood by the audience they lead to participate in it. Yet if the language of persuasion is the collective voice of man, the originative movement it discloses seems as opaque, and as arbitrary and contingent as human responses, beliefs and opinions. The Sophist who intends to speak in the terms of ultimate things is reduced to the inarticulateness of the forces his techniques evoke.

When delivering a speech in the style of the Sophists, Socrates, in the *Phaedrus*, covers his head to indicate that in such a language, the reference to man's true nature is lost. But in doing this Socrates accepts the essential principle of the thought of the Sophists; that the reorientation of those human expressions which are contributions of man's originative powers to language provides the key to an adequate language. Where the Sophists understand this reorientation as an interpretation of such expression in the terms of a human nature defined by man's needs and interests; Socrates understands such a reorientation in the terms of a human nature defined by man's implicit commitment to completeness. Thus Socratic discussion relates human expression to man's nature as itself oriented toward the Whole and constitutes a redetermination of the structure of language. Socratic discussion guides and interprets the expression of human beliefs and opinions, and human response by the standard of the whole.

The formulation of the structure of Socratic discussion (as Plato sees this) makes evident a second important difference between this language and that of the Sophists. The exercise of the technique of persuasion determines the way in which language begins; that is, persuasion begins by evoking a variety of responses and expressions from an audience, by encouraging human contributions to language. The significance of this evocation for the structure of the language of persuasion is not merely that these human expressions are to be interpreted in terms of man's nature defined by his needs and interests; but that the requirement for this interpretation is to be found in their variety and confusion. Sophistic speech is initially provocative of human expression, thereby forcing the reductive interpretation of human expression in terms of needs and interests. By showing initially that the beginnings of speech are found in unsuspectedly deep movements of origination, an audience is led to accept participation in these movements through an interpretation which seems to define them.

Socratic discussion also accepts human expressions and encourages disagreement; but in Socratic discussion disagreement becomes the condition requiring the interrelation of human expressions which refer to the Whole. The conflicts of human expression are so sharply presented in Socratic discussion as to require resolution in the Whole. Thus for Socrates the human nature underlying the pattern of discussion is that of an originative movement implicitly oriented toward the Whole. Such a human nature is defined by this orientation, and its accessibility guarantees the possibility of Socratic discussion. But such a human nature evidences no love for human originative contributions as such, and it can only support a language which does not release the powers latent in human originative movements. The structure of Socratic discussion provides no means of accepting the originative powers which the use of language by men often releases; the transindividual powers of social expression, and even the powers of *physis* itself. If the structure of Socratic discussion is able to guide the development of intellectual originative movements whose expression can be formulated in sharply conflicting or contradictory ways, it achieves this only by ignoring what the Sophists emphasize, that is, the capacity of language to afford access to more fundamental creative movement. One aspect of Plato's criticism of Socrates is just this underestimation of the capacity and the task of language.

The function of the language of dialogue, then, is to do what Socratic discussion cannot do; to encourage and show the way of access to all levels of originative movement, and hence to creation as such. At the same time dialogue must do what the Sophists' technique of persuasion cannot do; that is, refer to the ultimate character, the standard, of the creative movement evoked. For just this reason, the form of a dialogue is drama. Human responses and expressions are held together loosely in the dramatic form of dialogue, and so permit the originative powers of the protagonists freer play. Dramatic form encourages originative movements first through spontaneous speech and then more deeply through the interplay of personality, temperament, and context which this makes possible. The clash and tension of personality and speech in drama is freer and deeper than the explicit conflict and contradiction in Socratic discussion, and it discloses beginnings which are inevitably hidden by the patterns *that* discussion weaves. Even Socrates himself may appear in a dialogue as one of several participants whose views provoke tension, and yet neither dominate nor guide the drama that develops.

As a drama a dialogue involves a number of protagonists each of whose originative contributions is presented as the disclosure of beginnings in which he participates. Dramatic structure, thus, changes human originative contributions, transmuting them from expressions as found in responses, beliefs, and opinions to a movement of acceptance of beginnings. This change makes of the protagonist a participant and constitutes his recognition of beginnings as ultimate, of their character as a standard. A dialogue develops through the mutual modification of the originative contributions of its participants, however. The recognition of beginnings as ultimate, as a standard, is to be found, not in a given disclosure, but in the development of the dialogue toward a balance of originative aspects. Such a balance is never quite achieved in any one dialogue. Thus in the *Republic* there is a distinct emphasis on the disclosures attained by placing the originative contributions of Socratic discussion of political theory in a dialogue. The development of this dialogue toward a balance is always somewhat weighted by the disclosures effected through the originative force of Socrates' radical love of the Whole. This dialogue requires a sequel which corrects this imbalance; and any one dialogue, for similar reasons, requires other dialogues. Properly understood the language of dialogue is to be found only in a dialogue series, for the recognition of the standard disclosed in beginnings is not to be formulated in terms of the acceptance of any particular origins.

What guides this movement of dialogue in its development toward the balance of originative contributions is the implicit contrast between its focus on origins presented in the terms of its participants and its focus on the nonhuman standard of the Whole presented through the incorporation of Socratic discussion. Human originative contributions to language ordinarily limit the capacity and power of language. The dialogue series is intended to overcome such a limitation by changing the nature of these contributions from the expressions found in responses, beliefs, and opinions to participatory development of the series as determined by the resolution of the opposition of these contributions in their multiplicity to the unity of the Whole. The language of dialogue takes account of ultimate things as these are disclosed in and through human origination by transforming and developing the significance of such disclosures in the linguistic movement which carries forward through the opposition of the human contributions to the nonhuman Socratic reference to the Whole; that is, in the terms of the necessity for their radical modification which this contradiction formulates in the language. This enables language to bring the multiplicity of human contributions to a balance in their repeated reformulation in a dialogue series. This reformulation of the human contributions to language as developed in the language itself carries the changes in human nature which man's possession by ultimate things both requires and makes possible. What ultimate things exact of man, Plato tells us, is that

[16]

repeated balance of the elements of human nature which defines orientation toward them.

But Plato's definition of this balance and orientation toward ultimate things in terms of the opposition between human originative contributions and the Whole is based upon a conception of contradiction which is both sharper than necessary and, indeed, belies the basis of dialogue in the drama. In art, in the language of the drama which the language of dialogue epitomizes, the function of human contributions is to open language to the infinitely rich background which it works to take into account. To balance human originative contributions in the movement of a dialogue series is to destroy the power of the drama to do this, for it transmutes human contributions into just and only those human elements which can be oriented toward the Whole. The significance of the dramatic basis of the dialogue must be understood as exacting of man not orientation toward the Whole, but an articulation of the significance of ultimate things. In this task a milder conception of contradiction is needed; and the transmutation of human nature, which such milder contradiction requires to further the movement of language, serves to disclose human nature as balanced when it reflects the infinite richness of ultimate things in the repeated particularity of their formulation. It is when language does this that it carries, in its own particularity, the ingression of perfection, and is adequate to its task.

[17]

HIRAM CATON

TRUTHFULNESS IN KANT'S
METAPHYSICAL MORALITY

Wenn mir einer von jemandem, den ich schon durch eine
einzige Probe als scharfsinnig erkannt habe, sehr ungereimte
Meinungen sagt, so glaube ich ihm nicht.

—Kant

Truthfulness is a basic and persistent theme of existentialist literature. But whereas truthfulness presents itself as an ethical category,
existentialists separate it from its ethical content in order to treat
it, as they believe, in a more fundamental way as a mode of human
existence. The peculiarity and problem of this manner of treatment can be indicated by reference to Nietzsche's "immoralism."

Unlike existentialists, Nietzsche begins with morality, and,
by interrogating its claims and its nature, traces its origin to two
different sources. On the one hand, morality is said to be a manifestation of what is truly fundamental: nature as the will to power.
Another line of reasoning concludes that, owing to the indifference
of nature to good and evil, nature cannot be the source of morality; rather, morality is an invention, or a posit of freedom. The
closest approximation to a reconciliation of these claims is the
view that nature supplies men a fundamental and unchangeable
disposition (will to power), although the opinions—the "world
view" or "ideology"—which constitute a given morality go far be-

yond nature; morality may or may not be in harmony with nature (according as it affirms or denies the will to power), but to some extent every morality dissembles its own natural root and also its character as a free posit by inventing fictitious authorities for its claims and demands. At the basis of every morality, therefore, is the conscious or unconscious "pious lie," whose function is to conceal the arbitrariness in the origin of morality. Accordingly, the highest philosophic virtue is truthfulness, as the probity to live without illusions and in the knowledge that moral choice has no ground but human freedom.

Seen from this perspective, it can be said that Heidegger replaces nature with Being and morality with human experience, while retaining freedom and taking it to its last extreme. For this reason, truthfulness becomes all the more important; it reappears as authenticity. Authenticity is not a moral obligation, but an ontological possibility of human existence; it is that experience of the truth of human existence from which all knowledge and morality are projected.

Two difficulties press the attempt to grasp truthfulness existentially. It is doubtful that Heidegger succeeds in divorcing authenticity from the moral claims characteristic of truthfulness. There is certainly no doubt that Heidegger believes authenticity to be more choice-worthy than the superficiality of *das Man*; and the basis of the choice is that when men are confronted with the alternatives of knowing the truth or of taking refuge in comfortable illusions, they cannot choose the latter without self-reproach. The second difficulty is that the phenomenological method can only describe what existence is like for those who believe that choice is a free project; it cannot establish that belief as true. For Heidegger, the question has evidently been decided by the successes and failures of others, among them Kant. The decisive importance of authenticity seems to be pre-figured in the prominence Kant gives to truthfulness. An examination of Kant's reflections on truthfulness may therefore help clarify its present status.

Kant makes a deliberate break with the traditional view of truthfulness, which derives from the Platonic teaching about the noble lie.[1] He is the first philosopher to teach that lying is the greatest ethical offense, and the propensity to lie, man's primary fault.[2] But the innovation has an air of paradox. Kant says that the *Critique of Pure Reason* imitates the Socratic defense of morality: it is strange that the only philosopher to condemn irony as unethical should take the most ironical philosopher as his model.[3] As for the noble lie, in Kantian morality it is a square circle.

This sharp divergence arises from the very different perspectives in which these judgments are made. The Platonic noble lie emanates from the lawgiver or founder who promotes amity among citizens by employing myth to conceal certain defects of the origin of society. But Kant, as a moralist, speaks from the perspective of "common human reason," or of the plain citizen. In this office he aspires to no more and claims no more than to have given the rational articulation of the sentiments and convictions native to everyman's breast. His defense of citizen morality against the sophistications of philosophy and politics goes so far as to deny that there *is* any moral wisdom other than the citizen's.[4] From this point of departure, Kant reasonably denies that virtue is knowledge, identifying it instead with courage: the fortitude to submit to the commands of the rational moral law. Consistent with the denial of philosophic virtue, he declines to speak of the origins of the state on the grounds that such matters may not justly be communicated to the multitude.[5]

For the citizen, justice is identical with the legal and virtue is piety toward the law. Kant's moral teaching is a "metaphysics" of this perspective; that is, it gives a metaphysical underpinning to the absolute or unconditional claims made by the law on the citizen at the practical level. It might be said that metaphysics raises the general "form" of citizen morality (law-abidingness) to the level of a metaphysical absolute. In any case, the law does present itself as the most grave and irresistible authority. It alone possesses the majesty to command the sacrifice of life and to take life openly. The virtue appropriate to the law wears the mien of solemnity; it responds to the absolute prerogatives of the law by attributing absolute validity to it. Citizen virtue is courage because it must brook no compromise with the blandishments of pleasure and the calculations of utility, knowing full well the weakness of such allurements in the face of the law's awesome demands. The essence of virtue is an unyielding resolve to obey the law because it *is* the law and without regard to consequences.[6]

Kant's asceticism of truthfulness grows in the soil of virtue as fortitude. Martial virtue is virtue's nature because man's moral nature is freedom from enslavement to the natural appetites, or man's capacity to subjugate his own sensible nature to the commands of the moral law. The honor of this soldier is the only genuine honor, human dignity as such, which is consciousness of oneself as his own lord (self-mastery).[7] Virtue ceases to be if it is conceived as a means, which is to say that it is essential to the being of virtue that it be willed for its own sake and without thought of any advantage it may bring. But since all action stemming from natural motives is for the sake of one's advantage, fortitude must consist in a self-examination that scrutinizes conscience for the purity of its motives, lest virtue be debased to a mere mercenary exchange. But the passions can be subtle; they know all too well how to insinuate themselves into actions by masking envy or revenge with honorable motives. Self-mastery thus demands the courage of self-knowledge which defeats the attempts of the passions to corrupt pure motives. No wonder that natural simplicity is for Kant the genuine nobility.[8]

In order to bring out the reason why truthfulness is the first duty to oneself, we must observe the role of conscience in morality. Practical reason, as the free submission to the moral law, is conscience.[9] The correctness of this identification, which at first is surprising, becomes obvious once the parallel between the structure of conscience and practical reason is noticed. Practical reason divides self-consciousness into two "persons," *homo noumenon* and *homo phenomenon*—legislative reason which gives the law, and the natural or sensible self to whom it is addressed as a command. The moral act as such consists in comparing the phenomenal self with the noumenal standard in order to ascertain whether they correspond. The two persons inherent in the structure of conscience emerge merely by change of terminology. The phenomenal self becomes the accused in the court of conscience. Legislative reason is the infallible judge who calls the accused before the law (and in so doing gives the law for cognizance) and who conducts the examination to determine guilt or innocence by inspecting the maxims and motives of the accused.[10] To lie to oneself is to lie to the judge in the very sanctuary of morality. It is an attempt to hide the phenomenal self from the scrutiny of the judge by creating an apparent self represented as being in tune with the law. The attempt to deceive the judge is an effort to cut off access to oneself in order that he might escape moral responsibility. The lie to oneself thus strikes at the very root of human dignity; it is moral suicide. It is therefore the extreme of moral worthlessness and the greatest violation of one's duty to himself.[11]

Unlike the lie to others, the internal lie cannot deceive fully, since in a way it is always known—the judge of conscience is an infallible searcher of hearts. Kant gives the impression that the phenomenal self lies to the judge's face only in desperation. For the most part the lie takes the form of evasion, of an attempt to keep out of the judge's sight. When this mode of the perpetration of the lie is stressed, the main function of conscience is altered from that of a judge to the permanent disposition to insist upon pure motives in the phenomenal self, or more simply, conscientiousness in fulfilling practical reason's law.[12] So understood, conscience is the fortitude to maintain the unremitting demand on the phenomenal self that it relinquish its attempt to evade the law; it is virtue as the will to truthfulness.[13]

By its nature the importance of truthfulness to moral life depends upon the strength of the tendency to deceive. Unfortunately, this tendency belongs to human nature as such; it is the "original sin."[14] The stamp of this view betrays itself to a mere glance at Kant's reflections on metaphysics, religion, and politics; we find him forever engaged in a relentless exposé of deceptions of colossal proportions. Not only is there a sham science that succeeds in passing as exalted and architectonic, even reason itself is by nature infested with illusion. Since these deceptions bear on self-knowledge, and in large measure are errors about the nature and powers of the mind, they have the most important consequences for morality: they thoroughly corrupt it. Genuine morality therefore requires a propaedeutic that clears the ground of the fundamental deceptions and self-deceptions; it requires a critique of pure reason.[15]

By far the most important illusions concern theology. The combination of dissimulation and self-deception that pervades theology manifests itself in the refusal of that "science" to submit to the conditions of free inquiry. Public utterance of doubts about the truth of theology, not to mention outright rejection of its claims, is a punishable offense. The external compulsion betrays a dissembled, gnawing inner doubt, which becomes explicit in the pious lie. It may be an inner lie, in which case it is typically the confession of belief, where closer inspection would reveal weak belief or even absence of conviction.[16] As a lie to others, it is a prudential argument. The premise acknowledges doubt, and hence the uncertainty of theology, but maintains nevertheless, that its teachings are salutary. In order that these salutary effects might be preserved, it is better not to disturb the conviction of others by revealing one's own doubts.[17]

The first step in purging the mind of illusion is to bring the doubt confessed in the pious lie before the court of conscience (the "tribunal of pure reason"). Under the court's interrogation, conscience is made to confess openly and candidly the doubts long concealed from public view. The confession is extracted from a reluctant witness by the "method of skepticism," which undermines the fortress of theological convictions by setting them in a dialectical combat with materialism and naturalism.[18] The war's function is to chastise pretentiousness, for it is pride of knowledge that dissembles the inner doubt and thereby conceals from consciousness true awareness of its limitations.[19] At the same time, by staging the combat for all the learned world to see, Kant destroys the credibility of theological pretentions and in that way destroys the conditions for the effective use of the pious lie.

The fundamental illusion that gives rise to the whole system of errors and spurious claims is a subreption of judgment whereby certain subjective conditions of thought are posited as objective, that is, as constituent of reality. The self that thinks, for example, as distinguished from the self that appears to inner and outer sense (homo phenomenon), never appears in the flux of change and for that reason is thought as simple and substantial. The subreption occurs when it is inferred that through such predicates the real existence of the self as simple and substantial is known; or, as one may also say, it occurs when the concept "soul" is hypostatized, i.e., posited as a real being and not merely as a concept.[20] This illusion is raised to its highest grade when it is believed that the concept is directly apprehended as an object through an intellectual intuition.

Belief in intellectual intuition is the most haunting metaphysical illusion. It is the ultimate support for that distinguishing mark of dogmatic (or rationalist) philosophy, belief in noetic principles as the cause or source of the material world.[21] The alleged intuition leads to the last consequence of metaphysical illusion. The "object" has the character of being passively apprehended, but it is manifestly not given through the senses. In order to explain these sudden illuminations, one comes to believe in divine knowledge or inspiration (Eingebung). Such beliefs, which Kant styles "fanaticism," are the highwater mark of reason's self-deception and the authentic link between metaphysics and religion. The most exalted mode of rationalist knowledge turns out to be indistinguishable from religious inspiration.[22]

The ultimate intention of reason's remote speculations is, in Kant's view, actually practical.[23] Theory and practice are related by the conception of morality that presupposes the existence of God and the immortality of the soul as its foundations. The defects of this conception are peculiar to all "theological ethics." Under the auspices of this conception, the voice of conscience is conceived to be divine, since the only infallible, all-seeing judge is God; speculative "fanaticism" is thereby carried into the moral sphere.[24] But this leads to that pride of knowledge or intransigent certainty that sanctions persecution of heterodoxy. Furthermore, God and

[24]

eternity in their "awful majesty" dominate morality, with the result that most actions conforming to law are performed "from fear, few from hope, and none from duty."[25] The ethics itself being almost always some particular revelation and not the rational moral law, the wrong law is obeyed for the wrong reasons. One might think that this morality would at least have the merit of taking morality seriously, but according to Kant it does not realize the full potential of moral seriousness. The responsibility of the believer extends only to the performance of duties that he did not himself impose. Responsibility becomes infinitely weightier if man undertakes to originate the law to which he submits. Only by elimination of all external sources of authority and dependence can man become fully moral and at the same time self-sufficient.

Such considerations lead to recognition of the more profound function of the Dialectic. The "vacant space" cleared by its destructive criticism is the demolition of the theological fortress for the sake of a new structure to be raised upon "humanity."[26] Humanity replaces the divine will as the criterion for the moral law by stipulating the perspective of the law as the perspective of mankind. This universality of perspective renders the law rational. So conceived, morality imposes on man the responsibility of acting as if he were a providential God. But since Providence embraces nature as well, the moral law must likewise be conceived as a law for nature: man must conceive his will to be the support not only for humanity but also for the universe.[27] By taking upon himself this infinitely weighty responsibility, man acquires "absolute inner worth": "the descent into the hell of self-knowledge prepares the way for deification."[28]

Since according to the official view[29] reason's illusions are natural, the pious external lie in metaphysics does not consist of the invention of sophistries but of the rather less promiscuous indulgence of errors that men have a natural tendency to make: that is, some metaphysicians have presumably discovered the illusory character of reason but neglected to communicate that discovery to others. Their reason for declining to purify metaphysics is that in certain matters practice takes precedence over theory. There are some illusions that ought to be indulged because they are "salutary."[30] In the case of the external pious lie, then, moral deficiency is a greater barrier to the exposure of illusion than deficiency of insight.

It must be supposed that those who were aware of metaphysical illusions possessed a non-illusory doctrine that they did not communicate openly to the public. Although it is not essential to the success of Kant's fight against illusion, one might expect an exposé of this "philosophia arcanae" and the manner of its communication. In fact he says little on the subject, although that little is considerably more than is usually noticed. Perhaps the most enlightening and least ambiguous remark is a statement of the policy that governed the procedure of the moral philosophers of antiquity with respect to paganism. These men renounced a frontal attack upon the gross fantasies of myth, but gave themselves a free hand to interpret the myths in accordance with sound morals and without regard to the sense that the myths were intended to convey.[31] This procedure, which Kant expressly approves, was, according to him, imitated by Christian and Jewish authors. He also accepts the venerable tradition according to which the Bible speaks "after the manner of men" (ad captum vulgi), which he styles "ad hominem" persuasion. This rhetoric ensconces the genuine moral teaching in an exterior (Hülle) of popular beliefs, whose purpose is to secure acceptance of the genuine teaching by smearing it with the honey of familiar prejudices.[32]

Brief though they are, these indications are very helpful for understanding Kant's own attitude toward the noble lie. Notwithstanding his many direct and indirect condemnations of that practice, Kant has not escaped suspicion of "hypocrisy." Perhaps the most important case is the rational faith or moral theology which, despite the criticism of "all [rational] theology," suddenly appears at the end of the Critique of Pure Reason.[33] It is gratuitous because the new theology does not at all differ in content from the standard rational theology of Kant's day. Moreover, it fills the empty space whose creation is the great labor of the Critique, thereby annulling the hard won gains for morality.

It has not been generally noticed, however, that the moral theology as a whole is said to be an ad hominem argument for use as a "weapon of war."[34] It is addressed to those whose moral "need" or "interest" is left unsatisfied by the negative result of the theological criticism, that is, to those whose morality depends upon belief in the existence of "objects" corresponding to the "concepts" of God and immortality.[35] Moral theology gives back to such persons what the theoretical critique took away by allowing them to "postulate" such objects as "actually existing."[36] These beliefs are sanctioned in order to supply an object for the will, that is, to rectify a deficiency of motive for obeying the moral law.[37] In this way it functions as a weapon to ward off the onslaughts of atheism and agnosticism. Once the farfetched and artificially complicated terminology in which Kant states this doctrine is penetrated, it seems evident that he imitates the procedure which he attributes to the ancient moral philosophers and Biblical authors. Herder testifies to both the need and success of this admittedly "unusual concept" of moral theology in saying that "precisely this back stairs of pragmatic doctrinal and moral faith ... is largely responsible for the acceptance of critical philosophy."[38]

Since the *ad hominem* argument is identified for what it is, Kant's imitation of the ancients is qualified. The very illusion the argument feeds tends to be destroyed by the explanation.[39] This procedure would be absurd but for Kant's view that mankind has now entered a decisive stage of progress, the stage of popular enlightenment, which will eventually eliminate the need for esotericism by gradually communicating the esoteric teachings to the multitude.[40] Thus, Kant can reasonably join moral condemnation of esotericism with a provisional esotericism of his own.

But even provisional esotericism requires provisionally withholding some doctrines from some persons, and hence a distinction between initiates and those who are taught edifying things. This distinction, as Kant draws it, is so extraordinarily artificial that it is difficult to apprehend. He ingeniously capitalizes on the necessity that he, as a university professor, observe certain officially prescribed limits in his lectures and writings to invent an a priori "quarrel among the faculties" as the vehicle for his statement of the restraints that critical philosophy observes.[41]

The dispute first comes to light in the Preface (2nd ed.) of the *Critique of Pure Reason* when Kant enters the ostensibly purely academic dispute between the skeptics and the dogmatic philosophy of the "schools." Since the *Critique* exposes the spurious claims of the dogmatists, it seems to favor skepticism; and since the dogmatists think skepticism is dangerous to morality, Kant feels obliged to defend criticism. His first retort is an enumeration of the several causes that prevent the dispute from reaching the ears of the multitude.[42] The second retort takes the offensive with a *tu quoque* argument. The metaphysical theology of the schools is itself harmful to morality; it is "despotic," not because of its exclusion of non-dogmatic philosophies from the schools, but in its relation to the multitude. The remoteness and obscurity of metaphysical theology enables the academicians to get themselves accounted by the multitude as "the sole authors and possessors of [theological] truths ... reserving the key to themselves and communicating to the public their use only.[43]

The commentary on this somewhat cryptic passage is presented in the *Quarrel of the Faculties*. The philosophical faculty (which Kant identifies with critical philosophy) and the theological faculty are in contention for the allegiance of the multitude.[44] According to philosophy, theology holds the multitude in thralldom by means of superstition. For the multitude believe that theologians are adept in knowledge of the fate of the soul in the afterlife, and in their hope for a good result, superstitiously attribute to the theologians powers that they do not possess.[45] Criticism would emancipate the multitude from their misguided obeisance by proving that the theologians possess no knowledge that is not also available to the common man. However, the dispute with theology is really secondary and derivative, for the theologians are servants of the sovereign, who ultimately prescribes what is to be taught. The interest of the sovereign is not the truth or falsity of some doctrines, but the tranquil guidance of the people.[46] Criticism thus cannot dispute the teachings of the theologians without setting itself at cross purposes with the will of the sovereign.

To negotiate this impasse, Kant proposes the following arrangement. In return for freedom to criticize theology, philosophy agrees not to address its criticisms to the multitude, confining its speech to the learned public only, the theologians especially. Their office is to judge these criticisms and to incorporate whatever seems fitting into the curriculum for pastors and other public servants, through whom they eventually reach the multitude.[47] One thus understands how Kant can explain the *ad hominem* character of moral theology without destroying its effectiveness: the theologians presumably will not transmit to the multitude the fact that the new theology is *ad hominem*. Philosophy thus clears its conscience of the burden of the pious lie by shifting it to the pastors.

Yet this arrangement seems to be quite unworkable. As King Fredrick William was curious to know, how can Kant keep his part of the agreement when his criticisms are accessible to all readers? His response to the King, which one may assume is his most serious answer, is that he has taken precautions to ensure that the multitude will take no interest in his books by shrouding his thoughts in the obscurity of academic jargon.[48] After the death of the King, however, Kant indicated, without saying it in so many words, that the agreement he made under duress is not to be accepted at face value. This he does by publishing his harshest criticism of theology in language that can be understood by everyone, and precisely in the work (*The Quarrel*) which promises that philosophy will not speak to the multitude: the very manner of the statement of the agreement effectively annuls it.[49]

The divergence of Kant's practice from his own moral teaching is best understood from that teaching itself. As a metaphysical doctrine, morality is "completely isolated" from the "phenomenal," i.e., real world of events and sensibility.[50] This retreat to the noumenal fortress brings two great advantages: morality is able to command absolutely, without reference to the troublesome problem of determinism, and it is freed altogether from any dependence on deliberation and prudence. The latter advantage is indispensable for the realization of moral equality. For if morality essentially requires deliberation, those who are naturally best at deliberating must in justice be set over those whose deliberate powers are naturally weak. But recognition of inequality in the sphere of morality would inevitably lead from approval of difference in orders of rank to approval of the noble lie, which Kant is at pains to eliminate for the sake of egalitarianism. Nondeliberative metaphysical morality is essentially for men of "happy simplicity."[51]

Even so, the fact remains that not all men are simple: "innocence is indeed a glorious thing, but ... it is very sad that it cannot well maintain itself."[52] The price of moral egalitarianism is the incommensurability of theory with practice. The formula expressing this predicament is that the well-ordered state is the condition for good morals, although that state itself is instituted by intelligent devils.[53] Morality, in order that it might be realized in the phenomenal world, must be preceded by the torch of prudence, lacking as it does the deliberative virtue which discerns what measures are appropriate to a given moral end at a given moment. Indeed, in the absence of good management by prudence, morality tends to become a fanaticism which insists upon the immediate realization of the moral condition, for example, the replacement of monarchy by a republic, when the circumstances are not auspicious.[54] In order to protect innocence from itself and the world, Kant is thus compelled to surround it by the mind of prudence, while yet keeping morality itself blissfully unaware of its compromising presence.[55] This peculiar arrangement is a temporary measure only. As men progress in moral improvement, that is, as morality occupies more and more of the real world, prudence will grow progressively less necessary until at last it becomes superfluous.

If deceit belongs to the original constitution of man, the clash of theory with practice should be nowhere sharper than in the disproportion between the moral demand for truthfulness and actual practice. "Every intelligent man," says Kant, "finds it necessary to conceal a good portion of his thoughts," and not even simple men are entirely candid.[56] This harsh exigency extracts from Kant the admission that it is morally permissible to conceal one's views by silence when it becomes necessary for preventing the abuse of one's candor by ill-disposed persons.[57] This dispensation will of course not suffice to protect those like Kant, who claim to speak exhaustively on all matters of importance. Not only are his themes just those to which the state prescribes limits (hence, they are the most dangerous themes), but Kant is in substantial disagreement with the officially prescribed opinions. The condition for the freedom to oppose the received opinions is then accommodation by means of *ad hominem* arguments. Viewed from this perspective, moral theology is *the* "weapon of war" which establishes the sphere of prudential agreement within which all opposition to received opinion must be oriented.[58] After all is said and done, it appears that individuals who would mix in affairs of state must imitate the conduct of the state, whose practice "flatly contradicts" what it says.

In order to bring out the reason for the universal dissimulation that permeates all human relations, especially among the most highly civilized, Kant performs a thought experiment. Imagine a species so constituted that its members could entertain no thought to which they did not give immediate utterance. What kind of society would such beings have? Unless they were angels, they would not be able to bear one another nor sustain society.[59] The natural, non-moral man cannot help harboring unfriendly thoughts about his fellows, because he is exclusively or primarily concerned with his own advantage. Prudence teaches him, however, that he requires the cooperation of others in order to attain his end. In terms of the *Metaphysics of Morals*, men ought to relinquish the "lawless freedom" of the state of nature; but they should also dissemble their true reasons for doing so, although on this point the *Metaphysics of Morals* is discretely silent.[60] The deceit that belongs to the constitution of human nature turns out to be the essence of man's social nature.

Fortunately for the species, man likes to be deceived as much as he likes to deceive, for he typically prefers fine and pleasant illusions to harsh truths.[61] The transition from deceiving to being deceived, from lie to illusion, is made by the suppression of consciousness of the deceptive intention of the original sociable dissimulation. This would occur in the following way. The natural man's deliberate misrepresentations are taken at face value and fixed by social sanctions—they become morals or customs (*Sitten*). Those brought up in the customs, however, are of course not told of their original intention. But since customs stipulate what man is and ought to be, to assimilate the customs means to mistake man's dissembled nature for his true nature. Thus, custom succeeds in hiding man's nature *from himself* by weaving a cloak of "beautiful seeming" which conceals its opposite lying more or less dormant in the suppressed natural appetites.[62] One is brought to the shocking conclusion that morality is the *Lüge an sich*.[63] Commensurate with this terrible result, in this context, and only here, Kant openly acknowledges the legitimacy of the noble lie, on the grounds that morality as a semblance is better than none at all.[64]

Only when the relation between morals (*Sitten*) and human nature has been grasped by anthropology can the genuine problematic of a "metaphysics" of morals be stated. We previously observed that metaphysical morality presupposes morals in the sense that it accepts the morality of common human reason at face value, waiving all investigations of its origin. This is so much the case that metaphysics does not consider human *nature* at all, which is exclusively the province of anthropology, but only human reason from a transcendental point of view.[65] Anthropology, however, reveals a discrepancy between morality as it is in its origins (its "*an sich*") and what it appears to common human reason to be (its "*für sich*"). The discrepancy, as we just noted, is that knowledge of origins destroys full commitment to morality by revealing the radical defect of the origins. Those who possess the intellectual virtues remedy this defect by occupying higher ground, as Plato shows in the *Republic* and as Aristotle shows in the *Ethics*. This route is closed to Kant because he intends his moral doctrine for the multitude. On the other hand, the intention to liberate the multitude from their servility causes him to reject the traditional indulgence of illusion. The *via media* between continued servility and destruction of the moral illusion by genuine enlightenment, which the multitude cannot assimilate, is an apparent enlightenment in the form of a metaphysics whose function is to appear to satisfy all rational objections to the validity and obligation of morality. The metaphysical noumenal world and its revived theology is an artificial barrier which arms the "realm of freedom" (the *für sich*) against destructive incursions from the "realm of nature" (the *an sich*).[66]

The long-range function and ultimate rationale of this seeming is explained when, in his writings on history, Kant views the genesis and perfection of the moral realm as a whole in its real setting *within* the realm of nature, that is, the relevant nature–anthropology on a grand scale or history.

History for Kant has a direction and therefore a meaning, which is the gradual reconciliation of nature and freedom via the victory of man's moral and rational powers over his unsocial nature.[67] This process occurs through the self-suppression, or better, through the sublimation of human evil into the good precisely by means of complete development of evil.[68] The paradigm for this "dialectical" transformation is the passage between opposites that founds human society. As we noted, reason discovers that the most effective pursuit of one's own advantage dictates that one ought to pretend to be good. But the pretense acquires independence in the form of social sanction, and in this capacity turns in earnest against self-aggrandizement and unsociability. This means, however, that what originally was only an appearance (*für sich*) is transformed into a reality (*an sich*)—morality effectively enters the realm of nature by making its claims felt. This is not to say that morality as such overcomes nature; there is nothing in the relationship between good and evil that points to a resolution of the tension. The factor that tips the balance is reason in the forms of the arts and enlightenment. The arts break the hitherto prevailing pattern of the rise, fall, and replenishment of civilizations from barbarian tribes by providing the means whereby civilizations flourish to the point that all peoples are contiguous and thus essentially members of one world; the arts, one may say, create the condition in which "humanity" becomes a practicable concept.[69] Since the few remaining barbarian nations will easily be subdued by their neighbors, who possess gunpowder, civilization for the first time has the prospect of an indefinitely long existence, uninterrupted by barbarian invasions and the ensuing return to primitive conditions. This of course presupposes that the light of civilization will not be extinguished by war among civilized nations, which is to say that the suppression of war through the establishment of a world-state or league of nations is necessary. Given the proximity of nations, and hence constant irritation, Kant surmises that the world-state might be established by roughly the same causes that moved individuals to enter society originally. The long reign of undisturbed peace makes possible the advance of morality by removing the harsh circumstances that hitherto necessitated struggle and antagonism. Under these auspicious conditions, morality will gradually insinuate itself more and more firmly until at last it becomes "second nature" or expels the original human nature.[70] The noumenal moral world thus *becomes* in reality what it appears to be (*an und für sich*), thereby reconciling nature and freedom.

The march of progress since Kant's time unfortunately gives us no warrant to modify his own profound skepticism about the possibility of mankind's advance to the perfect moral condition. Indeed, the very notion of progress has become doubtful, partly because the dangers of technology are at last manifest, but also because all morality now appears to be baseless. The enthusiasm and supreme confidence of the eighteenth-century enlightenment has been transformed into a self-consuming doubt that wavers between moral relativism and fervent commitment to the inherited enlightenment ideals. Or one could say that the erratic and increasingly irrational behavior of the contemporary heirs of rationalism arises from the combination of an inherited allegiance to the ideals of the enlightenment with lack of conviction that those ideals are inherently superior to any other ideal or non-ideal. Owing to this circumstance, the enlightenment ideals undergo a great variety of transformations. Progress deprived of belief in goals becomes a celebration of "process" or novelty for its own sake. Intellectual and moral self-sufficiency, which in the enlightenment is already a vulgarization of the original notion, is debased to an undiscriminating approval of all ways of life, except those that are undemocratic, or those that are incompatible with the production-consumption machinery, or those that are not chosen in the anguish of the knowledge that one's choice is groundless, depending on one's view of what is fundamental. Reason comes to mean exactness and efficiency, from which results an incapacity to distinguish between wise counsel and the machinations of scoundrels and even the incoherence of fools. The belief that all behavior and conviction is conditioned by stimuli of the environment is accompanied by an extraordinary reverence for the integrity of personality and disapproval of all restraint as suppression of individuality. I spare the reader further enumeration of these sad irrationalities.

The asceticism of truthfulness is both an effect and cause of the moral paralysis. In terms of Kant's projection of progress, the demand for truthfulness has been assimilated far in advance of the assimilation of morality to the human reality, with the result that uncompromising truthfulness leads to the popular exposé of all moral ideals—ultimately, even the will to truthfulness—as so many dissimulations of the will to self-aggrandizement understood as the enhancement of the feeling of power. One could say, as

[33]

Nietzsche in fact claimed, that Nietzsche's thought destroys the dialectic of progress by bringing forth from that process the self-suppression of the good in the form of an exhibition of the immorality of morality that destroys the "moral illusion."[71]

The perturbation which explodes in Nietzsche is already well established in Kant. It is perceptible in his smoldering anger with the excesses of religion, in his doubts about the soundness of philosophy, in his estimation of the potential of the multitude. Like other modern thinkers, Kant's thought about the multitude is a perpetual struggle between what we in fact see and what might be hoped for under radically new social conditions. This hope explains why Kant dared situate morality between its temporal genesis in human nature and its historical outcome in transmitted institutions; or, it explains why Kant dared join Hobbes' state of nature doctrine with moral idealism and utopianism. The attempt to fuse Hobbes and Rousseau into a new moral-anthropological teaching is the main source of Kant's misinterpretation of the role of dissimulation in morality. The state of nature doctrine requires him to believe that the noble lie is necessary to *establish* morality, whereas the *Second Discourse* furnishes the premise for belief in progress and hence belief in the historical contingency and ultimate dispensability of the noble lie. But an enlightenment which is assimilated, through institutions, only as true opinion remains mere opinion. The noble lie remains necessary because no amount of proxy effort can erase the difference between opinion and knowledge.

NOTES

Roman numerals followed by Arabic numerals indicate, respectively, the volume and page number of citations from *Kants gesammelte Schriften.* "A" or "B" followed by Arabic numerals indicates citations from the *Critique of Pure Reason.*

1. The philosophical, moral, and historical importance of this teaching has been articulated by Leo Strauss throughout his works. The reader will observe that the author has examined Kant's philosophy in the light that Strauss has shed on the interpretation of philosophic texts.

2. VIII, 267, 422.

3. B xxxi; IV, 404; IX, 29.

4. IV, 404–04; VIII, 370ff.

5. VI, 318, 339–40, 371; VII, 23–4, 29, 33; VIII, 304.

6. VI, 380, 383, 405.

7. VI, 408.

8. II, 218; also VIII, 268, IV, 222.

9. VI, 400.

10. VI, 186, 429–30, 438; VIII, 268, n.

11. VI, 429.

12. Apparently this movement is responsible for Kant's both asserting and denying that to have a conscience is duty. When it is denied, he thinks of conscience as practical reason; when it is affirmed, he thinks of it as conscientiousness. Compare VI, 185–6 with VI, 400.

13. The will to truthfulness, or conscientiousness, seizes the foreground because, owing to the fact that we know ourselves only as an appearance, it is impossible to know one's own motives with certainty. IV, 407, 451; VIII, 284–5.

14. VI, 39, 33.

15. A 319; V, 146–7.

16. VI, 186–90; VIII, 268–9.

17. K. Urteilskraft, par. 90; IV, 278; A 748–50.

18. A 423–4, 486.

19. A 470, 455–7.

20. A 580, 673, 598.

21. A 466.

22. A 638, 68–9, 277–8, 384–5, 546–7, 566–7. That this connection between metaphysics and religion weighed heavily in Kant's thought is evident both from the pre-critical Träume and the post-critical Von einem neuerdings erhobenen vorhehmen Ton in der Philosophie.

23. A 797ff; K. Urteilskraft, end par. 91.

24. VI, 194–5; 439–40.

25. V, 147.

26. A 259, 702; IV, 354; V, 49, 103.

27. V, 69–71, 44; IV, 337ff.

28. VI, 441.

29. A 339, 407, 422, 581, 642. Kant equivocates on the official view in several ways, the most important of which being perhaps that the ideas are inventions or fictions (A 320, 580, 584, 639, 673). These equivocations give force to Schopenhauer's assertion that Kant elevates mere sophisms to the rank of natural corruptions of reason and that he identifies Judaism with reason. Apparently Schopenhauer thinks this connected with restrictions on Kant's freedom of speech. World as Will and Idea (London: Routledge & Kegan Paul, 1948), pp. 90, 96, 98–100, 121–2, 129, 132–3.

30. K. Urteilskraft, par. 90.

31. VI, 111.

32. *Ibid.* Hypocrisy in religious teachers is allegedly the rule rather than the exception (VIII, 268). See VII, 45–48.

33. In addition to Schopenhauer, cited above, and Herder, cited below, see Schelling, *Werke* (Munich: Beck & Oldenbourg, 1928), V, 132; Nietzsche, *Götzen-Dämmerung*, par. 18 and *Der Antichrist*, pars. 10–12. Cohen's procedure with the postulate of the highest good typifies the manner in which Kant scholars normally deal with this problem. Although he admits, with Schleiermacher, that the postulate is "only political," the admission is diluted by interpreting it as a survival of Leibnizean optimism. Had Cohen faced the problem directly, he would have been compelled to admit that the postulate cannot be separated from the Kantian rational faith, as he attempts to do. [Hermann Cohen, *Kants Begrundung der Ethik* (Berlin: Dümmler, 1877), pp. 326–8.] Even Gerhard Krüger, to my knowledge the only scholar who has recognized that truthfulness is fundamental to Kant's morality, fails to consider whether Kant's practice conforms to his theory. [Krüger, *Critique et morale chez Kant*, tr. M. Régnier (Paris: Beauchesne, 1961), pp. 166–72.] The common fault of such authors is that they do not consider practice in sufficiently practical terms.

34. A 828–9. Also A 739, 742–3, 746, 777. At A 828–9, Kant does not use the term "ad hominen," apparently preferring to allow the reader to infer that the argument has this status from his statement that the argument is valid only when formulated in the first person. However, in the posthumous *Fortschritte* essay, it is expressly said to be *ad hominen* (XX, 305–6). In *Misslingen*, the argument is called a "Machtspruch" (VIII, 262). See also *K. Urteilskraft*, par. 90 and VII, 52, n.

35. The entire "Canon of Pure Reason," of which the moral theology and postulate of the highest good are parts, is introduced under the rubric of practical concessions to practical "needs" or "interests" (A 795ff.). This point of view is consistently maintained in all later treatments of the subject.

36. V, 134.

37. A 811, 813; V, 126, 142–3. When pressed by Garve (VIII, 278–80), Kant simply denies ever having said, as he plainly does at A 811, that deficiency of motive is the reason for the moral theology. The reason he gives—the need of an "object" to guarantee the coincidence of virtue and happiness—is however merely a round-about way of saying the same thing.

38. *Metakritik zur Kritik der reinen Vernunft* (Berlin: Aufbau Verlag, 1955), p. 296. See V, 144.

39. In his popular survey of Kant, for example, Reininger, defending Kant against the allegation that his famous statement that he does away with knowledge in order to make room for faith is a deliberate misrepresentation designed to enlist the support of the very persons he attacks, says that Kantian faith is a means whereby "von den religiösen Vorstellungen allmählich ganz von selbst wegfallen, was für eine bestimmte Zeit an ihnen überflüssig geworden ist." [*Kant: Seine Anhänger und seine Gegner* (Munich: Reinhardt, 1923), p. 259.] Precisely. Yet Kant admits that his "pure moral religion" is the "euthanasia of Judaism," i.e., Christianity (VII, 53), and that the Bible may be inter-

preted to teach the pure moral religion even though a moral religion may have been the furthest thing from the thoughts of the Biblical authors (VI, 111).

40. Enlightenment is nothing but the revelation of the esoteric teaching: "Aber in den religiösen Darstellungen den zur Moralität, welche das Wesen aller zwar einige Zeit hindurch nützliche and nötige Hülle von der Sache selbst zu unterscheiden ist Aufklärung; weil sonst ein Ideal . . . gegen ein Idol vertauscht und der Endzweck verfehlt wird." VII, 192. On the ripeness of the time for enlightenment, see VI, 84, 132, 165–7.

41. Karl Vorländer, *Immanuel Kant* (Leipzig: Meiner, 1924), II, 40, 56; *Kant: Philosophical Correspondence.* ed. & tr. by Arnulf Zweig (Chicago: The University of Chicago Press, 1967), 186, 213, 249–50; VII, 6–7.

42. B xxxii–xxxiii, xxxiv–xxxv.

43. B xxxiii.

44. VII, 30.

45. *Ibid.*

46. VII, 8, 21–2, 28.

47. VII, 28–9, 34–5.

48. VI, 14, 206; VII, 9; IV, 14.

49. By prefacing the *Quarrel* with the King's reprimand and his reply, Kant plainly indicates how one should interpret the "peace treaty" the *Quarrel* draws up. See also VII, 33, 31, and Herder's comment on the casuistry by which Kant sought to deny that he broke his promise to the monarch (Herder, *op. cit.*, p. 347, n. 1).

50. IV, 410.

51. IV, 404; V, 36; VIII, 286.

52. IV, 405.

53. VI, 366. Although, as mentioned above, Kant does not speak of the origin of the state in any of his ethical treatises, he does reveal its origin in the historical essays.

54. VI, 373, also 372, 377–8; V, 126.

55. To my knowledge no commentator has noticed the crucial role Kant assigns to prudence, even as he condemns it as immoral. In the later writings its function is concealed by the interpretation of the moral theology in terms of the providence of nature, i.e., history. For the relation of the theodicy to prudence, see VIII, 25, 262, 264, 362 n.; VII, 329.

56. VII, 332.

57. Kant sometimes (VI, 190; VIII, 269) distinguishes truthfulness (*Wahrhaftigkeit*) from sincerity (*Aufrichtigkeit*). The relevant difference is that truthfulness is compatible with concealing one's views by maintaining silence, whereas sincerity is a completely open heart, which is found only in children. In the *Metaphysics of Virtue* truthfulness and

[37]

sincerity are first identified (VI, 429), and then distinguished (VI, 471–2). In *Ueber ein vermeintes Recht aus Menschenliebe zu Lügen*, Kant purports to prove the *injustice* of the benevolent lie, although the *Metaphysics of Justice* expressly permits lying (VI, 238). Actually, the argument of *Verm. Recht* is drawn entirely from grounds available only to the doctrine of virtue, augmented by illegitimate appeals to positive law.

58. VIII, 146.

59. VII, 332.

60. *Ibid.*

61. VII, 152; VIII, 113, 376, n.

62. VII, 152.

63. Concealment, i.e., insincerity, is "the real basis of all true sociability." VIII, 113.

64. VII, 152–3.

65. IV, 410–12; V, 97.

66. B 310–11; A 643–5, 670–71; V, 174–76; VIII, 332–3.

67. VIII, 17, 362, n.

68. *K. Urteilskraft*, par. 83; VIII, 29–30, 367.

69. VII, 81; VIII, 21, 24.

70. VIII, 117.

71. The connection between the transvaluation of values and its mode as popular enlightenment is precisely intellectual honesty. *Der Antichrist*, pars. 38, 44, 47, 55–6, 62.

JOSEPH C. FLAY

HEGEL, HESIOD, AND XENOPHANES

Martin Heidegger has invited us to return to the Greeks and to
rethink the history of philosophy which followed from them. His
purpose is to reorient us toward this history in order to ask the
question of being in a way which is faithful to its original and
authentic meaning, a meaning which has been concealed from us
since Plato.

Hegel, on the other hand, affirmed the validity of the path
which has been taken and founded his own philosophical thought
on the historico-philosophical dialogue which began with the
Greeks and continued through Kant, Fichte, and Schelling. His
own task was to recall the fruits of this dialogue and, participating
in it, to bring it to a culmination. The moment in which completion was to be realized was that in which man would surmount the
separation from being entailed by the attitude of consciousness,
i.e., by that stance toward what is, in which being stands over
against thought as an object.

These two thinkers have recognized that man both belongs
to being and is separated from it. Further, both agree that philosophy has sought its goal by attending to beings in objectification.
Finally, both agree that the ultimate task of philosophy is rooted
somehow in the thought of the pre-Socratics.

Their difference lies in the question whether or not this at-
tention to beings has eventuated in access to being itself! Whether

[39]

attendance to beings and the consequent objectification of being has been a necessary positive—as well as negative—moment of the philosophical task. It is a question of mediation in opposition to immediacy.

It lies beyond the scope of any short essay to settle such a question. Perhaps we could not even properly ask it. But it might be further clarified. Since both thinkers accept the thought of the pre-Socratics as foundational, it is possible to see the question as a dispute over the meaning of the original beginnings. The question then takes the following form: did the beginnings point to the necessity for a mediated access to being rather than to immediate access?

With this limited question in mind I shall argue that the task as undertaken by Hegel and his predecessors, was not the result of a misinterpretation of the original task, but was precisely that set by the pre-Socratics. Within this context, then, this essay is an attempt to determine the justification for a mediated access to being.

I shall limit myself to a consideration of Hegel, Hesiod, and Xenophanes in so far as they deal with the problem of access to being and to truth. I have chosen Hesiod and Xenophanes because the former, together with Homer, is recognized by the Greeks themselves as the teacher of men and the latter is the first to significantly challenge Hesiod on the question of access. After first discussing briefly Hegel's view of his own project and his interpretation of the beginning, I shall turn to Hesiod and Xenophanes in an attempt to justify this interpretation. However, I shall not involve myself in a dispute with Heidegger directly; for if the conception of the necessary mediation of being is justified, his position will at least indirectly be brought into question.

I

Hegel formulates his task as tripartite. The first part consists in an examination of the manifold modes of being in and toward the world in which finite human beings find themselves. The purpose of this task, undertaken in the *Phenomenology of Spirit*, is not simply to catalogue these modes of being, but also, by means of a consideration of them, to lead us to the threshold of philosophy as science. The *Phenomenology*, then, is a *Bildungsprozess* by means of which we are led from the most simple and straightforward mode of conscious being in the world to the mode of being which grants us the possibility of a complete articulation of the meaning of being.

Such a complete articulation constitutes the second and third part of the task. It includes not only an analysis and critique of the intelligible structure of being but also, on grounds established by this analysis, an ontological knowledge of *concrete* being. The former is accomplished by the *Science of Logic*, the latter in *Philosophy of Nature* and *Philosophy of Spirit*.

It is the first part of this system which interests us here, for its presence entails a mediated access to the meaning of being.[1] We are led through a variety of concrete modes of being, each of which is shown to fail to grant access to the being of beings and to unconditioned truth. The goal of this "journey of despair" is the comprehension of being itself, and Hegel attempts to show that if the finite modes of being are properly understood, we are released from them into an infinite mode in which access to being is in fact achieved. The essence of this dialectical phenomenology is *release from finitude through attention to that which binds finite man and separates him from being.* Entailed is a claim that there is something not already explicitly present, which is nevertheless there and which must be *made* present. That is to say, there is a hiddenness which hides its own hiddenness; and it is the task of philosophy first to reveal this hiddenness and then to reveal the nature of that which is hidden.

The dialectical and mediated nature of the process of overcoming man's separation from being is not, according to Hegel, his own invention. It is grounded in the historical process and his own contribution to that process is to make that process explicit by recalling this labor of world spirit.[2] Our own understanding of Hegel's mediated access to being is thus grounded in an understanding of his view of philosophy and its history; and this understanding is in turn grounded in his understanding of the beginnings.

Philosophy begins, Hegel tell us, with the Greeks. With the Greeks man is lifted out of an immediate, submerged existence in the world and into reflective objectivity. They "placed their existence before themselves, separated from them as an object," and "made a history of everything they had possessed and of everything they had been."[3] This original act of recollection (Hegel refers to it as a *mnemosyne*) gave philosophy its beginnings and man came home to himself "as this presented being-with-self."[4]

But this at-homeness was not complete, for it had its stimulus from something foreign to them. While they recreated their existence they "at the same time unthankfully forgot the foreign origin, perhaps to bury it in the darkness of the mysteries which they kept secret from themselves."[5] The at-homeness harbored within itself a secret, hidden strangeness.

This understanding of the beginnings of philosophy reflects a polydimensionality of belonging to and separation from being which entails a necessary hiddenness. There is, on the one hand, a belonging to being established by the objectification of spirit. Finite man comes to be at home with himself by establishing in objective form the ways in which he belongs to what-is. On the other hand, this act of objectification dialectically entails a separation from his spirit in its immediate existence, for the act which brings him home to his spirit is an act which separates his existence from him. Thus the mediated, presented spirit necessitates the concealment of the original, immediate relation to what-is.

But now man's separation from being is possible only on the basis of an original submergence within it. Thus the separation from being which made it possible for him to be at home with himself was itself possible only on the ground of the original belonging to being which constitutes everyday, submerged existence. But again this original relation to being, sundered in the act of objectification, harbors within itself a separation from being, in so far as man *first* comes to be at home with himself in the objectifying act. On this view, then, what originally constitutes belonging to being (immediacy, submergence) is in fact a separation (qua reflexive and reflective consciousness) and what comes to be a separation (objectification) constitutes a belonging to being (being-at-homeness). The bidimensional constitution of reflexive being destroys the original bidimensionality by transforming original separation from being into a belonging and, conversely, by transforming original belonging to being into a separation.

There arises, then, an extraordinary world (the world of poetry and philosophy) which is hidden from man as he originally belongs to being. But, in turn, this original mode of belonging is now hidden from the reflection of objectification. What is lost is the original, immediate belonging to being; and the "secret," the immediacy now mediated, is firmly established. The question arises: *how are we to have complete being-with-self, total at-homeness, in spite of this separation from the original relation to being?*

According to Hegel it is this question which philosophy has attempted to answer. It is the task of the *Phenomenology* to recall this labor of world spirit and to transmute it into a form which is completely intelligible. The moment of world spirit which culminates in the *Phenomenology* is that in which the separation from being necessitated by the act of objectification is transcended. By exemplifying and manifesting the ways in which both immediacy and reflectivity bind man in his being in and toward what-is, we are released from finitude and the attitude of consciousness.[6]

It is clear now that Hegel's argument for the necessity of mediated access to being rests on his understanding of the "beginnings." It is only by presenting and overcoming the separation from being entailed by presentedness that we can have access to being. We must now turn to the question of the justification of this interpretation.

II

The crux of our question is this: "Is there a separation from being which occurs in the beginning and about which a consciousness arises such that there is an attempt to overcome it?" The form and content of Hesiod's *Theogony* will affirm that there is.

Hesiod begins by addressing the muses: "These things tell me from the beginning, ye Muses who dwell in the house of Olympus, and declare to me which of them came to be."[7] This passage exemplifies the form which Hesiod's teaching takes. *There is an immediacy which is structured by separation.* Those to whom Hesiod addresses himself dwell in the house of the immortal, away from the habitation of men. Their presence before Hesiod is unexpected and inexplicable and simply to be accepted. The form of the discourse thus reflects a separation, a discontinuity recognized by both Hesiod and the muses. There is a communication through discourse about the origins and structure of what-is, and thus a presented immediacy which reveals what is constitutive of being; but the speech is oracular and is a revelation from a source which is separate from Hesiod and finitude.

This formal separation is indicated further by the monological form of the discourse, something to be recalled and repeated by the poet, but not questioned. Hesiod is informed that he is "a wretched mortal, a mere belly," and that he has no way of judging the truth or falsity of what is revealed in the discourse.[8] The discourse which articulates the nature of being concerns the extraordinary and Hesiod does not himself have access to this realm. It is only through the mediation of the muses that he can be approached by being in its immediacy.

[43]

Finally, the remoteness of the muses and the subsequent lack of identity between what is undergone by Hesiod as a finite mortal and what is revealed by the muses is further stressed when we are told that the speech is a *perikallea ossan*, spoken by the muses who walk in the night, veiled in a thick mist.[9]

Thus the muses and what they speak are ultimately hidden from Hesiod as a mortal. He wishes to know the ground and origin of what-is, is told of a ground and origin, and yet has no way of judging the truth of what is spoken because he is one among mortals. The hiddenness is revealed to him in the form of a hidden speech and the impenetrable ultimacy of what-is is freely admitted as hidden. Yet there is a revelation, and thus the separation entailed by the form of discourse issues in a belonging to being. Poetic speech, which is extraordinary speech, holds together this subtle revelation of being in a way that does not brook the questioning of the authenticity of the content.

This immediate, inexplicable form of the beginning reflects and is reflected in the content of the revelation to Hesiod. The act of genesis (in which bringing into being and coming into being are not distinguished from each other) is singular and by fiat and involves nothing other than the *archē* itself. But this generates an incommensurability between what is brought into being and the *archē*, in spite of the fact that there is no distinction made between them. For coming into being is seen as a process of birth and thus as a process of differentiation, separation, and limitation; while the birth of beings (including *Chaos*) is the result of non-limitedness, non-separation, and non-differentiation. The *archē* itself embraces both itself and what is generated; at the same time, they are distinct. There is here both an incommensurability and an overt disregard for this incommensurability.

We have here an ultimate distinction. There is that which is manifest and that which is not manifest, and the latter is the ground for the former. What-is, what comes into being, is beings—separated off, determined, delimited. Beings are distinctions which appear first as *moirai*. The ground and origin of these *moirai* is the self-differentiating, unconditioned, non-differentiated process. The *archē* itself is not a being, but is being itself as process. Being itself stands in relation only to itself and therefore not in relation to beings *qua* beings. But for this very reason it is not distinct from them either. The *archē* is not revealed as either being or not being, but as the source and ground for the being and non-being of conditioned beings. This ultimate distinction is displayed in its ultimacy by being both marked as a distinction and disregarded.

III

We have found in Hesiod's poem both a presence and a hiddenness in what appears as a hopelessly entangled distinction between beings and their *arche*. The secret revealed to human intentionality about human existence is itself manifested and accepted as secret. Human intentionality and existence are opposed by the *arche* and its *moirai*. The recognition and acceptance of the *arche* as encapsulating what-is is made possible through objectification; but at the same time, because of the nature of the form and content of the revealed, the *arche* remains separated from the beings which it encapsulates.

I suggest that the situation of immediate presentedness found in Hesiod reveals the bidimensionality which lies at the basis of Hegel's explication of the meaning of hiddenness. As undergone, what-is is hidden from man in so far as its origin and ground are concerned. As a consequence, Hesiod must ask after the ground and origin in order that they might be revealed to mortals. Thus, in belonging to what-is, man is separated from being. But through the speech of the muses and the immediate presentedness of the *arche*, man comes to be at home with himself, and therefore he achieves a belonging to being which is the goal of his quest and which he does not possess as immediately immersed in his existence among other beings.

But what is made manifest is that being at home with himself in this manner also depends upon his immersion in what-is as it has come to be from the *arche*. His immediate immersion is an original belonging to being as a being which has come to *be* through the *arche* and thus as in community with what-is. Therefore, the moment of presented immediacy, achieved through the hidden muses, represents a moment of separation. Man has been separated from being as immediate existence through an understanding (uncertain as it is) of the nature of that immediate existence at its origins.

But secondly, the ultimate problem of the accessibility of what-is in its being is therefore revealed. As immediately immersed in existence, man belongs to what-is; and his ground is in the *arche*. But he is also separated from himself and what-is because he fails to understand what-is in its being. What-is, as such, remains hidden from him; its nature has not yet been made explicit.

When he stands before a presented immediacy, on the other hand, an *arche* has been asked after and revealed; but by that very fact, what-is is made objective. Thus *the belonging to being which is man's in his immersed immediacy is given up for a belonging to being which makes this immersed immediacy an object for man, grounded in hiddenness.*

Finally, in so far as the muses are able to present this immediacy, transmuting original immediacy into presented immediacy, the ultimate ground which was sought after is recognized and accepted as hidden. This aspect of the situation in Hesiod reflects the fundamental separation from being which governs both immersed, original immediacy and presented immediacy as well.

The result is a tension between existence and being, between what-is and the *archē*. And the *archē* itself holds this tension within itself. At this juncture both the speech which reveals the *archē* and the *archē* itself remains a mystery, albeit a mystery revealed as mystery.

IV

No philosophical problem arises if the mystery is accepted as mystery and adopted on faith. The problem of being remains enshrouded in the matrix of religious experience and speech. But if the divine speech is reflected upon, then the philosophical problem arises which, for Hegel, was the problem of a preparation for a complete articulation of the meaning of being. If we begin with Hesiod, as we have, then it was Xenophanes who originally recalled the speech of the muses and who formulated the question which according to Hegel molded philosophical thought in the West.

The problem receives the following formulation. The very pronouncement of the mystery as a mystery entails, as a precondition, an accessibility to the *archē*; but the accessibility is essentially an inaccessibility in respect to the separation from being which governs the discourse, the content of the discourse, and man's own immersed immediacy. *How is it that the inaccessible is accessible?*

In response to this question, Xenophanes does not merely offer another conceptual framework for the intelligibility of what-is, but questions our very access to the divine speech. He thereby directs our attention to the tension we have discussed and recognizes that what was sought after, namely the *archē*, was neither revealed nor not-revealed. That is to say, he calls into question the very revelation of hiddenness itself.

Xenophanes examines the two poles of the tension, the human and the divine. On the one hand there are mortals who are seekers; on the other, the divine. Seekers are mortals, *thnētoi*, who

[46]

themselves belong to what becomes and therefore are limited and temporal.[10] On the other hand, the divine thinks, sees, and hears the whole of things and is not in any way like mortals.[11] That is to say, the divine is neither limited nor temporal and does not come into being through the *arche*. The divine "moves things" simply through mind, from afar (separated), and does not itself participate in change and becoming.[12]

This is clearly a reflection upon and repetition of the speech of the muses. That which is mortal and that which is divine are separated off from each other. Yet the divine encompasses all, "moving" what-is, yet unmoved itself. But through this repetition Xenophanes seeks further to explain why it is that mortals are not given a revelation of the *arche* in a presented immediacy.

On the one hand, those who seek are incapable of effecting a revelation except through mediation by an other which transcends beings; for they themselves are imprisoned in becoming, having come into being. As Anaximander had said before, for *thnetoi*, necessity and time govern the emergence and existence of beings. The whole and its *arche*, being neither limited nor sequential, cannot be grasped by what is itself limited and temporal, i.e., by those who themselves come into being and pass away.

But neither can the divine reveal anything other than the become; for *there is no distinction between divine thought and what results from it.* If a revelation concerning what-is and the *arche* of what-is is to be intelligible, it can only be in the form of the appearing of the appearances. Thus, only the grounded and originated, but not the ground and origin itself, can be revealed by the divine. The becoming of what becomes is, in fact, already the revelation.

The gulf between appearance and its ground, between the *arche* and the created, is set as an absolute contrast. Even if by chance what is sought for approximates truth about the ground and origin, there can be no recognition of it as truth. I can neither know that I know, nor know that I do not know.[13] What is said can, at best, be taken as resembling the actual.[14] The philosophical problem has been set at this juncture; for *Xenophanes has brought into full view a noetic negativity which, of necessity, derives from the ontological negativity established by Hesiod.* It is no longer possible to rely upon the form of presented immediacy as mediation. The demand has now been for an *elenchos* which is to be judged by reason.

Xenophanes' stance toward the question of the *arche* is not one of skepticism; for he too speaks of the divine over against the mortal. He has simply asserted the problem of access to the *archē* as a problem. But at the same time he has thrown into question his own pronouncements, and thus has fallen into a problem identical to that faced by the skeptic when his skepticism is challenged on skeptical grounds. What is this *archē* which is cognized as a hiddenness? How is hiddenness itself recognized as hiddenness? In other terms, how is it possible that the distinction and tension between beings and the *archē* is manifest? How can that which does not appear be distinguished from that which appears, when the former does not even appear as a non-appearance?

V

The explicit realization of the need for mediation was already present in Hesiod in the form of the muses. The form which this mediation took there was that of a divine revelation issuing in a presented immediacy. Xenophanes has shown, however, that such a presented immediacy is in principle impossible. Yet he too acknowledges some access to primordial being in so far as he also discusses the nature of the *archē*. His analysis of the problem introduces a crucial notion: the notion of *the necessity for a mediation which will at first bind us to beings*. He has argued that what is revealed from the beginning, whether its origin is in the divine or in seekers, is what has become.

> outoi ap' archēs panta theoi thnētois' hupedeixan,
> alla chronō zētountes epheuriskousin ameinon.

"The gods have not revealed all things to men from the beginning; but by seeking men find in time what is better."[15]

The necessity of mediation through attention to beings and the consequent objectification of being is grounded in this primordial philosophical insight: in seeking the ground of what has become, we are always already over against the become itself, both as what-is in general and as those who seek to know. What has become, if taken in its immediacy, reveals nothing but the emergence and subsiding of being. The ontological and noetic negativity established by Hesiod and Xenophanes ground the recognition of a belonging to separation-from which Hegel took as the basic dialectical structure of the philosophical project undertaken in the *Phenomenology*.

If, then, being and unconditioned truth are to be made accessible, there must occur a transformation of what-is as it exists for finite consciousness into an immediate confrontation of being, mediated by this transformation itself. The argument justifying Hegel's dialectical view of this access can now be put in the following form. As a result of the beginnings we have just reviewed, access to being presupposes that we have overcome the gap between our immediate relation to being as it is in itself and our mediated relation to it as it reveals itself in its creative activity. But given the inescapable finitude revealed by Hesiod and Xenophanes, we cannot achieve this overcoming in any way free from finitude and from our participation in the realm of becoming. The immediate beginning of the complete speech about being will therefore be a mediated beginning.

NOTES

1. G. W. F. Hegel, *Science of Logic,* trans. Johnson and Struthers (New York, 1929), Vol. I, pp. 80–81.

2. G. W. F. Hegel, *Phenomenology of Mind,* trans. Ballie (New York, 1949), pp. 90–91.

3. G. W. F. Hegel, *Lectures on the History of Philosophy,* trans. E. S. Haldane (New York, 1955), Vol. I, p. 151.

4. *Ibid.*

5. *Ibid.,* pp. 150–51.

6. *Phenomenology of Mind,* pp. 804–5.

7. Hesiod, *Theogony,* 11. 114–15.

8. *Ibid.,* 11. 26–8.

9. *Ibid.,* 11. 9–10.

10. H. Diels, *Die Fragmente der Vorsokratiker,* ed. with additions by W. Kranz (Berlin, 1954). Xenophanes, fr. 18. (Fragments will be cited according to the arrangement of this edition.)

11. *Ibid.,* fr. 24.

12. *Ibid.,* frr. 25, 26.

13. *Ibid.,* fr. 34.

14. *Ibid.,* fr. 35.

15. *Ibid.,* fr. 18.

STANLEY H. ROSEN

HEIDEGGER'S INTERPRETATION OF PLATO*

I

Since this paper deals with some fundamental aspects in the thought of both Heidegger and Plato, it is essential that I state from the beginning the limits of my intentions. From the viewpoint of both, no study of Heidegger's interpretation of Plato could pretend to be adequate that had not mastered *their* work as a whole. As both would agree, the "work" of the philosopher is to think the whole; one therefore "masters" the work of a philosopher by himself thinking the whole in itself, and not merely as it appears in the work of others. A peculiarity of philosophical thought, as both would perhaps again agree, is that, although in one sense a part of the whole, it is that part which mirrors or reveals the whole *as* a whole.[1] By virtue of the synoptic character of philosophical thought, one may see an image of the whole through a consideration of some of its parts. The most I dare to hope for is that this paper is such an image; I shall be quite content if the reader regards it as a *mythos* rather than a *logos*. It is an inquiry (*historia*) that "looks for" (*zētein*) as it "looks at" (*theōrein*).

In these obscure regions I am guided by the words of Heraclitus: "If one does not hope, he will not find the unhoped-for, as not to be found and inaccessible."[2] I take "hope" to stand for the *pathos* or *Stimmung* which opens the soul to the otherwise unseen light of Being. The mood of hope is frequently called "wonder" (*thauma*) by the Greeks; both Plato and Aristotle tell us that it is the origin of philosophy. In my own interpretation of Plato's image of the cave, Socrates silently alludes to wonder when he asks Glaucon to suppose that one of the cave-dwellers, "having been released (from his chains), is forced instantly (*eksaiphnēs*) to stand up, to turn his head, to walk toward and look at the light (of the fire)."[3] The *periagōgē* or "conversion" is not originally *paideia* or "education," but the instantaneous illumination of wonder which permits *paideia* to occur.[4] It is this instant of conversion which drags the released man up into the light of the sun. Wonder opens man's eyes to the light of the good through the divine spark, the *theia moira*, the *mania*, or gift of the gods, as Plato variously calls the horizon of instantaneous vision.[5]

The image of the cave is central to Heidegger's interpretation of Plato. I refer to it at the beginning of this paper and will return to it at the end in order to suggest that Heidegger's interpretation, for all its help in reading Plato, is a very serious *misinterpretation*. But I shall try to do this in a way which does justice to Heidegger's intentions as well as those of Plato. My procedure is therefore somewhat different from the one which has often been taken by classicists and historians of philosophy. In my view, this procedure is at bottom inadequate, not merely because it rests upon the circular acceptance of conventional hermeneutics, but more specifically because the traditional picture of Plato as painted by modern scientific and *geistesgeschichtliche* scholarship prevents us from seeing important resemblances between Plato and Heidegger. Apparently Heidegger himself has been influenced by that traditional picture, even in the "oddity" of his approach to Plato. At least he shows no awareness that the differences between himself and Plato may be viewed from within the horizon of a common endeavor. Let me give an introductory sketch of the balance of this paper with a few more words about the image of the cave.

The "releasement" of the cave-dweller by the instantaneous agency of wonder is reminiscent of what Heidegger calls *Gelassenheit*. Wonder leaves man free to let beings be, as they are, independently of his subjective *Vorstellungen* of them in the world of *doksa*. The difference between the sunlight and the firelight is the Platonic analogue to the "ontological difference" drawn by Heidegger between *Sein* and *Seienden*. Heidegger's "lighting-process of Being" (to use Father Richardson's translation of *Lichtung des Seins*) is in Plato the light of the good, and the things in the sunlight are the Ideas, accessible to *noēsis* or instantaneous vision.

The cave represents *doksa* ("seeming" in the sense of "opinion"), and vision by flickering firelight, that is, of the images cast by the fire, and is the moving, i.e., temporal, or discursive thought of *dianoia*. These images, we must remember, are the shadows of puppets, presumably made as well as manipulated by men, an aspect of his own image which Socrates strangely ignores in the balance of his exposition. I suggest that the puppets and puppet-masters stand for what Heidegger would call the *Vorstellungen* of *Subjektität*, and so the unrecognized ground of dianoetic thinking, in which must be included what Socrates calls *pistis* and *eikasia* when he discusses the divided line prior to introducing the image of the cave. *It is thus man or man's thought which moves,* and neither the Ideas nor the good. The real problem in understanding the image of the cave is the unstated relationship between sunlight and firelight, or between *noēsis* and *dianoia*.

In other words, the openness which characterizes man in the "cave" of the world is not the same as the openness of the good in the domain of the Ideas. Man shares in the openness of the good thanks to his share of the divine *Nous*, or noetic intuition. In order for man to become aware of this divine gift, he must understand the direction of his striving or intentionality, which Plato calls Eros, or more fundamentally, the daimonic.[6] And yet he cannot see that direction without the gift itself: hence the circularity of existence[7] which is the ground of the so-called "hermeneutic circle." Eros is the Platonic version of *Sorge*, or the directed openness of Time. But within the interstices of the moments of Eros, another transcendent or ecstatic "place" or "clearing" is opened up: *to eksaiphnēs*, within which man sees the Ideas, and to the degree that he can see it reflected in their visibility, the good. Being or the good conceals itself as revealed in the forms of the Ideas, in the formlessness of mind, and in the flickering quasi-forms of spatio-temporal individuals. Mind, one may say in this connection, is that aspect of Being which stands for the whole by standing to its thoughts as Being stands to beings. But the minding, caring, or Eros of mind, and so the light in and by which it speaks, although it derives the luminosity of its light from Being, constitutes a difference within Being, as is clear from the fact that the Ideas do *not* speak.

Socrates calls Being "the good" and, still more erotically, "the sun,"[8] not because he has "objectified" Being, but because of what may be explained as a fundamental disagreement with Heidegger about Being itself. At first glance, the "sun" is at least in some crucial respects surprisingly like Heidegger's *Sein*. It is the giver of life as well as light, and thus of man and speech. Its light can blind as well as illuminate, and hence "truth" as "presence" or "unconcealment" is inseparable from "absence" or a hiddenness by virtue of light itself. Its rising and setting may be understood as defining Time and so, too, historicity: the sun's motion thus opens up the horizon within which, and only within which, we see it. In these and similar terms, Heidegger's *Sein* is even more like the sun than is that of Plato, or so I would suggest. For Heidegger, thanks to the temporal nature of the horizon of man's vision, Being is a process or *Bewegung* that "occurs" (*ereignet*) as a show in and through man or *Dasein*. Whatever may lie "behind" the horizon of temporality as an unseen source or unity, Being as presence or emanation from that unity is confined by Time in the very act by which Time opens the showplace within which Being presents itself to man. In the most fundamental sense, the Time within which the show occurs and man views it are one and the same; that is, the openness of *Sein* and the openness of *Da-sein* are one and the same. Given his special etymologies of the constitutive terms, Heidegger accepts the Parmenidean utterance that *to gar auto noein estin te kai einai.*[9] *To auto* is the *Zwiefalt* within Being between itself and thought; but at the root of this duality is a unity which one might call their need for each other.[10] For Plato, on the contrary, *einai* has no need of *noein*. There is a difference between "sunlight" and "firelight" corresponding to the double duality between Being and beings on the one hand, and *noesis* and *dianoia* on the other. Thought needs Being, but this need can be gratified only by way of beings. In sum: Being is the good, and beings (*ta ontōs onta*) are the Ideas. Being is visible/concealed only as or in the form of Ideas or beings, which in turn present themselves to man as appearances (*ta phainomena*).

Since Being and thought are not united in Plato by a reciprocal need, it is less fruitful to speak of a "duality" here than of a "harmony of opposites." The unity between the One and the many has reference in Plato to the structure of beings, and so to mind only as *a* being, but not between Being simply and Thought or Mind simply. Mind is opposed to Being as the living or thinking to the non-living or non-thinking. Of course if we consider such passages as *Timaeus* 35aff., we may say that, for Plato, Ideas, mind, and spatio-temporal particulars are related (*syngeneis*) by the common elements of the unchanging, indivisible, or eternal *ousia*, sameness, and otherness. But this is merely to render somewhat more precise the structural relation of beings as beings. The recipe in question fails to explain why one kind of being is alive and thinking, whereas the others are not. The problem is re-emphasized rather than resolved if we take seriously the figure of the demiurge as an ultimate principle of unification, since again, there is an opposition between the demiurge and the Ideas on the one hand, and the demiurge and the receptacle on the other. This is scarcely a problem which is peculiar to Plato; in the history of philosophy, one finds a variety of proposed solutions which cannot be examined here. Perhaps I may simply mention the situation in Kant because of its relevance as an intermediate situation between Plato and Heidegger. In Kant we have the three "dimensions" of transcendental ego, phenomena, and things-in-themselves or the noumenal. The distinction between phenomenal and noumenal is maintained by the schematism, or generally Time as the product of the pure productive transcendental imagination.[11] As the form of inner sense, Time is the form of the phenomenal world, which is consequently temporal, as the noumenal world is not. Furthermore, since Time is the product of the transcendental imagination, it defines a "horizontal" dualism between the transcendental ego and the phenomenal-noumenal, which we may call the "vertical" dualism. In other words, as a function of the transcendental ego, the transcendental imagination is obviously not itself *in* Time.

Restricting our attention to these three Kantian dimensions, may we not say that the openness of the phenomenal is different from the openness of the transcendental, and that both in turn differ from the closure of the noumenal, which reveals itself, so to speak, only in the domain of practice? And as is the case with Plato's demiurge, if we look to God for the ultimate principle of unification of the three dimensions, a problem arises. God cannot properly be said to have "created" the transcendental ego, which Kant thought of as a logical condition binding even God in the creation of an intelligence conforming to sensible extension. So far as such an intelligence is concerned, its own activity is the ground for every instance of combination or unity in its objects.[12] I can only suggest here that unity in the world of human thought seems finally to emerge from the production of Time by the transcendental ego; and this, of course, is Heidegger's own conclusion in his first Kant book.[13] Since the same cannot be said of the transcendental ego or of God, the result is as follows: the openness of the eternal is not the same as the openness of the temporal. Differently stated, the eternal is atemporally "present" as the ground of temporal presence or of temporality altogether. But the manner of "atemporal presence" is not the same in Kant as it is in Plato.

God is something more than the Platonic demiurge. Nor can the transcendental ego be equated with the Ideas. If we restate the three dimensions in Kant as God, transcendental ego, and the activity of the human mind in its spatio-temporal form or bond, we may say that in each case the principle of unity is a kind of mind or thinking, whatever the difficulties which arise in attempting to unify, or even harmonize, the three different kinds. Kant, despite his concern for morality or practice, is on the way toward identifying Being and Mind: even morality is grounded in the autonomy of thinking mind. And thanks to the root function of the transcendental imagination, he is on the way toward making Time the horizon within which Being, even atemporal or eternal Being, "occurs."

To return to Plato and Heidegger, they differ radically in this respect: for Plato, Time is not the horizon of openness within which Being lights up beings (and thereby reveals itself as concealed). Instead, Being is the horizon of openness within which Time occurs as the intermittently illuminated twilight of man's existence. Second, openness in Plato is only partly mental: *ta eidē* are not the same as *ta noēmata*. However, Heidegger's formulation of the correlation between Being and man, or his "phenomenology," is unmistakably Kantian in its development of thinking, and so of Time, as the structure common to both. Heidegger differs from Kant in that, even in his later works, he attempts to eliminate every trace of the transcendent from his phenomenology or *hermeneutic* of the world. For Heidegger, to name "man" is to name residence in the fourfold unity of heaven, earth, divine and mortal, and with things.[14] Thus the heavenly or divine is immanent in man's worldly life, very much as in Greek thought; it does not refer to the transcendent Christian God, as He is in Himself apart from His revelation to man. At the same time, the complete immanence of human existence provides a link between Heidegger and Christianity. Since the world is bounded by temporality, and Being emanates from a hidden source, it is possible for the Christian reader to find in Heidegger both the contingency of human existence and the *Deus absconditus* of his own faith.[15]

Let me recapitulate what has been said thus far. The most general way to state the error of Heidegger's interpretation of Plato is by observing that Plato recognizes the difference between Being and beings, between the light and what is uncovered or illuminated. For this reason, Plato sought to avoid a speech which would temporalize, objectify, or rationalize Being itself.[16] The openness of Being, as prior to distinctions of beings, particular speeches, kinds of measuring, and the subject-object relationship, is the unstated luminosity within which the dialogues are themselves visible. The dialogues become intelligible only when we perceive this unstated luminosity, which is directly present as the *silence* of Plato. The spoken voice of the dialogues occurs always within the cave (if not always in the language of the cave). We may emerge from this cave at any instant that we hear the silent accompanying voice of Plato. In my opinion, Heidegger goes wrong because he is not sufficiently attentive to the silence of Plato. Still more specifically, he never confronts the significance of Socratic irony or the dramatic form of the dialogues.

Heidegger is resolved in the face of *Angst*, but never playful. I suggest that this may account for the surprisingly conventional character of Heidegger's unorthodoxy in the interpretation of Plato. It is true that Heidegger inverts the conventional or obvious interpretation of the Platonic Ideas by rendering them in a Kantian perspective. But an inversion of orthodoxy, as Heidegger himself has reminded us in the case of Sartre, is still grounded in convention. In Heidegger's treatment, the Platonic Idea becomes more radically an epistemological concept than in the work of the most ordinary of analysts. Like the most professorial of philologians, Heidegger normally ignores the dialectical context of those sentences, which he abstracts for analysis, as though they were independent, technical propositions instead of the speech of irony. His procedure in this vein is also reminiscent of the way in which Rudolph Carnap casts positive scorn on one of Heidegger's negative utterances. Even when Heidegger seems to be aware of the dramatic context, as in *Platons Lehre von der Wahrheit*, he refers only to those aspects of it which seem to serve his purpose. He ignores the details even when insisting upon an individual nuance. In proceeding abruptly to the voice of Being, Heidegger does not do justice to the Platonic view that it can be recorded only via the infinitely subtle echoes in Becoming.

Heidegger's account of Plato turns upon his interpretation of the Ideas as a distortion of beings by the rational or categorizing function of mind, and so as the decisive step in the veiling over of Being. As he states it, in the original and authentic Greek teaching, Being is understood as the presence of visibility, in the dual sense of "sprouting" or "opening forth" (*physis*) and "gathering together" or "collecting" (*logos*).[17] The appearance or presentation of beings within the openness (*Lichtung*) of Being, is a process, happening, or eventuation whereby Being both diversifies itself by spilling out from an unknown and silent source, and also collects or gathers itself together in the common bonds of sight and hear-ing.[18] But the happenings or events of this process (beings) draw our attention away from the process itself (Being); we are tempted into the description of beings in their heterogeneity and specificity, into the technical activity of sorting and measuring in accordance with kinds. Being is then conceived as a general property of beings, instead of as their ground or source. We consequently fail to observe the difference between Being and beings. Being is not thought in its own terms but as an abstraction or derivative from beings.[19]

Plato renders Being invisible by sundering *logos* from *physis* and thereby creating the two realms of the super-sensible and the phenomenal.[20] Whereas previously "truth" or "uncoveredness" was the same as "Being" or the process of sprouting forth and gathering together in the openness of presence, it is now conceived as a property of statements *about* beings. "Truth" is now defined as "correctness" in the sense of similarity or correspondence be-tween propositional speech and the separate Ideas.[21] Man is thus sundered from lived intimacy and integrity with Being. Truth is no longer an activity of manifestation or uncovering in which man participates and by which he is "in touch with" what presents itself.[22] Wisdom no longer retains its authentic meaning of "know-ing one's way about in that which is present as the uncovered and which is the continuous as that which appears."[23] Philosophy is no longer life, but a preparation for dying; or more accurately, it is the death of *physis* through the instrumentality of the sundered and so altered *logos*.

The Platonic murder of *physis* is perpetrated in the name of the Ideas. In his concern with the visibility of beings, Plato mis-took their "look" or "face," how they seem to man, for what they genuinely present themselves to be.[24] According to Heidegger, the Ideas are "appearances" in the sense of subjective projections rather than the presentation of presence as it is allowed to be by a think-ing which is not wilful but marked by *Gelassenheit*.[25] This is the nerve of Heidegger's conventional orthodoxy: he completes a line of argument which goes back through Nietzsche, Marx, Hegel, even Kant, to the beginnings of the modern era. What we may call the "historical individual" (an individual bud or sprout of *physis*) first points itself out as a that (*to hoti*). This is the facticity, as well as the finitude and temporality of beings, which emerge from the aperture of openness in the bonds of Time: mittence is intermittent. Plato covers over the *that* by transforming it into a *what* (*ti esti*).[26] The facticity of *Dasein* is replaced by the Idea of man, or the groundless playing of Being is replaced by the technical principle of the ground.[27]

The idea or picture by which Plato designates the *what* is in fact a photograph, a categorial re-presentation that hangs over and so renders invisible, the *that*.[28] I suggest that the Heideggerean "that" has its own proximate historical origins in Kant's *Ding-an-sich*, and so in the *Empfindungen* as prior to synthesis by the transcendental imagination.[29] The deepest concern of Heidegger's thought is to bypass the machinery of the transcendental ego, in order to stand before the pre-synthetic *Empfindung* or individual moment of the temporality of Being.[30] There are two implications associated with this concern. First, Heidegger accepts the Kantian conception of reason as ordering, synthesizing, projective or positing structure, even while condemning these activities as the obscuration of Being.[31] From this perspective, the Platonic Idea is a primitive version of the principle of modern epistemology. The Idea is the first product of the will to power, or the will to will, whereby man makes use of the buds of Being while himself attempting to replace the plant. In addition to this, the unique historical individual, the *that* of beings apart from the subjective *what*, is analogous to a moment of time conceived as existing independently of the formal properties by which a moment is designated: as the "pure stuff" of Time, something in itself, but not deriving its self from categories which express mental unifications imposed from outside the moment.

II

In the first part of this paper, I began with a general comparison between Plato and Heidegger (formulated in terms of the image of the cave and the sun), gave the example of Kant as an intermediate position between them, and then summarized the particulars of Heidegger's treatment of Plato throughout his writings. In this part, I shall try to combine generality and particularity by taking up certain pervasive features of Heidegger's interpretation of Plato. As I have already indicated, the issue which is common to these features is the problem of openness: that is, the relation between Being and Time, as it emerges from a consideration of thinking, speaking, and doing. Once again, my account is in no sense intended as complete; I hope merely to sketch out the broad picture of what is involved in a genuine comparison of Plato and Heidegger.

According to the Platonic dialogues as they have always been understood, the presence of visibility or intelligibility is the timeless presence of Ideas as ungenerated, unchanging, neither spatial nor temporal, both general and particular, somehow accessible as both *that* and *what*, or in the visibility of the instance (the temporal shadow of the instant) as both same and other. In addition, the dialogues say nothing of a noetic structure which constructs or projects formal unity from or by operations upon a previously indeterminate manifold. Instead, *Nous* "sees" or "grasps" the manifold *as* formally determined or differentiated. Noetic vision as described in the dialogues is in fact the "letting be" of beings as they present themselves within the light of the good.[32] I am tempted to say that it is Plato rather than Heidegger who genuinely counsels *Gelassenheit* in the presence of Being. For Plato, the noetic "activity" is a *pathos* in the sense of self-surrender to the presence of the visible, an *absenting* in this presence of the self-ish projections of *dianoia* or (in Heidegger's sense) *ratio*. It is discursive reason (*dianoia*) which performs the temporal activity of gathering or weaving together in *logoi* what has been remembered of the instantaneous (*to eksaiphnēs*), trans-temporal, and in that sense ecstatic vision of the Ideas.[33] The *logos* of *dianoia*, or human speech, is self-ish, or what man brings to the self-less vision of *noēsis*. *Dianoia* is the *Bewegung* which speaks or categorizes, and so obscures as it re-presents, the stillness of *noēsis*. One of the most difficult problems in Plato is whether this "stillness" is also a "silence," and in what sense one can say what one has seen in the ecstatic instant.[34] Here Plato comes very close to Heidegger's view that "language speaks as the ringing of silence.[35] Perhaps the difference is this: for Heidegger "thinking is a hearing that sees,"[36] whereas for Plato it is a seeing that hears.

If I may speculate further in this vein, vision seems more appropriate than hearing to instantaneous occurrence. Hearing "takes time" just as does dianoetic thinking. Whether we hear words or the ringing of silence, there is a sequence constituting the message with an internal structure that is temporal rather than spatial. Within this metaphor there can be an instantaneous look which we then translate into speech by means of temporality. In hearing there is a gathering-together of one word after another, or a movement of thought that may be "measured" by the "before" and "after" of the words. In seeing, the before and after of the spatial elements of the vision may be simultaneous, as in the *Gestalt* of a single glance. As I understand Heidegger, noetic vision is for him a looking-around-at or circumscribing of what has been gathered together in hearing. For Plato, on the other hand, it is hearing which moves or *follows after* the visible in the dimension of recollection. Speech then arises from the erotic striving after the completeness of the Ideas. We remember temporally, and so selfishly, the vision of completeness in the ecstasy of the instant. The transcendence of Time is thus for Plato immanent in the sense of *interstitial*: instantaneous vision occurs in the interstices between the moments of Time, and serves to hold these moments together as the visible world.[37] The wholeness of what is held together can be spoken only in *myth*, or with respect to the paradigmatic function of vision, the attempt to speak in spatial and visual terms.[38] Since it takes time to see as well as to speak in the spatiotemporal world, there can be no complete vision or speech within that world.

Human speech is for Plato a "moving image of eternity."[39] Consequently, man is not needed "to guard or watch over (*hüten*) the unhiddenness of every essence (*Wesen*) on this earth," as Heidegger puts it.[40] Watching is not watching over; we must distinguish between the presence of Being and its appearance to man. In other words, Plato is not a phenomenologist; the distinction between Ideas and *ta phainomena* corresponds to that between two kinds of visibility. Man is peculiar in his ability to move *between* these two domains, but his movement is not an integral component of the mode of visibility of the Ideas.[41] For Heidegger, however, there is no Being without man.[42] One might express the difference between the two thinkers by saying that the movement of intermediacy, or *doksa*, in Plato is not the *Geschehnis*, or *Geschick*, of *Geschichte*. It is not the voice of Being, but the voice of man. Although Heidegger frequently emphasizes that Being occurs independently of man's acts, choices, or will,[43] this occurrence is *as such* to and for man and consequently is described in formal or structural terms which derive their meaning from the role of man as participant. As the teacher says in a difficult to translate but important passage in *Gelassenheit*:

> Human nature is released to that-which-regions and used by it accordingly for this reason alone—because man has no power over the truth, and this remains independent of him. The truth can abide independently of man only because human nature as releasement to that-which-regions is used by it in regioning-to-man (*Vergegnis*) and for the preservation of the conditioning process of things (*Bedingnis*: i.e., the process by which things become visible in the region). The inde-

pendence of truth *from* man is evidently a relation *to* human nature, which relation rests on the regioning (*Vergegnis*) of human nature in that-which-regions.[44]

To comment on this passage: openness occurs, or *is* open, as open to or *around* man, and man himself is a region *of* that openness: namely, the region within which openness shows itself. Man does not make or will openness, nor the truth that shows itself in openness, but he is needed *in order that there be a show*. Openness in Heidegger is therefore equivalent to man's "visual" field, in the language of sight. In Plato, on the contrary, the openness of man's visual field is into an openness that transcends what man can see.[45] Since both Plato and Heidegger are men rather than gods, they can only speak the language of men, and say what men can see. But for Heidegger, man's speech brings *das Seiende* into openness.[46] The structure of openness can be appropriately described in terms of openness-to-man, however difficult the task of forging an adequate terminology. What looks like the anthropomorphic dimension in Heidegger's language is then not myth but the speech of Being. Differently stated: both Plato and Heidegger might agree that openness to man is only the visible "side" of the horizon or Being. For Heidegger, however, nothing can be said about openness-away-from-man, beyond referring to it as the source or origin of the occurrence of the Being-process. Being emanates *unto* man out of an invisible "opening." *But it is Being which so emanates*; in speaking of the phenomenological unity between man and openness-to-man, we are speaking of Being. Our speech *is* the speech of Being: i.e., Being speaks.

In the language of *Sein und Zeit*, man is radically in-the-world: that is, in *this* world, the *Lebenswelt* of *doksa*, and so of temporality, which functions as boundary in the double sense of delimiting and defining. For Plato, on the other hand, openness-to-man as a being-in-this-world is like the opening into a cave, an openness of flickering shadows rather than of the lighting-up process of Being, but one in which by a divine fate or madness we are enabled to discern the visibility of Being as open away from man. The discernment of Being in this world enables man to exist ek-statically in *another* "world."[47] The opening *into* the cave is the horizon of our vision, but as such it is also visible as an opening *out* of the cave. This vision or recognition, that there can be no cave except as enclosed by an external horizon, is the first step in the upward motion away from human openness.[48] Even as a resident of the cave-world of *doksa*, man may intermittently leave or transcend that world for "another place." But the step up is also a step down, namely, by the light from the external horizon which illuminates and in turn, identifies, the opening of the cave.

To terminate this line of speculation, we see that when Heidegger makes man the shepherd of Being, he suppresses the fact that shepherds are ultimately the agents of butchers and woolmerchants. As a recent interpreter, Father G. S. Seidel, puts it:

> But since being gives itself ('*es gibt*') to *Dasein*, it is man that comes to determine the course which being is to have in history. It is *Dasein* that comes to determine the fate not only of mankind in this regard, but even of being itself, since it is *Dasein* that first brings being along a way that is in the open (*Weg des Entbergens*).[49]

In other words, if "letting-be" is also a "grasping" or "taking in" analogous to the gathering up of the harvest, man's activity, as distinct from the *pathos* of *theōria*, does not merely tend to or watch, but *imprints*.[50] Man plays a part in forming both the shape and significance of the crop, which *is* a crop only thanks to man. The ambiguity to which I refer is clearly if unintentionally revealed in the following passage from Father Richardson's highly sympathetic account of Heidegger. He says that the function of *Dasein*

> is to gather into concentration the overwhelming power of Being and thus contain (*noēin*) its dynamic advance in such a way as to force it into the disclosure through which the non-concealment (truth) of beings comes-to-pass . . . in forcing Being into disclosure, There-being must let-be (manifest) the negativity as well . . . .[51]

Perhaps it is true that Heidegger, as he and his disciples claim, has escaped the relativism implicit in the subject-object relation.[52] So far as I can see, there is still a strong component of what must be called "anthropomorphism" in his portrait of Being. And the reason for this is the immanence or this-worldliness of openness as radically inseparable from the openness of man *to* Being. To the immanence of openness *qua* thinking there corresponds an immanence of openness *qua* speaking. At the same time, Heidegger's lack of sympathy for the Platonic mode of speech leads him to accuse it of what amounts to subjectivism, in however preliminary a form. In so doing, Heidegger replaces the playfulness of Platonic dialectic by the utter seriousness of history. Thus for Heidegger, the nature of Being varies at different times because of its dependence as visibility upon how it looks to the great thinkers of a given epoch,[53] whereas for Plato visibility endures in and as itself at all times, regardless of how it is seen by anyone. The fundamental "timelessness" of the Platonic dialectic is a denial of the philosophical relevance of history in any but its literal sense of "inquiry." I playfully suggest that Heidegger's doctrine of radical historicity is in part the consequence of an excessive seriousness or "realism" which prevents him from appreciating the playfulness of Plato's "idealistic" dialectic. The very few instances of Heidegger's irony that I have observed are bitter rather than playful. In general, Heidegger makes no jokes: his is a *spiel-los Sprache von der Spiel des Seins.*[54]

Heidegger's seriousness was evident from the popular sections of *Sein und Zeit,* in which he analyzes the "fallen" condition of human existence in unmistakably Christian tones.[55] One has only to contrast his *Daseinsanalytik* with the equivalent surface-stratum of the Platonic dialogues, with their "pagan" portrait of daily life, to see the difference between a timely and timeless account of time. Just as melodramatic essays on the philosophical significance of play are no substitute for the dramas of a playful psyche, so one cannot understand irony by translating it into the *List der Vernunft* or the speech of Being. It is not Being, but man, who is ironical. According to Heidegger, western philosophy since the time of Plato may be called *dialectic.*[56] But Heidegger interprets "dialectic" as *katēgorein* or "addressing something as something," which is in turn a "thinking through and discussing of the *genē tou ontos*"; i.e., "dialectic" is for Heidegger exclusively the *technē* of division and collection in accordance with kinds. "Dialectic," as Heidegger understands it, is essentially *Logic,* as he indicates in reference to Hegel.[57] Heidegger ignores the playful or ironical dialectic of man: specifically human speech is almost at once replaced by specifically divine speech, by "metaphysics" or "onto-theo-logy" (and then, in turn, by the utterance of Being). Therefore he seems to be quite deaf to the possibility that there is a note of irony in the dialogical speeches about the techniques of division and collection. Despite his "unusual" etymologizing, Heidegger's interpretation of Platonic dialectic is, in its own way, as inadequate as that of orthodox classicists. Heidegger "epistemologizes" Plato.

Although Heidegger says next to nothing about "dialectic," he is quite loquacious on the subject of *logos.*[58] By considering very briefly his treatment of *logos,* we are able to see the Heideggerean replacement for human dialectic: namely, what I am tempted to call with very little irony "the silence of agriculture." The simplest translation for the Greek word *dialektikē* is "conversation." We might also say "through" or "by means of speech," thereby indicating the sense of an activity or directed motion. The verb *legō*, as Heidegger has continually emphasized, means "to pick up," "to gather," or "to choose," as well as "to say." Thus "dialogue" or "dialectic" might be defined by "collection," as well as by "conversation." Dialectic, in a Heideggerean mode, would then be a turning-toward, and hence an attending-to, which is also a living-with what has been gathered together. In an essay on *logos* Heidegger gives as its original and authentic meaning "the collecting, laying-down and laying before of what collectively presents itself."[59] Thus speech is derived from the activities of selecting and collecting, and still more fundamentally, from the simplest acts of human life, such as gathering the harvest or selecting the best grapes for wine-making. That which has been collected lies before us and so displays itself or appears, in a *rest* which is consequently a derivative—and a temporary derivative of the *motion* of collection.

There are a number of observations to be made with respect to this interpretation of *logos*. To begin with, it makes the silence of doing into the ground or paradigm of the speech of thinking.[60] Instead of human dialectic, we begin with pre-philosophical silence. No mention is made of the fact that this silence is already defined by speech. But apart from this, the kind of silence which functions as paradigmatic is especially instructive. So far as I am aware, the Greeks made love at least as frequently as they made wine. And yet, if I am not mistaken, Heidegger never mentions the sexual meanings of such related words as *synousia* or *dialegō* when he etymologizes upon the existential senses of Greek words for "being" and "speaking." Why is agriculture ontologically superior to Eros? Is that superiority ontically evident? Not to me.[61] I should also say here that the act of gathering in the harvest relates man silently to the mute plants, whereas Eros normally relates human to human in a situation in which speech is a natural component. Performatory utterances are proper between lovers ("with this ring I do thee wed") but not between man and the grape ("with this press I do thee crush"). It is true that the power of the grape may move us to an ode to Bacchus, but Heidegger is not concerned with this "humanization" of viniculture in his etymologizing. Man brings speech to the soil, whereas speech emerges from *within* Eros.

By returning to the "founding," or *geschichtliche*, senses of technical philosophical terms in archaic ordinary speech, Heidegger gives the impression of moving back from the rationalizations of metaphysics to authentic thinking and hence to the origins of thinking in its initial harmony with Being, prior to the disjunction between *noein* and *einai*, or the sundering of *logos* from *physis*. But everything depends upon the kind of motion by which we are returned to the origin, and so to the relation between motion and rest *within* the origin. Throughout his writings and in a variety of ways Heidegger treats rest as a "tarrying in" or derivative of motion.[62] And motion in the ontological sense (e.g., in his analysis of the worldliness of *Dasein*) is always understood to be primarily temporal rather than spatial.[63] His interpretation of *Anwesenheit, parousia* and the like as "presence" in a sense derived from the verb-tense or temporal present is thus essentially related to his etymology of *logos* as a "gathering together." The unity of thought (*noein*) and speech (*legein*) conceived as the "taking up," "preserving," or "taking care of" what has been "gathered" or "stored up" is grounded in the conception of *physis* as growth, and so as birth and death: it is grounded in temporality and in temporality conceived in terms of human activity. This latter point is perhaps more evident in *Sein und Zeit* than in the later works, since in the former, *Zeitlichkeit* is grounded in the "*Da*" of *Da-sein*, or the worldliness of the world as a referential structure of human significances.[64] But it remains true in the later works, even though *Zeitlichkeit* seems to be replaced by *Geschichtlichkeit* as the *Geschick des Seins*. In each case, by conceiving of Being within the horizon of Time, Heidegger never takes seriously the possibility that the temporal present is itself a derivative of the trans-temporal presence of visibility.[65]

The discussion of thinking and speaking has taken place in terms of a contrast between dialectical and (radically) historical speech; that is, with respect to the difference between Plato and Heidegger concerning speech as uncovering or opening, and hence as regards its temporality. The whole discussion serves as an anticipation of the third term which, as I mentioned at the beginning of this part of my paper, is relevant to an account of the problem of openness: *doing*. The role or meaning of human doing is implicit throughout any adequate analysis of Heidegger's conceptions of thinking and speaking. The question of that role emerged explicitly in my discussion of the difference between Platonic *Eros* and Heideggerean *Sorge*: for Heidegger; Being needs man (even if only occasionally[66]), whereas for Plato, it is only the case that man needs Being. Allow me to restate this question: to what extent does man as agent share in the process by which Being occurs or presents itself? The answer to this question also determines our attitude toward history, that is, to the question whether there is such a thing as *historicity*. In other words, the whole issue of historicity is subordinate to the problem of whether or in what sense "opening" is a human "doing." I shall sketch the difference between Plato and Heidegger on these problems by returning to the question of the relation between openness and Time.

Even if *physis* in the sense of *eidos* should be historically posterior to *physis* in the sense of growth, there is no reason to assume an inverse identity between the order of history and that of authentic thought or the uncovering of truth. If there were, then we should have to agree with Pindar that "water is best" and become disciples of Thales, the original instrument of the *Seinsgeschick* that has determined western *Geschichte* (and whom Heidegger never to my knowledge discusses[67]). Here as elsewhere we may note the cryptic influence of Hegel on Heidegger's teaching.[68] Of course, like Hegel, Heidegger does not mean to suggest that Being is temporal in the way of beings.[69] For both, the structure of Time is meant to escape the transience of its moments. In *Sein und Zeit*, the non-transient nature of the structure of Time was evident in the form of the existentials of *Dasein* (the immanent counterpart to the structures of the transcendental ego of Kant). In one of the latest works of Heidegger with which I am familiar, the same point is expressed in a more fundamental manner. In an unpublished lecture from 1962 entitled *Zeit und Sein*, Heidegger speaks of *Zeitraum*, or the structure of Time itself, rather than of the structure of the temporality of *Dasein*. The situation now seems to be as follows: in order for Being to be characterized by "there" (and so of course by "here"), or by ecstatic location, directedness or intentionally structured openness must be established. Previously, this openness was grounded in *Dasein*.[70] But now Heidegger resituates this "ground" in the source or origin of the Being-process: "*Zeitraum* names the openness that clears (*lichtet*) itself in the joint self-sufficiency of future, past, and present."[71] Being as *Anwesenheit* or Presence occurs as a giveness within this clearing. It now looks as though Heidegger distinguishes between *Sein* and *Dasein*, but as we shall see, the look is deceptive.

I have just used the phrase "occurs as a givenness"; Heidegger says "*Es gibt Sein*" and "*Es gibt Zeit*." The "*Es*" is to be defined out of "*geben*" (like the "that which" in *Gegnet*), or the sending of Being within the clearing of Time, and thereby as what defines Being and Time in their togetherness (*zusammengehören*): as

Ereignis, which normally means "event" or "occurrence." In this key term, there is already a suggestion of the ambiguous relation between Being and man in the "late" Heidegger. As is often the case, Heidegger employs a word which normally carries a temporal, historical, or even human meaning, but in what he insists is a special or extra-ordinary sense. Thus, although we are told that *Ereignis* is a unique term, which in its special sense can no more be adequately translated than *logos* or Tao, Heidegger explicates its significance by speaking of both *Eigenen* and *eignen*: one's own or proper possession (somewhat reminiscent of the definition of *Dasein* as "my own Being"[72]), together with the notion of suitability or fitness.[73] Or again: "In the sending of the *Geschick* of Being, in the sufficiency of Time, a dedication, a transferring points itself out, namely of Being as Presence and Time as Reach (scope, range) in *Ereignis*."[74] *Geschick* normally means "fate," but Heidegger employs it in the sense of "order": namely, the order whereby Being consoles man by clearing itself, or filling up the *Zeit-Spiel-Raum*,[75] i.e. as the "over against each other" of Being and man.[76]

If we try to combine these representative passages from the later Heidegger, the result, as I understand it, is this: openness is implicitly and intentionally structured in a way which reveals itself to man as Time.[77] Being presents itself within this openness, and its presence is thus radically temporal. In speaking of "presenting," "giving," "sending," "consoling," "appropriate," and indeed of "past, present, future," we acknowledge the inseparability of the unity "openness-presence-within-openness" from man (or *Dasein*). As Heidegger says in his preface to the Richardson volume:

> if we replace 'Time' by: the lighting of the self-hiding of *Anwesen* (presence as holding itself together and before), then Being defines itself out of the projective scope of Time. But this results only in so far as the lighting of self-hiding puts to its use a thinking that corresponds to it. *Anwesen* (Being) belongs to the lighting of self-hiding (Time). Lighting of self-hiding (Time) produces *Anwesen* (Being).[78]

That is: Being belongs to Time as that which hides itself within it: as hiding, it appears (i.e., presents itself) as the structural process of temporality.

This "appearance" is not an illusion, but now Being presents itself to (human) thought. Man can never cease to think temporally, any more than he could cease (while still a man) to see beings.

Being can only be "seen" as the masked self-presentation, masked by beings in temporally directed order (*Geschick*). This temporally directed order, the unity of Being and Time with respect to openness, visibility, and presence, i.e. with respect to thought, and so to man (who also stands in the lighting of Being), is *Ereignis*: the *logos* or Tao of Heidegger's teaching.[79] It is the rest of the total assemblage of motion, and thus is reminiscent of the transcendental *Bewegung* of Hegel's Absolute. Thus we read in *Gelassenheit*, apropos of the occasion for releasement:

Scholar: But that means, such an occasion brings us to the path which seems to be nothing else than releasement itself . . .

Teacher: . . . which is something like rest.

Scholar: From here on it is suddenly clearer to me the extent to which movement (*Bewegung*) comes out of rest and stays within rest.

Teacher: Releasement would then be not only the path, but the movement (along it).

Scholar: Where does this strange path go, and where does the movement along it rest?

Teacher: Where else but in that-which-regions, to which releasement is what it is?[80]

In other words, the "resting" or "abiding" of man, things, and region, or of openness altogether in its regionality, is also a "tarrying" or motion which Heidegger again expresses in his later writing as *das Geviert*: the fourfold assemblage of man and gods, heaven and earth, whose reciprocal excitation defines the structure of "the thing."[81]

Thus I agree with the following remark by Father Richardson in the conclusion to his long and useful study:

Heidegger's perspective from beginning to end remains phenomenological. By this we mean that he is concerned only with the *process* by which beings are lit up and reveal themselves as what they are for and to man.[82]

Such a process necessarily requires as an integral element the doing or acting of man. As I previously suggested, the inseparability of mind or thought from Being or beings is evident in the attribution of "future, past, present" to the play of *Zeitraum*. This directional structure, whatever it may be "in itself," is described from the outset in terms of thought which finds its way about in the clearing of temporality. What I am urging is this: there is no such thing as "future, past, present," and certainly no significance to that order of the tenses, *except to Dasein* or its equivalent. The structure of Being, Time, *Geschick, Ereignis*, or what you will, is *from the outset* expressed in terms of the structure of human time. *Ereignis* (to use this word as a summary of the rest) is *how Being looks to man*: the face of Being, or exactly what Heidegger says about the Platonic Idea. Nor is this consequence altered by the fact that the "look" is not conceived in terms of the subject-object relation but in terms of the horizon of that relation.[83]

There is of course this radical difference between *Ereignis* and the Platonic Idea. *Ereignis* "occurs" within the horizon of Time, whereas the Idea does not "occur" or is not itself an instance of temporal structure, even though visible or present *through* time. Furthermore, at least so far as the exclusively phenomenological domain of Heidegger is concerned, openness in the triple sense of "clearing" or "light," "viewer," and "the viewed" is temporally, and so humanly, understood: not perhaps in a subjectivistic or relativistic sense, but certainly in a way deeply akin to that of Kant's transcendental ego. For Plato, as I have already pointed out, this is not the case. The three domains of man, light, and Ideas are distinct if related.[84] Heidegger seems to present us with a more coherent or unified portrait of Being than does Plato; on the other hand, this unity is subject to continuous dissolution because its binding structures are defined or articulated in terms of human time. That is, Heidegger's doctrine of Time is inadequate because immanent time serves as the paradigm for transcendental Time. In fact, as is especially clear in *Sein und Zeit*, Heidegger used "transcendence" and "ekstasis" in a specifically *immanent* or intra-temporal sense. There is literally *nothing* to hold open the "clearing" which provides the theater for the various activities of Being, activities inseparable from human doing.

Heidegger's "clearing" is defined or held open by the directionality internal to the illumination of self-concealment. But this directionality can hold itself together only by structural referentiality which directs temporal flow without itself consisting of that flow. Differently put, the openness of a horizon is not the same as the transformation or sequence of illuminations thanks to which we can see *in* that openness. In quasi-Platonic language, the configuration of the sequence defines a form or *Idéa* which is not equivalent to the flow of the members of the sequence.[85] Whereas in the Heideggerean teaching, the unity of *Ereignis* leads finally to the identity of light, viewer, and viewed without being able to account for their differentiation, in the Platonic teaching, the difference of the three is the starting-point. Whether or not Plato can account for the harmony of the three in one cosmos, his teaching seems to me more accurate to the very phenomenological situation which Heidegger is ostensibly explaining. As I understand Heidegger, there is nothing anywhere in his account which allows for the phenomenological presentation of the eternal or transtemporal; such a possibility is ruled out from the very beginning, ostensibly in obedience to the "facticity" of human existence. But the whole question concerns the nature of that facticity. Heidegger ultimately reduces all phenomena to a process of illuminations, which is at least reminiscent of the reduction of the cosmos to atoms moving in the void, but which he paradoxically describes in anthropomorphic terms. Plato comes closer to saving the phenomena.

To conclude this section of my paper: for Heidegger, the intentional, directed, and so directing or illuminating structure of Time, derived from the phenomenon of visibility-to-man, provides the "space" within which Being occurs as the fourfold or reciprocally defining *Bewegungen* of heaven and earth, men and gods. The simplest way to contrast the Platonic teaching is by summarizing the defects which it would ascribe to Heidegger's account of Time: (1) the ontological account of Time is actually an articulation of the "ontic" facticity of *Dasein's* temporal existence as intentionally directed within the tridimensional unity of past, present, and future. But *to on* is *in advance* regarded as *to phainomenon*. Although Heidegger interprets *to phainomenon* as "presence" of Being itself rather than "appearance" or "illusion," "presence" is "presence-to-man" as the abiding or tarrying of temporality. Heidegger's "phenomenology" is no longer concerned with "essences" but with "facts" in the sense of "occurrences." (2) Even as an account of how Time looks to man, this phenomenology is defective, since it rules out the possibility of the presence of the eternal or genuinely transtemporal within the very structure of *to phainomenon*. One of the most important results of this procedure is to blur, if not to suppress altogether, the difference between man and Being. (3) More specifically, Time cannot supply from within itself the structure of its own Being. That is, Heidegger fails to explain how Time holds itself together within each of its moments, let alone as the opening or clearing within which Being occurs, since that opening is itself an occurrence. (4) Heidegger singles out Time as more fundamental than Space, but this assumption seems to hold only if we accept as fundamental the temporality of man's existence. In fact, Heidegger cannot speak of Time except through Spatial terms: the least one could say is that both dimensions seem to be equally necessary in an account of human existence. And the necessity of space (i.e., of *human* space) is a clue to an inadequacy in Heidegger's otherwise excellent discussion of openness as the horizon of noetic vision. (5) Finally, it is hard to see how Heidegger, despite his distinction between *Geschichte* and *Historie*, makes it possible for man to take a responsible stand toward history. One must seriously question the adequacy of the resolute acceptance of tradition—i.e., what happens—as a criterion for human conduct. An ontology which cannot assist man in his struggle to preserve himself from his own actions runs the risk of Nihilism, which I regard as the consequence of the claustrophobia of complete immanentism masquerading as freedom.[86] But the problem of Nihilism will be reserved for the next part of this paper.

NOTES

* This paper was delivered in a lecture to the graduate philosophy club at Yale University on January 13, 1966, and was also read to the philosophy department at C. W. Post College on May 11, 1966. It is a preliminary study for my recent book: *Nihilism* (New Haven, 1969). I wish to acknowledge the contribution made to this paper by my colleague, Richard Gotshalk, in the form of many conversations over the past several years, which helped to clarify for me my own thoughts as well as the meaning of Heidegger's writings. I am also indebted to the editors of *The Journal of Existentialism* for permission to reprint this article, which appeared in the Summer 1967 issue.

1. *Republic* 537c7; *Was ist das—die Philosophie?* (Pfullingen, 1956; henceforward *WPH*), pp. 21ff.

2. *Diels*, Fr. 18.

3. *Republic* 515c6ff.

4. The elaborate program for educating philosophers in the just city depends for its enactment upon the prior existence of philosophers. The way up is not quite the same as the way down, which precedes it.

5. E.g., *Phaedrus* 244a5ff.; cf. *Epistles* VII. 341cff.

6. *Symposium* 203a6: Eros is only one of the daimons.

7. In Plato, the wholeness of human existence is "circular," as prefigured in the myth of the circle-men in Aristophanes' speech in the *Symposium*. I have discussed this elsewhere at some length. Cf. *Sein und Zeit* (Tübingen, 1953, 7th Ed.; henceforth *SZ*), pp. 152–3.

8. Cf. my "The Role of Eros in Plato's *Republic*" (*Review of Metaphysics*; March, 1965).

9. Diels B3; *Vorträge und Aufsaetze* (Pfullingen, 1954; henceforth *VA*), pp. 249ff.

10. Cf. *Was Heisst Denken?* (Tübingen, 1954; henceforth *WHD*), pp. 114–26; 146ff.

11. *Kritik der Reinen Vernunft* B179–80. This also resolves the dualism within *Verstand* between intuition and the categories.

12. *Ibid.*, B130: ". . . we cannot represent to ourselves anything as combined in the object which we have not ourselves previously combined . . ."

13. *Kant und das Problem der Metaphysik* (Frankfurt-am-Main, 1951; henceforth *KPM*), pp. 127ff.

14. *VA*, p. 157.

15. Cf. W. J. Richardson, S.J., *Heidegger* (The Hague, 1963; henceforth *Richardson*), p. 640 and *Identität und Differenz* (Pfullingen, 1957), pp. 70–71.

16. In this connection, one should consider carefully *Phaedrus* 229c4ff.

17. *Einführung in die Metaphysik* (Tübingen, 1953; henceforth *EM*), pp. 11, 131–4, 142; *VA* pp. 269ff. At p. 274, Heidegger says that *physis* means the same as *zōē*: "life" is here defined as "stepping out" or emerging into view. In *EM*, p. 11, however, he states that physis includes as instances the course of the heavens, the waves of the sea, etc. We see here the beginning of his interpretation of Being as the fourfold: heaven and earth, human and divine, which are explicitly mentioned.

18. "Process," "happening," and "eventuation" translate *Bewegung, Geschehen*, and *Ereignis*. For the unknown and unthought character of the "source," cf, *ID*, p. 44; *Nietzsche* (Pfullingen, 1961), Vol. I., p. 471; Vol. II., p. 484; *Unterwegs zur Sprache* (Pfullingen, 1959; henceforth *US*), p. 31. For the common root of sight and hearing, *Der Satz vom Grund* (Pfullingen, 1957; henceforth *SG*), pp. 86ff.

19. *Nietzsche* II, pp. 211, 486.

20. *Ibid.*, pp. 430ff.

21. *EM*, p. 142; *Platons Lehre von der Wahrheit* (Bern, 1954; henceforth *PLW*), pp. 41–2, 49; *Über den "Humanismus"* (Same volume; henceforth *UH*), p. 106.

22. *EM*, pp. 134, 146; *WHD*, pp. 73–4, 122–126; *VA*, pp. 208ff.

23. *PLW*, p. 47.

24. *Vom Wesen des Grundes* (Frankfurt-am-Main, 1955; henceforth *WG*), p. 41; *WPH*, pp. 16, 24–27; *PLW*, pp. 34, 46; *EM*, p. 139.

25. Cf. *PLW*, p. 51 with *Gelassenheit* (Pfullingen, 1959) *passim*; *Nietzsche* II, p. 452.

26. For the discussion of *to hoti* and *ti esti*, cf. especially *Nietzsche* II, pp. 400ff. (Here and elsewhere, e.g., *WG*, p. 41, Heidegger erroneously makes the *idéa* equivalent to *Möglichkeit*.)

27. *SG*, pp. 59, 90, 185ff.

28. *Nietzsche* II, pp. 72ff.

[73]

29. Cf. Gerhard Krüger's brilliant essay, "Über Kants Lehre von der Zeit" in *Anteile: Martin Heidegger zum 60. Geburtstag* (Frankfurt-am-Main, 1950).

30. Such is my understanding of *Gelassenheit*.

31. *Zur Seinfrage* (Frankfurt-am-Main, 1956: henceforth *ZS*), p. 9; *SG*, p. 125; *Kants These über das Sein* (Frankfurt-am-Main, 1963), pp. 9, 12, 16; *Die Frage nach dem Ding* (Tübingen, 1962), pp. 114–15, 171–3, 178, 186. Throughout his writings, Heidegger gives "histories" of thinking as *ratio, percipere, Vorstellung*, etc. as obscurations or "objectifications" of Being; e.g., *Nietzsche II*, pp. 229ff.

32. A good example of this is *Sophist* 248d4ff., where the activity (*poēma*) of knowing is related to the psyche or mind: the changeless objects of knowledge cannot undergo a *pathos*.

33. Cf. *Sophist* 248d10ff., 250cl, 259e5: it is life, *nous* or the dianoetic *logos* which move, not the *megistē genē, to on* and the *symplokē eidōn* (*kinēsis* is here treated as an *eidos* or *genos*). For *to eksaiphnēs*, cf. notes 5 and 37.

34. In this connection, one should consider the various remarks in the dialogues about dreaming and divining; e.g., *Republic* 505el–506a5, 523a8; *Theaetetus* 201d8ff., *et passim*.

35. *US*, p. 30.

36. *SG*, p. 86.

37. The problem of the Instant and the relation between "Being and Time" is treated by Plato in the *Parmenides* 156cff. In discussing the hypothesis that *to hen esti*, i.e., that it *is* or *exists*, and so partakes of time, Parmenides derives the consequence that *to hen* must both move and rest, and that the change from movement to rest, as identical with neither, cannot occur in time, but must occur in *to eksaiphnēs* (the instant): *alla hē eksaiphnēs hautē physis atopos tis enkathētai metaksy tēs kinēseōs* . . . (Cf. Aristotle's doctrine of actualization). If the Instant occurs between any two moments of time (within which there may be either motion or rest, but not a change from one to the other), then either (1) the Instant both *rests* (between mk and mk+1) and *moves* (from or between one pair of moments to another), or else (2) time passes discontinuously through the Instant. That is, the Instant makes time discontinuous; it makes the "rest" of mk and the "movement" from mk to mk+1. As the context shows, the Instant is neither Being nor non-Being (and so, neither is *to hen* when in it); Being and non-Being are co-ordinate, and as such, subordinate to what we may call *Actuality*, for want of a better name (= the Instant). Cf. *SZ* p. 338 (on *der Augenblick*).

38. *Phaedrus* 246c6: there is no *logos* of a deathless thing, and no *noēsis* sufficient to operate independently of imagination. Consider in this connection *SZ*, p. 6, where Heidegger objects to myth that it speaks of *Sein* as a *Seiendes*.

39. *Phaedrus* 247dl: *dianoia* goes round with the moving world, and sees the hyperuranian beings *dia chronou*; cf. *Theaetetus* 206dl, *Philebus* 17b3: speech *flows*. See also *Sophist* 263e3ff.

40. *VA*, p. 40.

41. *Symposium* 202e3ff.

42. Cf. *SZ*, pp. 212ff. and *Der Ursprung des Kunstwerkes* (Stuttgart, 1960; henceforth *UK*), p. 100.

43. E.g., *PLW*, p. 50; *UH*, p. 75.

44. *Gelassenheit*, pp. 65–66. I have modified a translation by John Anderson and Hans Freund, published by Harper and Row.

45. *Phaedrus* 247b6ff.: the surface of the hyperuranian visible is still, whereas *dianoia* moves: this is Plato's "version" of *Gegend*.

46. *UK*, p. 84; cf. *ZS*, p. 28.

47. *Phaedo* 109b4ff.

48. Cf. *Theaetetus* 176bl.

49. *Martin Heidegger and the Pre-Socratics* (Lincoln, Nebraska, 1964), p. 24.

50. Cf. *WHD*, pp. 124–5.

51. *Richardson*, p. 296; cf. *EM*, pp. 131ff.

52. E.g., in "Hegel und die Griechen" (*Die Gegenwart der Griechen im neueren Denken*, Tübingen, 1960), p. 55.

53. E.g., *Nietzsche* II, p. 257; cf. pp. 37, 43–4, 98, 332 and *Nietzsche* I, pp. 173–4; *SG*, pp. 158, 176; *ID*, p. 65. These are only examples of a theme which appears continually throughout Heidegger's work.

54. Consider here *Theaetetus* 145b10ff., where Socrates indicates that mathematicians do not joke. There is something "mathematical" about Heidegger's approach to and account of Being.

55. Cf. Otto Pöggeler, *Heidegger* (Pfullingen, 1963), pp. 35ff. and *US*, p. 96.

56. *Nietzsche* I, p. 529.

57. *Ibid.*, p. 530.

58. Representative discussions may be found in *VA*, pp. 208ff.; *WHD*, pp. 122ff.

59. *VA*, p. 212.

60. Thus, e.g., in *SZ*, theory is regarded as an abstraction from the concrete use of beings as "tools" in daily life. It is true that Heidegger makes *Rede* an existential in *SZ*, but even there, speech is given a primordial interpretation similar to the one in his later writings.

61. In Plato, farming is praised by Eryximachus, the spokesman in the *Symposium* for technicism (186e4ff.); in the *Laws* (889c5ff.), the Athenian Stranger associates farming with materialism. In the *Symposium* speech *replaces* drinking (agriculture-viniculture); in the *Laws*, however, it is pointed out that drinking serves to test man's psyches by making them talk freely (649a4ff.). Heidegger seems to recommend viniculture, but not symposia or drinking.

62. For some representative passages, cf. *Die Frage nach dem Ding*, pp. 33ff.; *Nietzsche* II, pp. 13, 485, 489; *SG*, p. 144; "Vom Wesen und Begriff der Physis Aristoteles Physik BI" in *Il Pensiero* (Part I,

May–August, 1958), p. 138. In *US*, p. 213, Heidegger says: "*Die Zeit selbst in Ganzen ihres Wesens bewegt sich nicht, ruht still.*" But *Ruhe* is for Heidegger self-constraining motion.

63. *SZ*, pp. 367ff.

64. *SZ*, pp. 350ff.

65. Cf. *Timaeus* 37e4ff. and note 33 above.

66. *Nietzsche* II, p. 486.

67. Cf. my essay, "Thales: the Beginning of Philosophy" in *Essays in Philosophy* (University Park, Penna., 1962).

68. Heidegger deals explicitly with the difference between himself and Hegel in *ID*, e.g., p. 43. He is not so explicit about the similarities.

69. *SZ*, pp. 18–19; cf. Pöggeler, *op. cit.*, p. 186.

70. *SZ*, pp. 133, 157ff.

71. The quotations are from a privately circulated copy of this unpublished lecture. Here the reference is to p. 8. For a very similar statement in the published writings, cf. *Unterwegs*, pp. 214–5: "Zeitigend-einräumend be-wëgt das Selbige des Zeit-Spiel-Raumes das Gegen-einander-über der vier Welt-Gegenden: Erde und Himmel, Gott und Mensch—das Weltspiel." The soundless, calling gathering of this Be-wëgung is "die Sprache des Wesens."

72. *SZ*, pp. 41–2.

73. *ID*, pp. 28ff. (Cf. the original sense of *ousia* as "private property.")

74. *Zeit und Sein*, unpublished text, p. 10.

75. *SG*, p. 109, 130.

76. *Ibid.*, p. 158.

77. *UK*, p. 58.

78. *Richardson*, p. xxi.

79. Cf. *Richardson*, pp. 638ff. on the ambiguity of *Ereignis*: it means (1) some third thing other than *einai* and *noein* prior to and unifying both; (2) Being itself as *Geschick*.

80. *Gelassenheit*, pp. 46–7; again I modify somewhat the translation by Anderson and Freund.

81. *VA* ("Das Ding"), pp. 163ff. For Plato, contrast *Phaedo* 90c2ff.

82. *Richardson*, p. 627.

83. Cf. A. de Waelhens, "Reflections on Heidegger's Development" in *International Philosophical Quarterly*: Sept. 1965, p. 490. In speaking of *SZ*, he gives a consequence of its teaching, not stated by Heidegger, and which he says would no longer correspond with the latter's thought: "If the time that is anterior to the World and the time that marks the course of things are but modes derived from the temporality that springs from our Being itself, then we must go one step further and maintain that the Being of beings, that which is time in them, is likewise a mode that has issued from the Being of that being which com-

prehends Being." With the appropriate shifts in terminology and emphasis, however, I suspect that this consequence *does* correspond to the later Heidegger's thought.

84. Cf. *Sophist* 248e6ff., *Timaeus* 34a8ff., *Philebus* 30alff.

85. Cf. the distinction between *Wesen* and *Sein* made by Oscar Becker in "Platonische Idee und ontologische Differenz" (*Dasein und Dawesen*, Pfullingen, 1965), pp. 157ff.

86. See *SZ*, p. 310 for a statement of the resolute, sober, and *angstvoll* acceptance of *this* world in its factic temporality. *Entschlossenheit* makes us *illusions-frei* but therefore excessively sober, in my opinion.

CARL R. HAUSMAN

THE ROLE OF FORM, VALUE, AND NOVELTY IN CREATIVE ACTIVITY *

It is fashionable today to study "the creative process" and to praise creative thought. Yet, to my knowledge, no one has seriously and systematically carried out a study of the meaning of creativity. In the following pages, I should like to begin such a study by suggesting a way of identifying "novelty" or "newness" as a basis for characterizing human creativity. In attempting to accomplish this purpose, I shall suggest several ways in which form, value, and novelty are interwoven within the product of creativity.

In beginning with a description of "novelty," I shall first be concerned with certain generic characteristics of creative acts. However, the final aim of this description concerns not routine acts of making or repetitive achievements, but rather those more dramatic productive processes which are often associated with genius and which are thought of as examples of what we call "originality" or, sometimes, the "genuinely creative." If we want to understand creativity, it seems advantageous to approach it in those instances in which it is most clearly evident. Surely the kind of creativity which has provoked inquiry is found in the more dramatic cases. If these can be understood, perhaps further light can be shed on creative acts of lesser interest. Accordingly, my plan is to begin with a discussion of the general features which mark an object as new. The relation of novelty to the created character of products will be considered after these general qualifications of newness have been identified. In order to accomplish this purpose, it will be necessary to introduce and to examine briefly what is meant by the concept of "form." Against this background, I shall then discuss various qualifications required to identify a process as creative. I shall contend that an act which is creative must, in a special way, be controlled and must issue in a product which is valuable and new with respect to its form. Finally, the suggestion about the requirement of value will be explored briefly as an adumbration of a theory of value in relation to a theory of creativity.

I

Novelty. It will be assumed at the outset that anyone who has considered the issue with which we are concerned acknowledges that some phenomena at least seem to be new. Thus there are occasions when things of which we are conscious, whether they be events, objects, qualities, or categories, appear in certain respects (though not in every respect) to be disconnected or dissociated from what went before them. The question of whether or not appearances of newness are real or only illusory will not be settled here. At this stage of the discussion, it is claimed simply that sometimes things *seem* to us to be different from the past. On such occasions, what occurs appears as irreducible and unprecedented in the light of what was known before it was encountered. It must be emphasized, then, that even if one were to insist that its irreducibility could be proven to be illusory, and even if the phenomenon could later be shown by causal explanation to have been predictable, the question of such a proof and explanation is distinct from the immediate issue at hand. Hence I shall provisionally maintain neutrality with respect to explaining newness. In short, I shall assume at present only what may be thought of as the phenomenological objectivity of the appearance of newness and inquire into its relevance for creative acts.[1]

On the basis of this assumption, we should expect one of the necessary conditions of novelty to be the presence in an object of irreducible and unprecedented difference. However, it is obvious that if novelty were nothing more than the difference between a thing and its antecedents, novelty could be ascribed to every discriminable thing. Each event or object in the world can be considered new with respect to its particularity. For example, no matter how much one penny may be like another of the same stamp, the first can be thought of as a particular object which occupies a different spatial location and, if inspected closely, must vary ever so slightly from the other penny. Similarly, the penny is different from all other things, including its antecedents. It is dissociated from its past and its present precisely to the extent that it is distinguishable from all other particulars. Even appearances of what we call the "same" penny under different spatial and temporal conditions can be distinguished as different particulars in the sense of difference at issue here. In this sense, all things are different, or numerically novel as particulars.[2]

Some things, however, appear to be novel in another, more radical way. The subtleties that mark a particular in its uniqueness may contribute to it qualitatively. Thus, radical novelty appears on those occasions in which there is difference not only of particularity, but also of form. This point may be developed by a consideration of how particulars may manifest qualitative uniqueness. Let us call the complex of qualities—or, more generally, the complex of properties—which appear to compose the particular, "the structure of the particular." Now, I want to suggest that sometimes a certain aspect of the complex of qualities, or the structure by which the particular is characterizable, may appear to be unlike anything known before. Further, what appears as different in this sense may function with the other properties so that the complex is intelligible in a different way than was identifiable before.[3] Thus the complex appears as a structure which is different or new.[4]

At present, what is important to see is that the uniqueness of a particular may exemplify a form different from the form with respect to which the particular had previously been classified as a particular. Thus uniqueness may be constituted in the difference of form or matrix of the particular in question. With respect to the different form, the thing is determined by an intelligible identity not discernible within established knowledge. Novelty of the more radical kind, then, is recognized in instances in which the determinateness of a special order or organization of a thing is new. Let us call this more radical novelty, "novelty proper."[5]

This characterization of novelty proper necessarily varies with respect to the kinds of processes from which novelty issues. However, all instances share a common and crucial character— the appearance of an exemplified form which is different from all prior appearances of exemplified forms. I shall mention only a few illustrations. Novelty proper is present in first occurrences of plant or animal species in biological evolution, for the differences between an old and "new" species are sufficiently radical and impressive for them to be recognized as new kinds of life. In citing the evolution of kinds as exemplifying novelty proper, I am, of course, assuming that a new kind or species is an instancing of a new form. And this assumption depends upon the insistence that what is identifiable as a kind is so identifiable by virtue of a form or definite character.

Other examples can be found in the history of art. Any work which manifests a different style within a tradition, such as that of Renoir within Impressionism, exemplifies a form different from the form with respect to which it is a particular art work, that is, a form different from previous forms of art works that constitute the tradition of Impressionism. Or an individual painting may exhibit a coherent structure which exemplifies a different form with respect to a style peculiar to the painter. Thus, in the production of art, novelty proper may occur in an object whose form serves to initiate a tradition or a style within a tradition; or it may occur in an object whose form is a variation within a style.

Novelty proper, then, appears with the first instancing of a form. Thereafter, it may be repeatedly noticed in every future occurrence in which that form is compared with what had been apprehended before its first occurrence.

In proposing the notion of novelty proper, I must presuppose that we have at least an intuitive understanding in ordinary experience of the nature of intelligible matrices or forms. As already suggested above, my appeal here is to a version of a Platonic view with respect to the presence in experience of intelligible objects of thought which are exemplified in things. However, it is necessary to discuss several considerations concerning the notion of "form" and its relation to novelty proper, for the concept of form is crucial for the defense of the thesis that we can recognize radical, as distinct from numerical, novelty.

I have said that a form is an intelligible identity, a pattern or matrix by which a structure is recognized. In order to avoid misunderstanding, let me point out that there is a sense in which the term "form" as I use it has as its model repeatable visual shapes. And it is true that the term as I use it may refer to patterns in the sense of what is exemplified in visual shapes. However, as already indicated, its meaning should not be restricted to the intelligibility of visual patterns. Other organizations or complexes—what I have referred to as structures—exemplify forms. Thus certain sounds may occur as complexes or structures which exemplify forms, as in the case of sentences exemplifying propositions. In the case of music, tones may function together so as to exemplify certain musical forms. Most generally, the term "form" refers to that in virtue of which an object has sufficient coherence to be recognized and identifiable. Once this coherence is recognized, the object appears to have a structure by virtue of the identity of character or the form which the structured object exemplifies.

It should be pointed out, also, that a form ideally is absolutely definite. As such, it would be perfectly coherent and would consist in a unity. On the other hand, the form may not actually be absolutely definite, but may only approximate ideal definiteness. As such, it manifests a degree of indeterminateness or vagueness. Degrees of vagueness may be present in both structures and the forms exemplified in those structures. In any case, vagueness cannot be so dominant that the matrix or form completely lacks character. Thus, the matrix must at least consist in a characterizable identity in difference—an identity which, I think, presupposes unity, even if the unity sometimes eludes exact specification.

If there may be degrees of definiteness with which forms may be exemplified, it should be obvious also that not every object or group of objects given to consciousness exhibits a pattern that calls for recognition in terms of an intelligible matrix. Not every aggregate is sufficiently coherent in structure to appear as exemplifying a form. And only on rare occasions are coherent structures sufficiently different as structures for them to appear to disclose *new* forms. Now, the point that coherence and unity are conditions under which forms are recognized suggests that the identification of a form depends upon a kind of valuation. That is to say, consciousness functioning cognitively exercises a kind of valuing because it occurs under those conditions in which the object of cognition is sufficiently attractive to call forth the cognitive activity. Thus, what might be called an epistemological valuation occurs when consciousness begins to function cognitively in consequence of recognizing sufficient definiteness in an object so that it simply is not only noticed, but, in addition, is recognized and identifiable.

Let me elaborate this point briefly. Everything and every combination or aggregate which is an object for consciousness must be discriminable. Thus, in order to appear for consciousness at all, the thing or aggregate must appear as at least partially definite. It must be definite at least as an appearance of a singular or an individual. And all things, in this minimal way, exemplify order, the order of appearing as singular. Yet if the object appears to have no more coherence than that supplied by the vague character which it must have in order to be noticed, the object does not have sufficient order to render it as intelligible in its character. It is not set off as an exemplification of a form distinct from, though related to, others. It would not exhibit sufficient character either to be classifiable or to be contrasted with classified objects. On the other hand, the thing which is not only noticed, but is also attended to and recognized as having specific character, must be valuable in the minimal sense that in its character it is selected for sustained attention. And it attracts attention because its coherence requires that it be noticed and compared.

This acknowledgment that a kind of valuation is required in the cognition of form might seem to imply that if the cognition of forms and, most significantly, new forms, is valuational in the sense suggested, then the recognition of new forms is relative to and dependent upon a subject constructing or constituting the form. Thus the recognition of new forms is relative to the observer. However, even though I do not accept this suggestion as it stands, it does not conflict with what has been said about novelty proper. If valuations concerning identity and coherence are required for the recognition of forms, the importance of forms for the appearance of radical newness is not thereby lessened. For even if forms—and, in turn, examples of novelty proper—were wholly dependent upon a form-giving and value-ascribing consciousness, what appears to be radically new would nevertheless be recognized in first appearances of forms. In other words, the recognition of these forms may be dependent upon conditions which make them sufficiently attractive to call forth attention from an observer. Thus, the thesis that what is conceived as radically new must exhibit a new form is not affected by the condition that discerning forms is a kind of valuation. And what is of utmost importance to my argument is the point that, in recognizing a form as new because of its attractiveness, we would need to differentiate this attractiveness from the attractiveness of those which were already familiar, and such a differentiation would depend upon discerning the differences in the characteristics of the things deemed valuable.

But it might be asked whether the occurrence of a new value rather than a new form is not, after all, what is intended by the notion of "novelty proper." Why complicate the account of newness by drawing on the notion of form and the many issues it raises? In response, I must suggest that if "novelty proper" is construed as "first occurrence of value," the recognition that a specific value is a first occurrence would nevertheless depend upon the recognition of the definite character of the value. Recognition of the value as different depends upon discriminating its identity, that is, the form which gives the value specificity and character.

Thus newness must initially appear in the difference of a form, even though the form is valued by virtue of its being selected.

However, the point about the role of valuation in recognizing novelty proper is important. There is a sense in which the notion of an object as created includes several distinct but related concepts of value, one of which is the initial and primary value attached to the coherence and unity which makes an object intelligible as a kind of thing. This point will be developed later.

The concept of novelty proper raises other issues, however, and some of these must at least be mentioned here before the concept can be used to help describe creative acts. For instance, it might be asked whether I am not assuming that forms are real entities in nature. If so, must I not defend this Platonism against the views that forms are conceptual entities in our minds or perhaps only linguistic utterances? For the purposes of our discussion, I hope to avoid the necessity of settling such questions. In introducing the notion of "form" in order to characterize novelty proper, it is unnecessary to make a commitment to a view of the status of forms in reality. And my reply to the question is that, whatever the status of forms, recognition of them does occur. Whether what is recognized must be described or explained in terms of realism, conceptualism, nominalism, or some complex of these theories is not a question which needs to be answered initially in this description. Agreement that modes of order determining structures at least appear for apprehension is all that is required for the argument. And even if forms were nothing but linguistic phenomena, those which appear for the first time would be characterizable as novelty proper.[6]

It might be objected, too, that if I am willing to admit that the presence of forms which are "new" might be dependent upon the observer, then presumably they may be created by the observer rather than some agent who constructed the things which exemplify them. And in that case, I shall be committed to a subjectivist view which cannot—or an idealist view which does not—distinguish between creative agent and observer in the cognition of objects. To this I must reply, first, that it must be remembered that I have not at this stage identified the act which is responsible for novelty proper with the creative act. Further qualifications are necessary before such an identification can be made. However, it should be noticed that if observers are indeed considered to be "creative" as form-givers, we can still inquire about the characteristics of these acts. What is crucial here is the point that newness is recognized as the result of certain kinds of activities, regardless of whether these activities are centered in an observer or an independent agent who constructs the objects which appear as new.

Nevertheless, I think a distinction between observer and creator-agent can be made. We must surely grant that observers sometimes recognize new forms for which they are not obviously aware of themselves as responsible. It is true that there are occasions when forms do seem to be the observer's invention—such as the interpretive recognition of a face, say in a cloud or ink blot. But there are other occasions when the form seems to be discovered—as in the case of encountering a form specified through the structure of a work of art or in instances of suddenly seeing the structure of an argument. Hence, even within an idealist interpretation of creative observation, it is possible to distinguish, in particular cases, forms for which the observer in some sense may be held responsible, and forms which, though they may require his form-giving consciousness, also appear to be made available, at least potentially, by another agent.

Yet a third and more formidable difficulty must be faced. It might be asked whether a pattern or ordered complex which appears for the first time can be intelligible upon its initial appearance. A form, one might argue, must be abstracted and repeated in more than one instance in order to be identifiable and to render a thing intelligible. The only reply which can be given, I believe, is that this objection poses a difficulty no greater for my study than for any view which admits that knowledge, whatever its object, can occur for the first time. To insist that what is identifiable by virtue of forms must be something repeated, as well as repeatable, is to imply that knowledge can only be a kind of recollection. Yet even the Platonic doctrine of recollection makes room for the learning of a form for the first time in the actual genesis of knowledge.

This objection to the claim that an intelligible structure—when intelligibility depends upon form—can be confronted "for the first time" presupposes the view that knowledge is gained by cumulative observations. Thus a form could only be the product of a generalization which elicits the form gradually. But notice that the difficulty posed by the objection also appears in the view that knowledge results from an inductive process. The reason why the puzzle is not avoided consists in the fact that, however long it may take to discern what is general, the moment at which the generalization is apprehended as a generalization is the moment of the first apprehension of what is repeatable—i.e., the initial recognition of an identity in difference. Thus, whether slowly or suddenly recognized, an intelligible structure, and thus a form, must be recognizable for the first time, otherwise it would not be possible to gain new knowledge.

There is, however, a related problem suggested by this issue. A form, if abstractable and characterizable in distinction from its exemplification in the moment of initial recognition, must transcend the instance in which it first appears. It must transcend the structure which exemplifies it. Thus, insofar as a form is intelligible, the temporal aspect of its initial appearance must be denied or at least ignored. And if temporality is ignored, the recognition of a form as appearing for the first time must be excluded from recognition of the form. Hence it would seem that novelty cannot be discerned within the form. In short, it seems that the appeal to form necessarily excludes novelty.

With this point I agree. However, it does not necessitate the abandonment of the concept of novelty proper. The point simply calls attention to the distinction between the concept of form and the concept of the newness of the form. The recognition of novelty proper is the recognition of a form as different. But the recognition of difference from all previous intelligible structures is not the same as recognition of the intelligibility of the different form. The intelligibility of the form does not depend upon the novelty proper. Rather, it depends upon the coherence present in the form considered in its own right. In short, forms are timeless, while occurrences of novelty proper are temporal. Novelty proper bridges the timeless and the temporal.

Of course it may still be asked how a form which is different or which is not characterizable in terms of familiar data can be intelligible or even recognized. And this question indeed raises a problem. But we must not seek to avoid it by denying that radical novelty appears for human consciousness. Suffice it to say here that if forms are eternal, they could be eternally familiar only for a divine mind. Surely our finite minds do encounter coherent patterns that are, in the moment of encounter, different and yet somehow intelligible.

One final point should be made about the use of the concept of "form" to characterize radical novelty. The complaint is ready at hand that the claim put forth about radical novelty does violence to what is taken to be the continuity in all processes, including creative processes. Thus, it may be said, all processes flow; change occurs through a definite temporal sequence according to a persistent continuum.

In response to this objection, it should be emphasized, first, that the concept of novelty proper does not imply that ordinary processes are not constituted by continuities. Most processes may very well be continuous from beginning to end and, in turn, they may be considered continuous with other processes. Moreover, the concept of novelty proper does not exclude continuities from those processes which terminate in new forms. Certainly an evolutionary process in which new forms are introduced is developmental and inclusive of many continuities, no matter how sharply its stages may be distinguished. What the concept of novelty proper does imply, however, is that at some point in the continuous development of a special kind of process—namely, creative process—there is a break in continuity, a break with respect to the structure of the process. Thus, unlike the steady development of an acorn into an oak tree according to a pattern of change, a process which issues in novelty proper is not in every respect continuous. It is not continuous with respect to its structure, that is, with respect to its instancing of the patterns which make it intelligible at the beginning and which make it intelligible at the end, or at the provisional terminus, of the process. If we do not admit structural transformations of this kind, we must, I think, deny radical novelty by assuming that we are deluded about what appears as a different structure in the outcome of what was, before the appearance of the structure, a continuous process.

Consider for a moment the claim that a process which issues in novelty consists in unbroken continuity. What exactly is continuous? The process considered as a whole? But surely the process is not identical with its continuity. Perhaps continuity is a characteristic of the process. But then the characteristic way the continuity qualifies the process must change. For if there is change in the process from its beginning to its termination in something new, this change must express changes in the nature of the process itself. If continuity were a character of the process, it could not be the same at the end as it was at the beginning of the process. Its form would be different.

Perhaps the continuity in question is not a characteristic, but rather a constant factor which determines what happens throughout change. In this case, continuity is a principle that remains the same while the process changes. And, it might be said, the characteristics of the process at the terminus and at the beginning would be related by continuity. The form at the beginning leads to the end, and the form at the end is conditioned by the manner in which the change occurs. While there is indeed a difference of form, a general developmental structure given at the outset of the process binds beginning and end in an unbroken continuity. The manner of development abides and continuity is sustained.

But does the same kind of continuity hold in processes in which novelty is introduced? I think not. For if we are serious about the introduction of novelty, and if we mean what we say when we admit that an increment of novelty enters the process, then the general developmental structure of the process could not abide as the same structure throughout the process. The continuity of the whole process is not smooth. Not only is the character of the process different at the end, but this character is not given according to the requirements of the developmental structure. Thus, I insist that the intelligible aspect present in processes which include radical novelty is different at distinct stages of those processes; and the continuities in the processes, so far as they are intelligible, are not the same throughout. Not only does the character of the process change, but it changes according to a changing principle of growth. If this point is denied, I believe that the appearance of radical novelty must be either denied or interpreted as illusory.

Let me make the point from a different perspective. The term "continuity," when referred to process, characterizes process as unbroken, yet unfixed—as manifesting identity in difference. To identify an aspect of process in this way is to give it character and to consider it in terms of an intelligible form. But once process is so viewed, it is viewed steadily. The fluidity we try to insist upon in the process is frozen under the steady reference of our characterization. To be sure, it remains frozen, we say, only so long as we conceptualize by means of the term "continuity." And the term itself is intended to call attention to the unfrozen, to the flow of process. Nevertheless, the terms used fix what is referred to, even if only provisionally. And most important, once a closer view is taken of that which is said to be changing yet continuous, that which is intelligible in it is marked off, is made to stand still to be recognized as different from what, at least phenomenally, was required by whatever structure gave specific intelligibility to the process prior to the change.

II

Novelty Proper and Creative Art. It is appropriate at this point, I think, to suppose that the concept of novelty proper can be accepted in its essentials, at least for the purpose of exploring its applicability to creative acts. An initial and obvious application of this concept suggests that an act or process which is creative is one which issues in novelty proper. This suggestion is a straight-forward application and, I think, reflects a conventional way of thinking about creative acts. Most of us would probably take this proposal as a reasonable or initially plausible attempt to describe created objects.

However, the mere presence of novelty proper in a product does not warrant our calling the product a "created object." Nor does the production of novelty proper guarantee that the process is "creative." Thus, the description needs qualification. It will be convenient to indicate the necessary qualifications by considering possible objections to it.

Someone might argue that to say that a creative act must lead to novelty proper is to imply the exclusion of the works of crafts-men and artists who, though they are called "creative," conform to a style already known to them. It might be said, for instance, that the reference to novelty rules out the possibility that much ancient Egyptian art is "creative," for most artists of that period con-formed to a familiar formula or pattern—a form already known and thus not new. This argument, of course, depends upon the assumption that craftsmen and artists who restrict themselves to one style do not produce novelty proper. I would suggest, how-ever, that the term "creative" is appropriately applied to these artists and craftsmen precisely to the extent that they or those leaders whom they followed have surpassed routine duplication of established forms. Thus the products of creative craftsmanship "invite us" (to use Robert Macleod's words) to recognize a new form in the subtleties of the finished work.[7] Similarly, our admira-tion of the "creative" ability of the Egyptian artist lies in our recognition of variations and nuances which disclose different forms within the established basic form. Of course, there are some of us with less discriminating eyes who may fail to see these vari-ations. In that case, what is it which we take to be "creative"? I think that in such cases we conceive not of individual Egyptian artists but rather of an entire age as creative, or as it might be put, of "the" Egyptian artist as creative. Even in this case, however, novelty proper is ascribable to the general form of a period with respect to its difference from forms of earlier periods.

Further, the point that craftsmen are believed to be original in the sense of producing radically new results is shown in our recognition that some of those artists we consider extraordinary in creativity, such as Michelangelo, looked on themselves as crafts-men. In short, I am insisting that artists who adhere to formerly realized styles are deemed creative either because their work is associated with a process which already produced the style for the first time or because each of their works done in accordance with the style has its own individual coherent unity, i.e., its own novelty proper.

In any case, even if the initial proposal that creative acts must produce novelty proper did exclude craftsmen, Egyptian artists, and artists who repeat themselves—and I think it does not exclude them—the primary issue here concerns those instances in which creation advances beyond what was previously known. And the use of the concept of novelty proper is an attempt to do justice to the latter kind of creativity. The objection, after all, is significant only if it is intended to show that all artists are creative by virtue of imitating the past. But surely there is a difference between "creative artists" who follow forms given to them and "creative artists" who initiate what is new.

Now, if the requirement that a creative process must yield novelty proper does not exclude craftsmanship, it does seem to be too broad; for it does not exclude certain kinds of accidental processes. For instance, an array of pieces of glass fallen from a window which was broken by an inaccurately thrown baseball would be "created" if it appeared as presenting an intelligible visual principle or order. And although the boy who threw the ball would be responsible for the array, he could hardly be called responsible for the coherent form or novelty proper in the sense that he would be deemed "creative" of it. In this case, then, it might be said that no human created the result; it would be an accident which the observer discovered.

But surely, someone will say, a person who happens to see the shattered glass and who discerns a form, a coherent pattern, deserves to be thought of as creative. Such a person would be a creative observer; and this is what all of us must be in our aesthetic responses to both natural and contrived, as well as accidentally produced man-made objects. The point of this objection has in part been dealt with already. It was suggested that even if observers are creative in being responsible in some way for the forms they identify, we can nevertheless specify the criteria by virtue of which this activity appears to be creative. Thus it would not be inconsistent with the characterization of creativity which has been given thus far to admit that an observer who discerns novelty proper in the array of glass is creative. Even the boy who inadvertently broke the window might be considered creative if he had the courage to survey the result of his deed and, in doing so, recognized novelty proper. In that case, the creative process, I take it, would not be the act of throwing the baseball, but rather the discriminating act of observation—an act in which a critical, controlled "seeing" operates in the recognition of form.

Yet surely a distinction needs to be made. It was said earlier that we do distinguish between forms for which observers are responsible and forms for which another agent is responsible and which are made available for the observer's eyes. It is the latter kind of form which is ordinarily associated with creative artists or, more generally, creative agents. Thus, if an observer can indeed be creative, he is not ordinarily thought of as a creative agent unless he at least communicates to an audience his recognition of novelty proper. Further, this kind of communication must be effected through some controlled use of a medium such as words, visual qualities, bodily motions, musical tones, etc. Accordingly, I take it for granted that the creative activity in question is the kind in which an agent is responsible for novelty proper by virtue of conscious manipulation of materials in a medium.

The first qualification needed for the definition, then, is that the process must manifest deliberation and direction on the part of the agent. A process which is creative cannot occur apart from some connection with a deliberate purpose that is relevant to the novelty which issues from the process. The agent must be responsible for the outcome, and the outcome must issue in novelty proper.

Thus R. G. Collingwood considers human creation to be generation undertaken deliberately and responsibly. And as Vincent Tomas has convincingly argued, the creative art process, though not directed in the way a marksman aims at a predefined target, is an activity in which critical control is clearly evident.[8]

This characterization of creative acts, however, is not sufficient. It is apparent that the assumption with which this paper began insists that the radical novelty in question marks a break in continuities—a gap between what was already established and what is new. From the standpoint of our understanding, the order and direction must be discontinuous and not wholly preconceived. Indeed, in some instances of human creativity, whatever direction is present may be unrecognized by consciousness throughout the course of the creative process. The sudden occurrence of a whole musical composition, or a substantial part of it, to the consciousness of Mozart can hardly be called consciously directed or ordered before it appeared. And long periods of forgetting a problem, followed by sudden illumination, suggest that the creator did not consciously control and direct certain phases of the creative process.[9] Further, cases in which serendipity is apparent, as in Pasteur's discovery of vaccine, seems to belie the qualification that creative processes must be directed and controlled.

Does this insistence on discontinuity and disruption of order and control reintroduce the admission of accidents as creations? I think not. For all that need be claimed is that critical control or direction enters at some point. Thus the traceable qualities of the created product can be seen as coherent with its past, while that which is untraceable, that is, the novelty proper, is not incoherent with an ordered development in its future. The direction given the process by the creator may be the critical control exercised once the creator has recognized the new form and decides to accept rather than reject it.[10] Or, if processes in nature are in question, direction may be in the relation of a new form—a species, in this case—to a process of evolution which leads to and gains meaning from the form. A change which remains only a "mutation," by contrast, would be a new individual that is not sustained and appropriated into biological evolution.

Another objection to the description given thus far raises a further problem. What are we to say about two or more processes which issue independently in similar or identically new forms— in products that could not both be examples of novelty proper, yet which issue from processes that surely demand to be called "creative"? The evolution of the same species of life in two different parts of the universe presumably would both be creative (if *any* processes in nature are creative). Or, in human creativity, it is well known that Darwin's theory of evolution published in 1859 did not exemplify a structural pattern which, without qualification, manifested novelty proper. A. R. Wallace, so we are told, had, independently of Darwin, originated a theory which is basically the same. Similarly, Leibniz and Newton are said to have developed the infinitesimal calculus, each without full knowledge of the work of the other. In these examples, the processes seem to be properly called "creative"; yet, because one of them in each pair occurred second in time, presumably it could not manifest novelty proper. If two theories have the same structure and one is constructed prior to the other, it seems that both cannot manifest radical newness.[11]

This objection cannot be answered adequately by saying that each agent can be called creative relative to his own knowledge and consciousness of novelty proper. For if we count as creative any process which only appears from the standpoint of the agent to yield novelty proper, then every discovery, that of a retarded child as well as that of a distinguished investigator, would be creative. All learning would count as creative, for the form learned would be a new form for the learner. But if a retarded child's learning process is creative, it is not creative as is the work of those who provide the model for creativity—in the way, for example, Darwin, Newton, Giotto, or Beethoven are creative. The learning process can be creative, at best, only in a derivative sense, and it is misleading, I think, to refer to it as creative.

There are two qualifications which distinguish creative activity from ordinary learning. The first will be introduced here, and the second will be discussed in the concluding section.

A process which is creative must be productive of a new form which is relative not only to the consciousness of the agent of the process, but also to the orderly development of processes leading to, and rationally relevant to, the particular act which is creative. What may be called "the vertical dimension" of the tradition of work prior to the creative advance yields a break after which novelty proper appears. Thus, given the data available to the agent, and given assumptions about the normal capabilities of agents, the novelty for which he is responsible seems unpredictable and not traceable to past data and the agent's ordinary capabilities. By contrast, given capabilities and data known to be available to the "non-creative" agent, the "novelty" for which he is responsible is precedented and seems predictable and traceable to the conditions and the process leading to the agent's achievement. We can predict what persons at various ages, given certain information, will learn. And we can trace what appears as novel for them to prior data and capabilities in their development.[12]

Thus if two processes lead independently to the "same" results, as in the case of Wallace and Darwin, the processes are perhaps less striking, but the creative character of neither is diminished as long as each in its vertical development yields novelty proper for its tradition—that is, as long as each is not only relative subjectively, but also objectively relative to a development of activity that does not necessitate a previously established possibility.

The description, however, needs an additional qualification. As it stands, it may be taken to include processes which yield sheer eccentricity—i.e., forms which appear to be unprecedented in a tradition but which, while not incoherent with the tradition, are nevertheless irrelevant to it. Another qualification, then, is called for.

III

Novelty Proper, Value, and Creativity. The final qualification of our characterization of creativity depends upon the requirement that a process which is creative must issue in something which is valuable. The presence of value as a condition of creativity was explicitly suggested earlier in the discussion of novelty proper. It was claimed that cognizance of form depends upon valuation in the sense of selection and that the form or identity in difference presents a kind of value insofar as its coherence makes possible the appearance and selection of what is discriminable and intelligible. The presence of value in created objects was also suggested, if not made explicit, in the requirement that control and responsibility enter creative acts and that creativity must yield products which are either contributions to, or at least not incoherent with, traditions in their futures. I shall conclude this essay by sketching a program for specifying the role which value plays, both in identifying created objects and in the development of creative processes. This program presupposes a general theory of value which I shall only adumbrate in closing.

In considering value and creativity, two features of creative acts should be emphasized. On the one hand, the agent does not begin a creative process with a preconception of the explicit structure of the end toward which his act is directed. On the other hand, the agent in some way is responsible for the new form which appears in relation to the creative process. Thus an artist struggles to effect something the exact character of which he does not yet envisage. Yet he knows when he has achieved that for which he struggled. His critical judgment determines the moment at which the process is complete and whether what has been completed is acceptable to him. These two features are mentioned here because they should be taken into account in the suggestions concerning value and creativity.

Creativity, then, is neither exclusively the discovery of what was familiar nor exclusively the production of what is unfamiliar. Creative processes lead to discoveries and the production of unfamiliar results which are also valuable. Thus, novelty proper does not appear as created in character unless it is accompanied by value. However, it may be asked, what kind of value is attributable to created objects? The answer may be indicated by distinguishing two familiar modes of value: namely, the instrumental and the intrinsic or inherent.[13] Both kinds of value are fundamental and indispensable for creativity; but one of them, inherent value, is more fundamental.

Although it is not possible here to enumerate the many senses of the concept of instrumental value, two of them should be noted: utilitarian and extrinsic. Utility is value for an immediate need or purpose. Extrinsic value is value as a necessary condition for the realization of another value which is not an immediate need. Now, a thing may be instrumentally valuable in its usefulness for some purpose; as such, it is of utilitarian value. Further, its utility may be different from the kind of purpose for which the useful thing is ordinarily the instrument. An automobile, for example, may be valuable for shelter during a rain storm. This utilitarian value of the car is not necessary to its primary function. The purpose of obtaining shelter would be fulfilled even if the car did not provide us with a mode of transportation. And a car could run without serving as shelter. The shelter value of the automobile, then, is different and unfamiliar with respect to the primary use of automobiles. Yet, this functioning as shelter is not an instance of novelty proper; for the purpose of obtaining shelter is familiar and could have been anticipated in connection with automobiles. Alternatively, the combination of the automobile and shelter value is not a synthesis; it is not at once a new and valuable form. The resultant does not appear to be more than the sum of its parts. There is nothing radically new about this shift from a primary to a secondary purpose. Thus, though having utilitarian value might be necessary for an object to be useful in "creative" ways, it is not sufficient for the ascription of radical novelty to the object itself.

Yet an object may also be found useful in a way which is different or unfamiliar with respect both to previously known purposes and to the object's primary function. Thus, its purpose would be an instance of novelty proper because it is a function of a form different from what went before it. And because of its novelty and its value, the object would be deemed created. Pasteur's creation or discovery of vaccine seems thus to be a creation. The use of a spoiled cholera culture to prevent the death of the chickens with which Pasteur was working was a use not originally primary to the culture. The relation of the new to the old purpose of the cholera culture, however, is not like the relation of the subsidiary purpose of the car used for shelter to the primary purpose of the car used for transportation. The use of the culture as a vaccine is an instance of both novelty proper and utilitarian value, and is an example of creativity. Pasteur's creative achievement consisted in recognizing as a primary purpose what might have remained an indirect function—a function of no value because it did not serve his initial experimental ends. That is, Pasteur was creative in substituting a different but valuable use, vaccination, for a familiar use, the use of a cholera culture to cause cholera. I should like to suggest, then, that novelty proper may appear as the manifestation of creativity when it occurs in an object whose familiar and primary utilitarian value is replaced by a different utilitarian value which becomes primary to the object, and which could not be routinely interpreted or predicted prior to its occurrence.

Moreover, it is essential to notice that, because of the kind of instrumental value realized, the new purpose served as a contribution to human knowledge. Specifically, in its function as vaccine, the cholera culture was also valuable to the development of medicine. Thus it had something more than an immediately useful utilitarian value. It was instrumental to knowledge, which is itself intrinsically valuable. The discovery itself was thus not only instrumental, but also extrinsically valuable in the sense in which it led to values not immediately occurrent in its future.

This last point leads to the suggestion that, if an instrumental value involves novelty proper, the new thing must be a contribution to a tradition. Thus a thing may be of instrumental value by serving its own kind. A member of a species may serve its offspring and, in turn, its species, without itself taking on immediate utilitarian value with respect to other things. And if its contribution exemplifies a new form, then it may be an example of creativity. The realization of this kind of value is, I think, sufficient to qualify a new object as created, even if utility or immediate instrumental value is absent. This kind of instrumental value of the created object is reflected in terms such as "fruitful," "effective," "important," which are often applied to new results which are also "created," and which are applied without specific reference to utility. Thus, the value by virtue of which the created object contributes to a tradition is instrumental in the sense that the creation is a means to some end defined with respect to the tradition. The value may lie in the creation's culminating or enhancing a tradition, as did the music of Bach; it may lie in the advancement of a tradition, as did the work of Giotto and Cézanne; or it may lie in prophesying and adding to a tradition far in its future, as did El Greco's painting.

Being thus extrinsically valuable, however, is not invariably the kind of value which marks novelty proper as created in character. A work of art, for instance, may be deemed created although lacking in a clearly defined contribution to tradition. Thus off-shoots from the main development of a tradition, such as some of the experiments of Picasso, do appear to be creative achievements. Yet they are neither sheer eccentricities nor major contributions to the tradition as a whole. Why, then, are they deemed created? The answer, I suggest, is that they issue from controlled processes and exemplify both novelty proper and a kind of value other than that which is either utilitarian or extrinsically related to a tradition.

Moreover, instrumental value is not something at which a creator necessarily deliberately aims. That the creator does not foresee a contribution before he has finished his work is surely true of the artist, if not always of the inventor or scientist. In art, at least, the tradition is open. The works which advance it determine its nature. Only after the fact can we look back on previous developments as somehow "leading to" the new creation.

But what kind of value other than utilitarian or extrinsic value may be attributed to created objects? This question receives an obvious answer once it is observed that if a created object may contribute instrumentally to a tradition, it must originate a value intrinsic to itself and, in turn, intrinsic to the tradition to which it contributes. Thus the new form of the created object serves as a model which may define future processes. And as a model, its value must be intrinsic or inherent. Let it be noticed here that if it be insisted with C. I. Lewis that intrinsic values are subjective, I am willing, at this point, to substitute for the term "intrinsic" Lewis' term "inherent."[14] The kind of value under consideration is that which is self-sufficient and attributable to the object rather than some end the object serves. The created object, then, must be valuable for its own sake. And its inherent value is the condition by virtue of which created objects may become instrumentally valuable in perfecting or advancing, or, indeed, creating a tradition.

I should like to suggest that inherent values may be distinguished into kinds according to the kind of specificity and complexity they have. Hence, the created object is intrinsically or inherently valuable in at least two ways: (1) as a new being and (2) as a new kind of being. First, it is valuable simply by virtue of its constituting a new being. I use the term "being" here in the sense of any determination or discriminable and identifiable object of consciousness. Thus the created object is valuable because it is a determination or coherent structure which, by exemplification, adds intelligibility to what was known. And intelligibility, I take it, is an intrinsic or inherent value. This requirement suggests why we sometimes place value on "novelty," "freshness," "originality" in art, without at the moment deeming it necessary to refer to the precise character of what is original.

This requirement, I think, is also the basis for the creator's directing the creative process toward something the character of which is not yet determined but which is recognized by him as something which ought-to-be. The as yet indefinite ought-to-be functions somewhat as Susanne Langer's "commanding form" in the articulation of an art object.[15] It does not provide rules; it does not display criteria for accepting or rejecting ideas or elements. But it does appear as a "requirement," a demand, that a specific form be brought into definiteness. Thus the origin of a form as such, before the specificity of the form is recognized, is an aim which lures the creator. The creator is lured by it because, as a vague and as yet undetermined form, it marks the beginning of intelligibility and the possibility of definite intelligibility and specific value. Thus, since the undetermined form is the basis for intelligibility, it may be considered as instrumentally valuable to the inherent value of the finished and intelligible form which marks the result as a created object.

Someone might, of course, object that not all new things are valuable merely because they are new. Surely the Nazi "innovations" are not valuable because they came into being. But this objection, I think, springs from the view that a thing, whether new or old, may be evil without regard to other things. I would suggest, however, that evil is distinguishable from the *being* of the evil thing and is identifiable only with respect to a conflict between the thing in question and some other reality. Thus I wish to insist that coming into being is in itself of value and that there is no disvalue without a conflict of beings.

That coming into being is of value has been suggested earlier. It was said that selective valuation is the foundation for the apprehension of form. In the sense that the determination of form appears as demanding identification and characterization, and thus intelligibility, all forms are valuable. They depend upon the value of intelligibility for their appearance to consciousness.

Yet there is a second way in which a created object is inherently valuable. It consists in the exemplification by the object of what Nicolai Hartman has called the ought-to-be which is a kind of "ideal being."[16] This kind of value is inseparable from the first. It enhances and fills out the value of simply coming into being. And it is essentially related to the specificity of the new form, that

[99]

is, the character of the novel being. Thus, this kind of inherent value is attributable to a new form by virtue of its determinate structure. It appears on condition that the specific and definite form in question is recognized as what ought-to-be, not simply because it is intelligible, but also because it is a certain kind of being which is intelligible in a definite way that ought to be. Unless there were an inherent value in the *kind* of form that occurs for the first time, created objects would be valuable only in the general way all intelligible things are valuable, that is, valuable simply for being. Thus there would be no new values. There would not even be new instrumental values, for there would be no special value attaching to a new kind of purpose.

Inherent value of kind is, of course, correlated with the creative agent's admittedly paradoxical critical direction of the process toward a *kind* of result the details of which he as yet does not completely envisage. Unlike the inherent value of being, value of kind cannot appear to the creator as an aim, since it is not yet determined in such a way as to be the target of that aim. Nor can it provide a set of preconceived criteria by which the process is controlled. Yet, after the fact, after the created object is complete, its value of form can be viewed as the conditions which fulfilled the creative agent's critical demands, and as that for which he is responsible.

What has been said about the distinct ways inherent values function in the creative process raises a host of questions. How, for instance, is it possible that a creator can critically select and be responsible for a definite form which he can envisage only vaguely before he knows and accepts it? Is the value of being, i.e., is the lure of form and intelligibility, in some way intimately related to and determinative of inherent value of kind? But these are questions which cannot be treated here. The chief purpose of this paper has been simply to describe the conditions necessary to identify an act as creative.

Let me conclude with a summary statement of the characterization of creativity which I have defended. I have claimed that an act which is creative must meet three conditions: (1) it must appear to be discontinuously directed or controlled at least in being found acceptable by critical selection; (2) it must issue in novelty proper relative to a tradition with which it is not in conflict or which it enhances, advances, or initiates; and (3) it must yield a product which is valuable in at least two ways; that is, it must be inherently valuable as a determination of a new being and as a kind of determination which merits sustenance.

NOTES

* A grant-in-aid from the American Philosophical Society for the summer of 1965 made the writing of this paper possible. It is a modified and expanded version of a paper read at the annual meeting of the American Society for Aesthetics, October 28–30, 1965. An earlier revision was presented at the initial session of the Society for the Philosophy of Creativity at the meeting of the Western Division of the American Philosophical Association in Chicago, May, 1966. I owe an expression of gratitude to a number of my colleagues. In particular, I should like to acknowledge the help of Professors John Anderson, Richard Bernstein, and Carl Vaught. Discussions with them enabled me to see where further development was needed. Of course, they are not responsible for any inadequacies in the paper.

1. My intention is to avoid facing here the difficult metaphysical issue of determinism which, I think, lies behind the claim that what appears to be unprecedented is an occurrence which is only surprising and which is, in the final analysis, explicable and traceable to antecedents. I have tried to face this issue in "Spontaneity: Its Arationality and Its Reality," *International Philosophical Quarterly*, Vol. IV, No. 1 (1964), 20–47.

2. It may be remarked in passing that novelty of particularity seems to be the kind of newness admissable and emphasized by one side of a Whiteheadian treatment of creativity as it is exemplified in human activity. Thus, newness is ascribable to the uniqueness of every event or actual entity. I have tried to indicate certain limitations in a Whiteheadian approach to creativity in "Spontaneity, Its Arationality and Its Reality."

3. Throughout, I use the word "intelligible" in a broad sense to refer to whatever is a recognizable specific determination, or an identity in difference. An object is "intelligible" if it is at least identifiable and characterizable. It should be acknowledged here that I hold the view that there are occasions of immediate, nondiscursive cognition. Accordingly, in some instances, an individual may be intelligible by virtue of a unique determination which is an object for cognition, but which is not, in the moment of cognition, relatable to other known objects. The possibility of immediate, nondiscursive knowledge is essential to any view which acknowledges that new intelligibility can occur for human knowledge. I think it is also essential to any view which interprets intelligibility as dependent upon identity in difference. (I do not intend to say that those individuals which are thus immediately intelligible are therefore fully intelligible. Indeed, it could be argued that there is an element of unintelligibility in them. Nor do I claim that every individual is intelligible as unique, but only that there are some occasions in which the uniqueness of an individual is intelligible.) In one sense, Dun Scotus' principle of Heccaeity is suggestive of the view I am proposing, for this principle calls for the possibility of a "contracted" form which gives intelligibility to an individual in its individuality. On the other hand, C. S. Peirce's view of secondness as what resists intelligibility in the individuality of things points to my claim that something unintelligible is present in individuals.

4. It should be noted that in this discussion a structure is like a form in the sense of an Aristotelian interpretation of form as immanent. Thus a form is conceived as a participant within particular things. As such, a structure is an ordered composite of properties which appear in a particular and which appear to be relevant to one another because of an identity or a determinateness which is the basis for their mutual relevance. However, because the determinateness or identity is an indispensable condition for the intelligibility of the structure, the identity has a status which is for cognition distinct with respect to temporal changes in the qualities of the particular. It is by virtue of the identity which makes the particular intelligible that the structure is recognized. The identity of a structure, then, is like a Platonic form which serves to render particulars knowable. Such an identity is what I call "form," and sometimes "matrix" or "pattern." These terms as I use them suggest that the status of what I refer to is distinct from physical and mental location. What is physical or mental is changing and ambiguous so long as a distinguishable identity—a form—is not discerned to make it intelligible. A particular which appears as having a new structure, then, appears so by virtue of exemplifying a new form. My interpretation of form will be discussed further below.

5. The term "novelty proper," like R. G. Collingwood's term "art proper" which distinguishes what is correctly from what is falsely called "art" is used to refer to a kind of novelty which is less pervasive and more appropriately called "newness" than the newness shared by all particulars. Thus the term is normative insofar as the word "proper" suggests how "novelty" ought to be applied. C. Lloyd Morgan's "primary novelty" comes close to the meaning I wish to suggest. See *The Emergence of Novelty* (London, 1933). Morgan's "primary novelty" refers to initial occurrences of unprecedented complexes or relations and is intended to distinguish between what "emerges" for the first time and emergents which are repetitions of what was novel in the past. The question whether novelty "emerges," comes from causes which are in principle knowable, or simply pops into the world spontaneously, is, as already indicated, waived for the moment. It may be observed here, too, that the notion of "novelty proper" should mark the common ground between my characterization of newness and one side of a Whiteheadian view. An eternal object which is exemplified for the first time would, indeed, appear as an instance of novelty proper. However, if an eternal object can be new for human knowledge and for the actual world, then some processes must be new in a more radical sense than that attributable to the uniquenesses of all processes.

6. Once again, it must be emphasized that these initial considerations of the identification of newness and creativity are proposed as metaphysically neutral. In a treatment of the problem of explaining creative activity, this neutrality would need to be abandoned.

7. Robert B. Macleod, "Retrospect and Prospect," Chapter 6, Howard E. Gruber, Glenn Terrell, Michael Westheimer, editors, *Contemporary Approaches to Creative Thinking* (New York, 1962), p. 182.

8. R. G. Collingwood, *The Principles of Art*, (Oxford, 1938), pp. 125–135. Vincent Tomas, "Creativity in Art," *The Philosophical Review*, Vol. LXVII, No. 1 (January, 1958), pp. 1–15.

9. Graham Wallas' widely accepted description of incubation as one of the stages of the creative process emphasizes the point that the creator is not in full control of at least some phases of the creative act. *The Art of Thought* (New York, 1926).

10. That acceptance or rejection of the final result is a form of critical control is argued by Tomas, "Creativity in Art."

11. It could be argued that no two theories are exactly alike, and no two creations exemplify the same form. Leibniz and Newton did have some knowledge of each others' work, as did Wallace and Darwin. Just to the extent that they did not have acquaintance with each others' thought, is the extent to which there are variations in their creation. If this argument is correct, it does not call for rejecting my characterization of creativity by means of the concept of novelty proper. However, duplication of creation in independent processes is a possibility, and some believe it has occurred. I believe my description can be defended while such duplication is admitted.

12. The claim about the irreducibility of novelty proper to antecedents within a tradition is not intended as an assertion that there are no rational connections whatsoever to be found between the new form and its past. As Norwood Hanson has recently argued convincingly, there are patterns of discovery in science. And similar claims have been made for art. *Patterns of Discovery, An Inquiry into the Conceptual Foundations of Science* (Cambridge, 1961). However, those rational connections or patterns which can be identified appear after the discovery has been made, when we can look back on the relation of the result to past knowledge. They do not disclose themselves to the creator or to us until the new idea is made communicable through a set of concepts or through the new forms which have advanced the tradition. Furthermore, there remains the irreducible novelty of the altered or new assumptions which are required for the formation of the new idea. And these assumptions break with the rational course of an established tradition.

13. The reason for using the alternative terms, "intrinsic" and "inherent," will be indicated below.

14. C. I. Lewis, *An Analysis of Knowledge and Valuation*, The Paul Carus Lectures, Seventh Series, 1945 (LaSalle, Illinois, 1946), pp. 551–554.

15. Susanne K. Langer, *Feeling and Form* (New York, 1953).

16. *Ethics* (New York, 1958), Vol. I.

ALBERT TSUGAWA

ART AND DEATH

Works of art come to life before us. We can grapple with them
(the text, the score, the canvas); and thus there is something durable
there that we can hold on to, relive in our memories and, in spite
of the inadequacies of our language, share with others. On the
other hand, art has a way of never fully existing. The experiences
that we try to capture are elusive and escape the net of words; our
comprehension of them keeps changing and moves farther and
farther from completion; and our talk about works of art reveals
differences in our apprehension of them, exposing a gap that we
cannot fill. Something is there, and yet nothing is there. This
messy paradox of existence and nonexistence in art is the theme
of this reflection.

I

Works of art come into existence, and in the course of nature they
also go out of existence. Things that come into being go through
a period of gestation. Similarly this must be true of art; and the
folklore of art has many tales of the worry and agitation of artists
who, as vessels, incubate artistic forms. They do not know what
marvels or what horrors will emerge (thus the unsettling distrac-
tions) and they suffer periods of uncertain agony. This suggests
the analogy of birth. Beethoven worked many years, for example,

evolving the themes of his symphonies in notebook sketches. Artists bide their time as apprentices, waiting for their time to come. The muses strike. Necessity goes to work. If, as it sometimes happens, the work of art simply materializes, the artist himself not having known what was to emerge, we still say he recognizes it as his own and sees that it is good. For there it is, fully realized to be claimed and espoused.

We mistrust works that we cannot confront, for such "works" most probably have not undergone the *labor* and pain of delivery. Yet we know that between what we think we think in our minds, and what we can fully apprehend with our sense awareness, there is an abysmal gap. Poems that we thought we sang, scenes that we wanted to capture, buildings that we imagined in our minds, when put to the test of realization, turn out to be inadequate to the demands of matter. In dismay we say that what we imagined was infinitely more expressive, more beautiful, more powerful; somehow something intractable and uncooperative in the medium or our technique had interfered, preventing the realization of our fantasies.

Croce was hardest about this, saying, "Intuitive activity *possesses intuitions to the extent that it expresses them*."[1] And this dictum has the power of an *a priori* judgment in these romantic days, for whatever else art may be, it must be embodied in a sensuous medium; and it must utilize that medium to its fullest expressive potential. It must say something that can be said only in that particular use of that medium.[2] Art utilizes an immediate mode of expression. A painting may have an elaborate preconceived organization (a triptych), intend objects (a table with fruit, the conspiracy of Claudius Civilis, Mont St. Victoire), involve symbols and iconic signs (emblems of saints, even words like "ma jolie"), contain elusive conceptual references (the descent of the holy spirit, the persistence of memory); but what makes it first of all a painting and an aesthetic object is its embodiment in colors, lines, figures, depth, all that is entailed in visual, sensuous material from which it cannot be separated without the loss of its own being.

A painting as a permanent object can be said to have existence (a specific location in time and space); yet nothing assures them permanence: buildings and libraries have perished in fire, war, or under the sheer pressure of time. And short of absolute destruction, pigments darken or liquefy and run, canvasses buckle or rot, metals tarnish, buildings tilt and marbles crack. Moreover, either human carelessness, sheer forgetfulness, or progress have changed the meanings of words, the pitches of musical sounds, our stan-

[106]

dard of technique, our taste, our sensibility. Thus even if we *can* excavate the persisting objects from the debris of time, it may have changed its aspects in important ways. We can resort to the principle that we must, as much as possible, reconstitute the original art. This presupposes that by some heroic effort, it is possible for the historical imagination to achieve objectivity (recapture the past as it was, as well as, in the case of works of art, respond to them with the sensibility of the proper period). This is historical sentimentalism and the beginning of the love of ruins as ruins. We want the past whole and real because we are drawn by the patina of time—the irridescence of excavated Roman glass, the oxidized surfaces of Shang dynasty bronzes, the forgotten symbolism of old idols, the exoticism of antique objects. The belief in objectivity and the connoisseurship involved cannot be separated.

It is difficult to capture the past and the task is never completed. Moreover, some of the arts, particularly the performing arts, are not repeatable. This raises problems because we also mistrust works of art that we cannot reconfront. And there is difficulty in the fact that our responses to a work of art keep evolving. Yet what evolves has similarities, and what we experience and what we say of it has resemblances. Thus we posit two ideas: that there are abiding forms and that these abiding forms have a generative relation to existing works of art. To understand works of art, then, is to apprehend these forms, and apprehending these forms is a necessary and sufficient (and therefore relevant) condition for the full comprehension of these works of art. The body of the work of art consists in its material manifestation before us. But its meaning and its importance lie in the abstract forms—and even if we repeat that the forms can *exist* only in concrete objects, they must, nevertheless, be abstracted. We have thus introduced into this dialectic the idea of something other than existing entities, whether we call it essence or being.

II

The kinds of existences that we recognize are various. (1) They may be material embodiments that persist, like paintings and statues. (2) They may be material structures that must be viewed dynamically, like baroque corridors and Japanese gardens. (3) They may be nonpersisting material events, like actions of persons in drama or the dance. (4) Or they may be immaterial events, like music or literature. In this list of the types of existences, attention is concentrated on what can be apprehended immediately and sensuously. When history and category, language and description are introduced into this context, the interest shifts to what is common among art objects—to the forms and types.

An unexperienceable, unapprehendable work of art is pointless and gratuitous. Nothing, on the other hand, insures the fact that our several experiences of a work of art actually resemble each other. The operations of our consciousnesses are volatile, inscrutable, and ineffable. How do we even know that they have aspects in common? It is intolerable to allow our experiences of art to maintain their separate aloofnesses, and so we construct our accounts to make them reflect each other.

1. Many works of art come into being in the wake of other works of art: literal copying,[3] imitation, allusion, variation, translation, extension. Our modern sensibility respects (and thus allows) the last primarily. A poet or an artist creates something. The treatment of the subject matter, the style, or even the logic of the movement of consciousness suggest a further step, and another artist feels compelled to take this step. (Increase in orchestral size, tolerance for more and more note clusters that were earlier felt to be dissonant. The increased fragmentation of space and motion in painting, or the shifts of perspective in painting and in the novel.) But the imitations go beyond the obvious elements to include even the effects of time. Many artists have been impatient that their work should look so new. Whole periods have hankered after the ruins of the monuments of the past and even made new things look old (archaizing trends, and all those movements modified by the prefix "neo"). What makes even more dramatic sense here is the role of negation. Copying, imitating, extending are forms of acceptance. Negation also needs a springboard, something to repudiate. Parody and ridicule are mild forms of negation. (These forms, like irony and satire, assume a larger context that intends a positive and better value.) Nor are the milder forms of anti-reason, like the prurient snickers of the Dadaists and the surrealists, the first in the line of nihilism. Some artists have found it necessary to violate the very ground of their art. Witness anti-music, anti-art, anti-creation. Tinguely's famous sculpture that destroyed itself on 17 March 1960 is metaphysically nothing new.[4] There are many tales of artists, like those influenced by Zen, who have willingly destroyed what they have created. How else also can we make sense of the black paintings of Goya, the blank pages of *Tristram Shandy*? Perhaps too, we must conclude that Leonardo in his heedless, careless experimenting, even in his art, did not

want to succeed. In the completion of art, there is a closing of a circle, a limitation. What one intuits is dynamic, limitless, purely there (the onrush of a flood, the eye of a whirlpool, the center of a storm, all carefully sketched in Leonardo's notebooks).

The first way to corral works of art is to hook them on to predecessors and to understand this relationship as essential.

2. A typology of art that admits negations is incompatible with the doctrine of natural kinds. Rules, if formulable for any genre, will be violated soon by someone. This makes the idea of genre nearly useless.

Old ideas, however, die hard. To save the idea, why not think of genre in terms of convention?[5] This gives it a suitably empirical turn. Genre are conventions that control the range of meanings in any act of expression and meanings might be defined as the expectations raised by an expression. Genre, then, properly constitutes the "sense of the whole by means of which an interpreter can correctly understand any part of its determinacy." On such a conventionalist view, however, it is difficult to decide beforehand which are the relevant and necessary features of a type, genre, or category. Given any set of entities displaying features in common, they will all show subtle and interesting differences: and we may be readily (and properly) seduced into finding the differences more important than the similarities. (This always happens when we scrutinize various members of a family.) We can assert the conventionality of the family roots, but we may be driven to positing types with unique members.[6] This final move does violence to the idea of types (and tokens) since the chief rationale of the idea of types is that the tokens would, in their essential features, mirror the defining properties of type and that the types would have many members.

3. Genre are conventions and they change in response to history. So it would be convenient to see them as historical phenomena. But this is difficult. The pattern of a historical period, its meaning, cannot be perceived easily as long as we are in the midst of it. History is written after the event, and rewritten every two or three generations. With respect to art, we can only safely formulate descriptions (and therefore write histories) of dead categories. A taxonomist must have great confidence that he has surveyed all the relevant samples and that he knows what is contained in this idea of relevance (what the features are of this class that determine its significance both intrinsically and as a subject for study). Definitions are difficult to generate. It is a common

observation that Aristotle's definition of tragedy applies best (if not only) to "Oedipus the King." Does this suggest the reappearance of a unique type?

Even the historicity of a genre is dubious. Do artists consciously follow rules? This seems unlikely, yet the idea of genre as convention is attractive because we want to explain common features of similar objects of art as having been intended by the artist because the artist was *following* the convention. In many cases the conventions are formulated after the event. How useful is this sort of knowledge? The convention, then, may be that of the critics and connoisseurs themselves, formed centuries later and may tell us more about the critics and their methods than anything else. Like the writing of history itself, conventions seen historically must yield the relevant and essential meanings of a work of art. This makes art contingent on history. If the types and genre can be perceived *post hoc* only, and the typology can give clues to the meaning and significance of a work of art, art and its history would be inseparable.

4. Art forms, it would appear, have life cycles. Does the work of art? Many works of art have changed and evolved. Are they the same work of art? If a painting (like most of those of Claude Lorrain) have darkened in the green areas, what Claude did, and what was seen two hundred years ago, a hundred years ago, and recently are significantly different. What was originally and presumably trees, ambiently breathing in an Elysian high noon, now looks like scenes at dusk, the trees permeated by shadows. The tone, the mood, the meanings differ. Of course, the original "forms" are there—the schema of the classical landscape where

> the land-and-tree mass at the left is disproportionately larger and heavier than that at the right, and the main weight of the latter is set back much further from the picture plane. Letting the eye be guided by the land alone, there appears to be a strong inward diagonal movement in the opposite direction by the river which creeps into the picture at the bottom right corner.[7]

The sensuous surfaces must make their impact felt. The medium and the object depicted are not separable, and the schema is affected by the changes in the medium and the surface. The progressive darkening, or the sudden "revelations" of the cleaning of paintings change what we see. Recent cleanings of El Greco have raised doubts about the effect of modern taste and sensibility on the restoration and even the reconstruction of the surfaces of paintings. Floods, air pollution, time itself, have eaten away at the surfaces of Tuscan frescoes, marring our enjoyment. The progressive changes are not an organically unified movement toward a final end, so that it cannot be called a life cycle. The experience of the event, fused into an incandescent whole is the work of art—and if there are two, three, or four such moments that can be seen to be the same (or sufficiently similar or readily seen to have a family resemblance) it is the synthesis of the critical imagination that forges the object of understanding. It is the beginning of a historical entity.

Works of art that survive the movement of time exist, of course—but essentially they are constructs of the critical and historical imagination. The idea of the "Mona Lisa" to Leonardo's contemporaries, to the eighteenth century, the generation of Walter Pater, and the circle of Modigliani (who was accused of stealing it from the Louvre) cannot be the same. Beyond the physical existence of the canvas and the frame, it is our synthesizing faculty that interrelates these different views, seeking the common and organic thread, using as the substratum of this synthesis our vision of the march and progress of western civilization. It belongs to the making of history. The painting itself "each generation must reinterpret."[8] History is not the mere chronology, the objective and physical relic of the movement of time. It is the significant pattern that makes sense of the past. It can be written only when events make sense, and for that one must see that there is a movement and a direction. *Art forms* can have life cycles because history is possible. Though historical accounts (and therefore art *forms*) project a future, that history can be formed only when things have passed. A history, in order to make the parts meaningful in the light of the whole, must show that events have a beginning, middle, and end. Genre, to the extent that they are historical phenomena, can be posited only when the art form has undergone a cycle. The cycle must have been completed, and thus they must be dead. We who must posit the genre must stand outside of it. We are somewhere else.

5. Yet we say types do not die. They are eternal. And this shows how genre as historical phenomena is not the same as a type.

6. Have not works of art gone out of existence? When they perish, does anything of it persist? Do works of art perish all in the same way when they do? If not, are there different modes of death?

[111]

III

1. Any of the performing arts, of course, perish. The score of a musical composition, no matter how minutely it may indicate the particulars of a performance, leaves a gap that the performers and the occasion must fill, and each of these performances, once done, is gone forever. Each performance will show subtle differences, and in important and vital cases, differences that indicate different meanings. Fuertwanger's Wagner and Toscanini's Wagner delineate significantly different worlds, both certified by Bayreuth. To say seriously that works of art perish is to imply that any work of art is a concrete, particular realization. Someone structures the forms, of course, writes the directions, prepares the recipes. But the mind of the artist-performer (Schikaneder producing Mozart's operas, later on Mahler, Fritz Busch or Jean Louise Barrault doing so) is focussed in the concrete act on the stage; and if things do not look right there, he will scrap any concept he might have had prior to the reality before him. The test is how the art-event before him jells. Time makes a difference, the bodies and techniques available make a difference, the mood of all those concerned, including the audience, makes a difference.[9]

A certain performance, in its shaping and its dynamics may be unfaithful to the spirit of the score. Yet, on its own, it may be a thoroughly successful musical experience—perhaps even more eloquent and interesting than other performances that adhere to the dictates of the recipe more closely. Any work "should have the perspective of history, and yet essentially they must be made modern."

> When I began to direct "Madame Butterfly," I conceived it as an identity problem. Cio-cio-San's concern with American life, with becoming an American woman, became the important consideration..... In the second act, Madame Butterfly becomes an American. She dresses like an American woman of that time..... In the crucial moment in the second act when she expects Pinkerton back, she reaches a point of crisis. "He must see me as I first appeared to him," she says, and begins to put on her Japanese wedding garb over her American dress. But then she hesitates. She says, "No, I will go to him this way, American."[10]

Purists (whatever that might mean) will object; but the art (performance) is what is there before our eyes, and although it may not be "what the original artist had in mind,"[11] it may have its own authenticity and worth. Perhaps we must endow these creatures with one of those unwieldy hyphenated names that signalize a hybrid: e.g., Beethoven-Fuertwanger, Beethoven-Bruno Walter, Beethoven-Toscanini.[12] These all have differing characteristics. In point of fact, however, any object of the performing arts is such a hybrid creature,[13] and it is only the slavishness and mediocrity of the usual performers that obviate such hyphenated names. (The truth of the matter is that, like most artists, most performers are products of their times, and their view and thus their execution of the work of art have many conventional aspects.)

Several works that individually can be said to be "faithful to the score" can show radically differing features. Only by petrifying the medium (e.g., on film, on tape, on phonograph records) can one approach identical repetitions; and even that is far from absolute. Each work of art dies gloriously, unstintingly. What is poignant about the endeavor of a performer (original or recreative) is that whatever he does, it must of necessity go into nothingness.

2. Of those works of art that do not exist, some have been destroyed by accident. But until their destruction, they lived in their full beauty, glory, and perfection, emblems of the divinity (immortality) of man. It is not true that there are no perfect things. The whole accomplishments of Helenic Athens, Tang and Sung China delineate realms of perfection, in having brought to full flower a canonic ideal of beauty. We may sentimentalize by thinking that such beauty and perfection (like the alliance of city-states) contained in them a weakness that destined them never to endure. The classic past, though much in ruin, or seen only in fourth rate copies, or in breathlessly ecstatic but thoroughly inadequate descriptions, can function as "classic" because it once actually existed. The slogan "once we were in Arcadia" sums this up.[14]

Leonardo's *The Last Supper* is an important example here. It has a crucial position in the history of art and in the life of the artist. It is one of the high-water marks of human skill in painting; it is beautiful and cunning beyond compare; and as a working out of the central event in Christianity, it manifests a spiritual significance that theology or homily alone could never have articulated. It is a testimony to da Vinci's Promethean quest and one of the examples of perfect art. But soon after it was finished, it began to deteriorate (apparently wholly Leonardo's fault) and today it is nearly a total wreck. When one first sees it in the darkened hall, he is shocked by its state of ruin. It fills one with despair that something so famous, so precious, should come to this. The shock, however, has also much to do with how anything so damaged, and for so long, could have preserved its reputation. (Everything else comparable has long been forgotten. One suspects with disgust a hoax on the part of art critics.) But there it is, in the only state that we can now have this work. One can stay and look, though few have the heart or the patience. Then something uncanny happens. When the eyes have gotten accustomed to the dim twilight of the room, here and there colors begin to coalesce. One is held fast. After half an hour of staring, walking about, scanning, studying, something appears there. Not the painting in its original state, but so to speak, its ghost, like a mirage, now hovering over the crumbling, corroded plaster. Has one read this into the blotches? Is one hallucinating? How has one coaxed this out of the faint walls? The doubts are painful. Yet the experience itself is also indubitable. There was at first the crumbling, rotten walls of the room. Now half an hour later, there floats an apparition, a mysteriously expressive, powerfully compelling form, part of whose attraction is related, no doubt, to the damaged state of the material. This apparition is Leonardo's painting. Existence and causes seem irrelevant.

3. Nonexistence seems to consist in an incompatibility between the work as matter and the work as intention. Body and soul are ill assorted. In a common vocabulary, though a misleading one, we may think of this as making immanent what is essentially transcendent. (The inside-outside model of this metaphor is disturbing.) It is common to read that da Vinci or Beethoven encountered difficulty in grasping an idea or an ideal, something which is elusive by virtue of its transcendence, but which is whole, perfect, unified, eternal, and unchanging. Interesting examples, however, indicate that lucidity and ideality are not the ends involved. The world of Bosch suggests it: nocturnal horizons in which gallows and gibbets are etched against the disastrous, cosmic bonfires beyond the horizon. In the foreground, St. Anthony mortifies his flesh in a surprisingly populous desert, among creatures, some half pig and half corkscrew, others flowering insects or damsels entrapped in tea kettles, all emitting inaudible, hallucinatory cries. Van Gogh: the apocalyptic landscapes of blazing wheat and menacing sky, filled with angry, batlike crows. Piranesi's imaginary prisons: ceilings, bridges, and stairways lost in drifting mist, walls picturesque with huge instruments of torture, suitable only for

giants. The nonsense verse of Edward Lear. Goya's caprices. These works manifest in body (the sensuous) something that is wholly anti-body, resulting in art that is peculiarly anti-sensuous. They grope into the darker reaches of consciousness; they express the density and intractability of human suffering and absurdity, the contingency, the messiness, and the dynamism of existence. Principally, these are concrete presences. As meanings, they are not abstractions like types or genre. Calling them beautiful would miss their whole point,[15] for beauty is limited, an experience of an event that has come to fulfillment, and as complete, stands free.

4. But going one step further, there are works which by their very nature refuse to come into being, their gestation evolving the seeds of their impossibility. They are never guided by an idea. Rather, the creation works out something endlessly, the results by their unlimitedness symptomatizing elusiveness. The artist never finishes, nor claims to, but simply stops. He often remains satisfied by the most spartan of materials, for the infinite is best generated by the least means. The most radical example of this is the Japanese Nō drama.[16] The stage is a plain of immaculately polished wood, devoid of sets except an emblematic pine tree and bamboo on the rear wall. If there are props, they are minimal, artificial, and symbolic. Three musicians, a chorus (four to six persons) and two or three performers stake out the confines of this world. In this charmed circle, by the use of music, chant, and ritual dance, they conjure up uncontainable apparitions: the fierceness, devotion, and regret of a warrior now blind who relives the final glorious battle of his defeat ("Kage-kiyo"); the agony, despair, and cosmic unforgiveness of an unrequited lover who acts out the expiation of his hate ("Kayoi Komachi"); or an earth spirit flowering in his infinitely various demonic powers ("Tsuchigumo"). What we as participant-spectators witness and undergo is out of proportion to the means used to effect them. In the shadowy, deep, measured intonations of the chorus, punctuated by the sharp cries of the drummers and the long calls of the flute, even the gorgeous costume and the dance become golden notes and echoes. Then, Nirvana itself seems to dissolve us at the moment when these spirits, enduring their chimeric destinies realize their justification and escape from the bonds of existence into nothingness. Though we feel their powers as presences, they are not there. Or if "there" they are best described as negations. Like *The Last Supper*, what is not present can make itself felt powerfully, and again like *The*

Last Supper, it can be experienced as an artistic paradigm, though in a terrible state of ruin.

We thus encounter nonexistence, negation, destruction and death.

IV

Death, it is commonly said, is the only reality of human existence. The religious treat all of life as a preparation for dying: the one event that gives meaning to life. Is death such an event?

Death takes place in time. It can be pinpointed. It can be fast or slow, instantaneous and merciful, or long and agonizing. But it is an odd sort of temporal entity for it has only one side—we do not emerge out of it. It makes no sense to speak of undergoing death, for that metaphor suggests that we go through something and get out of it. Death, however, is not a portal but a terminus which leads nowhere. Such an absolute cessation cannot be an event. At most it is half an event, one which has a beginning but somewhere soon after that ceases to be. Events, on the other hand, make sense because they round themselves off and can be apprehended as wholes; in principle, they can be transcended and viewed externally. In this strict sense, death is not an event. It also follows that we cannot know what death is. It can happen to us, but there is something *a priori* about it as a notion. We *say* we all die because we define life in that way. Even if death is a final curtain, we are not actors on a stage, in spite of that famous analogy. Personages in plays do not experience the final curtain; the actors do. And the protagonists in the play (or novel) do not live happily ever after. There are no events after the falling of the curtain, the closing of the book.

Going out of existence might be compared with destruction. A man can be put to death, but he can also be destroyed. Dying is absolute. It is the permanent extinction of the light of his awareness. Destruction is different. This can be seen if we compare destruction with harming and damaging. A man cannot be damaged: but his hearing, his eyesight, or his kneecap can be damaged.

You'll ruin (harm, injure) your eyes, reading in the dark.

He ruined (harmed) his health by excessive drinking.

His hearing was damaged at the explosion.

He has a damaged heart.

He hurt himself (his toe, his fingers).

He was ruined in the crash of 1929.

He ruined (hurt) his chances.

We can formulate a clear and definite account of the form and function of the eyes, lungs, or kneecap. There is a system (a whole) in terms of which these parts can be said to be functioning well or not. The context sets an extrinsic standard that allows one to decide that the organ has been damaged, harmed, or ruined. We can see that, as means, these parts are not fulfilling their ends. (Such ends are not internalized.)[17] The case is the same with wealth. Not everyone is wealthy nor would we claim that wealth was among the essences of a man; but given the fact that he has wealth, a man can be ruined financially by things that he does or things that happen to him.

It is not easy to say what man's normal optimal condition should be as a whole, and it seems unlikely that we can establish an extrinsic norm. This is why it is impossible to speak of harming or damaging a man as a whole, for these verbs relate to specific ills.[18] The term "destroy" can apply to man as a whole—for example, an evil man can deliberately set out to destroy someone (say in revenge, as Iago did). Experiences that deprave and corrupt people destroy them—slavery, prolonged torture, a criminal environment, drugs, pornography.[19] Destruction, then, can come about although life goes on. Anyone who has been dehumanized has been destroyed, and that means that their integrity (their integratedness) and what is a requirement for integrity, a fully sensitized awareness, have been obliterated. He has lost his sense of being a person. A destroyed man can continue to exist but he ceases to *live*. He is not a human being.

That human integrity can be destroyed and in death be obliterated, can illuminate our fear of death. Lucretius obsessively tells us that it is the unknown that we fear and there is nothing to fear in death. Still this fear is not only a perfectly human failing, but an important one. While we cannot really contemplate a nonevent (nor really fear it) our deaths can cast a doubt upon the quality of what precedes it—and what we contemplate and agonize over is whether our life itself has the quality of an event—a meaningful coherence that makes having undergone it worthwhile. If we are fortunate, our lives can become biographies—stories with a unity radiated by a central meaning that draws in all the disparate, perhaps irrelevant occurrences, endowing them with significance, the early events prophecying what is to come, later ones echoing this theme poignantly and memorably. We want a life that we can call fortunate and happy after it is over, and even if not a hero, to have been a person. The life of Socrates is the paradigm here, and the lives of some artist-heroes. Dying is indeed fearful if the life it closes will fall apart, nothing really making sense of it, or if existence has no meaning intrinsically so that the moments after death alone can reveal the meaning of life in a set of rewards and consequences. Without awareness, pain or death have no reality nor any significance. In contemplating one's life, if one is unaware of the possibilities that life might have held (what a calling, a vocation, a great love might have done to it) one senses no loss. It is wholly true in this instance that ignorance is bliss.

We fear death also because its causes are often painful. We think existence in itself is a good, that it is worthwhile being alive at all costs, even if it is the life of a slave, a cripple, an idiot, a victim of malignant cancer. A cynic would say it is human delusion that accounts for this: in secret, even unconsciously, we expect a cure to be discovered tomorrow—a cure for terminal cancer, mental deficiency, an unfortunate existence, an ill-lived life. But one need not be so cynical about human motives and self-deception. It is not true that being alive in itself is worthwhile—the quality it has makes all the difference. At the hedonistic level of physical existence, perhaps breathing and the rhythm of vitality in themselves yield a kind of pleasure, but not without qualification, for example, the provision that some factor (like discomfort or disease) does not cancel it out. Death is not painful, but the conditions that bring it on are often painful—illness, decrepitude, a weakening of our mental faculties. A decline is always painful to contemplate so that death as a termination may well be a blessing. This is why we can contemplate suicide. Naturally, we cannot contemplate something which is nothing, if contemplating suicide means contemplating death. We cannot put an end to something like our stream of consciousness which phenomenally has no beginning or end. It has been going on forever—we experience it so—since we do not witness its coming into being or its going out. Though selective, our memory gives us a sense of infinitude. In envisioning death, the best we can do is to imagine it as endless darkness, endless sleep, (all metaphors) or in terms of how the places we vacate will be filled in. We *can* contemplate the method of taking our life, and *weigh* the "reasons" pro and con that might justify the act. Are there nonpainful ways to bring about death? Is there one that would not look like suicide so that the world might be deceived? In what way is nonexistence better than the quality of the consciousness that I suffer now? What of the responsibilities that my death would prevent me from fulfilling? We might envision what the consequences of our nonexistence would be for those who survive us (this is what gives plausibility to those who say, implausibly, that all acts of suicide are attempts to punish those who love us). Unlike death itself, the causes and after-effects of death can be studied. Suicide thus may be a rational act, whereas for most of us, death is just a piece of behavior.

One is tempted to say death is very personal. One suffers alone. But suffering as well as its subjectivity are here metaphors. Death as sleep reduces it to something familiar and comfortable (thus giving plausibility to the view that we awaken from death). We may think of it as a journey to a distant land. We can picture it as instantaneous, or as slow, thus comforting ourselves that it is a temporal phenomenon that is thoroughly familiar. Everything dies: love dies, hope dies, inspiration fails, talents dry up, opportunity goes away.

Strictly speaking, death cannot be known. But there are three ways in which we can talk about a knowledge of death. (1) We can externally live through someone's death. Friends and lovers die and the losses may be very great. But the suffering and particularly the loss is ours—we who do not die but survive. (2) We *share* someone's death when the spiritual relationship between two persons and the physical proximity are so close that one large experience results. The suffering, the pain, the indignity, the smell of death, the defiance of the dying person before death or his willing participation in it—all of these are combined in an intuitive, immediate whole. In such instances, a sense of loss or grief are not the natural consequences of the death but a profound exhaustion, accompanied by a sense of relief; for death has been a struggle and now there is release.[20] Such intuitive experiences are rare. For most of us, even the death of someone we love involves merely close observation, not a sharing. (Even Horatio was refused his share of death by Hamlet.) (3) What would it be like to know our own deaths? Camus made much of being condemned to death. The plague outside, the stranger inside. We will face the firing squad in fifteen minutes. When we are confronted with our own death in this dramatic way, what happens? All manner of things: some cry, some perspire, some become incontinent, a goodly number face death with courage and dignity. Of what does this courage and dignity consist? In accepting death as a matter of course? Facing a firing squad is not a matter of course. In not being afraid? It seems wholly natural to be afraid, to be outraged, even if one's crime has been monstrous.[21] One is told to prepare for one's death. Though praying and confessing seem to be meant, the only real form of confession is to review one's life. Only if one can accept one's life as it has been lived, can one face death with courage. Otherwise, there would be regret, confusion; and if the case is bad, panic. We may not be ready for death; we may be too young with little in our lives to justify it. Everything may exist in the future as possibilities to be savored. For the rest, faced with it, death becomes nothing, and that is why, often, to the dying, love and forgiveness alone matter. Having surveyed their lives (being up against it) they find that what was most precious, most worthwhile, was some variant of these. Soldiers in battle and civilians in sudden disaster have often displayed extraordinary courage and devotion. The courage and the will to sacrifice, it would seem, spring from the fact that the death they face for their country, their fellow soldiers, or for humanity endows, at that unexpected moment, a meaning and a worth to their lives singly or as a group—a meaning which they might not have quite chosen in this way but which death brings about. We can view our lives as events, just as we might a work of art, our lives being a not so dramatic epic poem. A fine death *is* a fine life; a bad death, the realization of a brutal, barbaric existence.

Death is reflexive. It has no other side. This is why it is said sometimes that our whole life passes before our dimming eyes in the moment of death.

The final words of Gertrude Stein: What is the answer?

Alice B. Toklas: (silence)

Gertrude Stein: In that case, what is the question?[22]

V

What survives when *objects* of art are destroyed and no longer exist? Against the existence that works of art enjoy, what notion may be introduced?[23] Being, I might have said. But that is thoroughly equivocal. Nonexistence, anti-existence, trans-existence: something, that is, that compels us, though even in its coming into being, it refuses to come into existence and it refuses to be limited. This is how the idea of non-existence enters the dialectic of thought about art. This dialectical node is still dark, and I have tried to cast light on it by introducing the idea of death as a form of non-existence.

What is the connection of art and death? There are a number that have interested others. *Ars longa vita brevis.* Art, like goodness and truth, is eternal. It survives death. If it is eternal, it must have being: and it must be this being (now translated into essence) which gives vitality and sense to the work of art. Even if the object of art is destroyed, the heroic creative activity (seen as an act of love by Plato) will give the lover immortality. And this again allows the artist-lover to escape the ring of existence.

Or again, dying itself might be seen as an art. Creation and death are one. So an art with death, or the possibility of death, at its core is the finest art. That is life itself: bullfighting as an art; death in the arena; Zen and the art of swordsmanship; flower arrangement of a morning glory that cannot survive the noon;[24] the dying swan.

Art also has revealed aspects of the reality of death to us: the death of Ivan Ilyich, Hamlet, "Memoirs from the House of the Dead," String Quartet in A Minor, Op. 132 (Beethoven), "Death and the Maiden" (Schubert), "Requiem Mass" (Mozart, Verdi), "Descent from the Cross" (Rubens, Van der Weyden, El Greco). The artists' visions in these cases mean more than the subject matter itself.

None of these happen to be my concern. The reality that works of art have which is independent of their existence, the ontological status of this reality—that is the theme. And not all things that masquerade as art are of concern to me.

Many works of art are satisfied to be locked in the realm of existence, first as matter, spatial articulation and sensuous surfaces; and second as phenomenal occurrences in our actively participating consciousnesses. Such art is sufficiently realized in the medium itself and is best exemplified in beautiful art. But not all works of art, and few important examples,[25] fall into this class. An artifact, we know, may exist and be thoroughly dead, just as a man may exist and be a relic of humanity. We also know that a work of art may not exist and yet make its presence felt powerfully. This reality is like death. It has no other side. So although we might feel that an intractable, dense work of art is attempting to reveal, to capture something that is on the other side of the fabric of the sensuous surfaces, there is nothing on the other side of them. The being of art is not a transcendent in any form, and extrinsic to it. So we are returned to the art itself. But we cannot then explain it pragmatically in terms of the action of the artist. The substance of the work of art cannot be his intentions, for there are works of art that "circumscribe" an unending (because unended and impossible) series of moves. Such series cannot be said to be intentional. The art, moreover, is not the historical moment that produced the object (existence again) nor its hypothetical, fictional essences and principles (transcendence again). Thus causes and motives are all irrelevant. There is, however, a double reflex in a work of art (unlike death that is only singly reflexive). It reflects back on what preceded it in the immediate experience, just as death reviews the life it brings to a close. *But in certain works of art (the anti-sensuous, anti-body) the being of a work of art points further at a domain of unpredictable possibility which is in the dense substance itself. What it signalizes, however, is not itself an existent. Nor is it the fully articulated, lucid, antecedent experience that we call its form. It points at the unlimited.*

One may find the reaching for the limitless in the most surprising places: in Shakespeare's torturing of English syntax and his heedless compression of time schemes;[26] in Poussin's geometrical landscape of the spirit; in Haydn's wit, particularly as it expresses itself in the startling harmonic shifts that are irreducible to principles; in Sharaku's kabuki prints; in Cezanne's apples. Like the melancholy of the slow movements of a Mozart concerto that so ineffably conflicts with its surface gaiety, brilliance, and assurance, or the skeletal simplicity of the seasonal images of a haiku by Basho, the *being* of such art reverberates in the mind, disturbingly, endlessly, having risen from the death of its material existences. One is tempted to say that the unlimited and the nonexistent cannot have anything to do with art. The reason seems to be that these features, being unpredictable and unmanageable, are meaningless. That, however, is the prejudice that only form and articulation can create meanings; that what emerges must be lucid and universal; that it must celebrate pleasure, affirm life and existence. But as death shows us, there are many forms of integrity.[27] The modern conceit of art as a machine, a machine that destroys itself, is nothing new. Having destroyed itself, Tinguely's sculpture has taken on a life of notoriety, both being and symbolizing that aspect of art that is narcissistic and auto-cannibalistic. Tinguely's example was too self-conscious, too conceptual, and too crowd-conscious not to betray insufficient integrity. But any work of art has always been willing to die. They were all willing to die and to die with dignity and courage because, being works of art, they possessed integrity and authenticity.

I have tried to elucidate the sort of being art has by discussing nonexistence and death as one way of understanding it. If that was an analogy, it is no longer clear to me which way the analogy points. I had thought that death was familiar and that it would light up the idea of art. But it may be, finally, that art was showing me what death—and thus man's life—is like.

NOTES

1. Benedetto Croce, *Aesthetic* (New York, 1953), p. 8.

2. This dictum can also be made to apply to literature with suitable modifications.

3. There is nothing bad about this. The copies may be better, more interesting, than the original. Provided the artistic tradition does not regard copying as in itself unrespectable (e.g., many artistic traditions in the Far East) the copyist may heroically try to relive and recapture the original impulse of creation. Many masterpieces of oriental art are known by copies. There is a genre, too, that contain in their titles the phrase "in the style of Master—" (though perhaps these are closer to imitations or even variations than copies).

4. K. G. Pontus Hultén, *The Machine as seen at the End of the Mechanical Age* (New York, 1968), p. 168ff.

5. E. D. Hirsch, Jr., *Validity in Interpretation* (New Haven, 1967). See pp. 71f, 86, 100, 106f.

6. This possibility is raised in a quotation which Hirsch presents with approval and he subsequently does not find it necessary to question this. Compare this passage, however, with p. 81 where he rejects the possibility of calling a particular meaning a genre.

7. Ellis Waterhouse, "Ascanius Shooting the Stag of Sylvia" in David Piper, ed., *Enjoying Paintings* (Middlesex, 1964), p. 211.

8. Kenneth Clark, *Leonardo da Vinci* (Cambridge, 1952), p. 117.

9. The situation is the same as when Mozart performs his own piano concerti (which requires the collaboration of an orchestra) or of one of his own piano sonatas.

10. Frank Corsaro, "A Small Matter of Survival," *New York Times,* 16 March 1969, p. D19.

11. Corsaro, in this case, has some psychoanalytic "evidence" to support his reading of the text (both the libretto and the "music" which he opposes to it).

12. I do not by this have in mind actual transcriptions such as Bach-Stokowsky, Bach-Ormandy, Handel-Harty, Ravel-Mussorgsky.

13. The case is most obvious in the ballet. A ballet by Martha Graham, danced by Miss Graham herself, is such a hyphenated object with a date superscript attached: e.g., "Appalachian Spring"—Graham-Graham (30 October 1944), Graham-Graham (1945), however often she

performed the work. The dance was revived in 1968 and these recreated instances are Graham-Ethel Winters (various dates). Much surprise and awe were voiced by critics reviewing the revival; they expressed surprise that Ethel Winters, dancing what was formerly Martha Graham's role, should look so uncannily like the reincarnation of Martha Graham of the 1940's. This is an extraordinary instance of the resurrection of a work of art.

14. This motto can be understood in two ways. See Erwin Panofsky, "Et in Arcadia Ego: Poussin and the Elegiac Tradition" in *Meaning in the Visual Arts* (Garden City, 1955), p. 295.

15. One may say that the beautiful is a symbol of the transcendent. A symbolic relationship, however, is usually conventional and external. A work of art can only *show* what it means *as a work of art*.

16. On the Nō drama, see Ezra Pound, "Noh Plays (1916)" in *Translations* (New York, n.d.); Donald Keene, ed., *Anthology of Japanese Literature* (New York, 1955), pp. 258–304; and Arthur Waley, tr., *The Nō Plays of Japan* (London, 1921). As another kind of example, I might have taken up African fetish figures: encrusted with pieces of mirror that look like openings in the body as they reflect light as a path for the soul, and decorated with pieces of red cloth and covered with scores of spikes that seem to nail down the spirit. The aesthetic function of silence, stillness, immobility, and boredom in the Nō drama, and the relation of these to transcendent art in general are topics that need further pursuit.

17. In most of these examples, human will seems to be involved (e.g., the hurt, the damage could have been avoided), but this does not seem to be true in all cases, e.g., financial ruin in a crash, or the possession of a damaged heart. Avoidability may be relevant to some difference between ruin and damage, but it is not of central interest here.

18. Of course, the word "destroy" *can* be applied to eyes, hearing, etc., where the obliteration is total. My point here is that the word "destroy" can be applied to specific entities like the heart or to processes like vision, and also to a human being as a whole. Harm, damage, etc. can be applied only to specific processes that involve external criteria. "He was hurt (harmed)" usually means some aspect of his body or his feelings. The colloquial expression "I was destroyed (wrecked) by what he said" fits my analysis here.

19. I mean by pornography, works of expression that are obscene; and by obscene, experiences that tend to deprave and corrupt people. Whether or not there are sexual-erotic experiences that deprave and corrupt, I leave an open question. (It would partly depend on the norms of a society: e.g., a rigidly Puritan one would have norms of health/corruption different from a more open society.) If there are sexual-erotic experiences that corrupt people, forms of expressions that embody them would be pornographic. It seems to me clear that certain forms of violence are clearly corrupting so that expressions of violence that are dehumanizing would be pornographic.

20. A sexual parallel is appropriate here, as in the *liebestod* or the climax of a sexual union.

21. Perhaps monsters commit monstrous crimes, but being monsters, they would not be capable of a sense of outrage.

22. Alice B. Toklas, *What is Remembered* (New York, 1963), p. 173.

23. If works of art can die, then they are created too. They are creatures then (e.g., in Spanish, *creatura* means a child). This reinforces the parallel between art and persons, being and human being.

24. Yasunari Kawabata, *A Thousand Cranes* (New York, 1968), p. 88.

25. Beautiful art is not as deeply rewarding as art that points toward death. In any estimation of a civilization, its height and depth are measured by works such as Euripides' "Bacchae" and "Trojan Women," Michelangelo's "Pieta Rondanini," "King Lear," "The Book of Job," Rembrandt's late self-portraits, the late string quartets of Beethoven. Against these, pleasant art, good taste, and decorative art are reduced to insignificance. When we protest that there is nothing wrong with beautiful art, since it enhances life, we have taken the first steps toward the evasion and opiate function performed so often by art, and we forget the need for seriousness, resolution, and non-self-indulgence that initiates artistic vision.

26. E.g., "The Winter's Tale," "King Lear," and even "Hamlet."

27. From art, the dialectic can turn to man again. We commonly feel it arrogant to think we can figure out a man completely. Yet in practice, we dislike mystery. We like people to be familiar—lucid, frank, amiable, loyal, harmonious, gracious, high-principled, moral—in other words, well-formed in his internal and external relations. But a person may be intractable, negative, rejecting, and unfathomable, and for all that, be *real*. We may feel that the strange, dark moves of his mind still spring from a man of integrity. And though we may be unable to "explicate" his form, we may yet feel a moving presence. Being able "to give an account" is not the only important thing, though, of course, there is a great difference between the unpredictability and incoherence of madness and the unlimitedness of an extraordinary person. (But in some cases, it may not be easy to tell which, for example, Marquis de Sade.) There are different kinds of art, and we now see, different kinds of men, and neither should be reducible.

HENRY W. JOHNSTONE, JR.

ON BEING A PERSON

I

Imagine an array of contiguous square jars forming a kind of grid. Each jar is filled with a different dye. A man has a handful of white pellets, and tosses the handful into the air over the array. Various pellets then land in various jars and are stained with various colors. The man fishes a pellet out of a jar. He then asks the following questions:

(1) "Why did this pellet land where it did?"

(2) "What would this pellet have been like if it had landed elsewhere?"

(3) "What would this pellet have been like if it had not landed at all?"

(4) "Was it a good thing that this pellet landed where it did?"

(5) "Was it a good thing that this pellet landed at all?"

(6) "Would it be a good thing if the color were removed from this pellet?"

These questions have various kinds of answers if they have answers at all. It might be argued that (1) has no answer at all; that there is no way of explaining where any particular pellet has landed, even though one might determine statistically the probable distribution of all the pellets throughout the jars. On the other hand, it might be maintained that (1) does have an answer, one that depends on the initial position of the pellet in the man's hand and the velocity and direction of the motion with which the man tosses the pellets into the air. The second question has an answer that it would be hard to dispute: if this red pellet had landed in the jar containing blue dye instead of landing where it did, it would have been blue. The third question needs some amplification. Why didn't the pellet land? If because the man didn't release it, or because it landed on the edge of one of the jars, then clearly it would still be white. If because the law of gravity has been suspended, there is no clear answer.

The answers to the fourth, fifth, and sixth questions depend on the purposes of the man. If he is attempting, by tossing the pellets, to dye a certain number of them red and a certain number blue, then whether he regards it as a good or bad thing that a given pellet landed where it did will depend on whether his attempt was a success or failure. If he is trying to dye all the pellets, then it is a good thing for all of them to land in the dyes; if he is, on the other hand, trying to keep some of them white, then each pellet that lands in the dyes reduces his degree of success. Neither one of these considerations quite touches on the question whether it was a good thing that some particular pellet landed, but presumably there is a criterion by which this question can be answered, too, and similarly for the question about removing the color from the pellet.

II

All over the world it is raining people. They can fall into different centuries, into different countries, into different social strata, and into different families. Someone asks the following questions.

(1′) "Why was this person born where and when he was?"

(2′) "What would this person have been like if he had been born elsewhere?" [For example, what if he had had different parents, as would have been the case if his mother and father had not met?]

(3′) "What would this person have been like if he had not been born at all?"

(3′a) "What would the world have been like if this person had not been born at all?"

(4') "Was it a good thing that this person was born where and when he was?"

(5') "Was it a good thing that this person was born at all?"

(6') "Would it be a good thing if this person died?"

To some extent, we can answer these questions in the way we have answered (1)–(6). If we say, for example, that a person was born where he was because his mother was there, our answer to (1') corresponds to the mechanical answer to (1). It is in fact often helpful to answer (1) in this way. Thus we say that Jesus was born in Bethlehem because his parents had stopped there on their way to be taxed. Yet if we have asked (1') about Jesus, this may not be at all the kind of answer we want. What we may instead have in mind is, "In the rain of people, why did Jesus fall in the Near East rather than Mexico? Why did he fall in the First rather than the Fifteenth Century?" When (1') is a question about an avatar it is open to this interpretation.

What I mean by an avatar becomes clear from the study of (2'). An avatar is the sort of person concerning whom it is meaningful to ask (2'), i.e., a person who might have been born at one place and time or another. Not that the answer to (2') will be as simple or straightforward as the answer to (2). Times and places may not affect persons in quite as predictable a way as that in which dyes affect pellets. We usually presume that the person will interact with his environment in complex ways rather than being passively colored by it. However, both in traditional Christian theology and in contemporary genetic theory it is assumed that the avatar is largely independent of his environment. At his second coming, Jesus will stand forth from the wicked world as exactly the same person he was before. And if we had had access to Mozart's genes, we could have produced another musical genius even in an environment in which the role and significance of music is vastly different from what it was in Eighteenth Century Europe.

It is precisely when we think of the person as wholly the product of his environment—wholly colored by it—that we find (2') a meaningless question. While the pellet can exist prior to landing in the dye, it makes no sense to say that an ordinary person could have existed prior to his birth or conception or could have been born or conceived under radically different circumstances. Thus (2') is not a meaningful question as applied to my neighbor Smith. Perhaps one can make sense of the hypothesis that Smith might have been born in Minneapolis rather than St. Paul. But what of the hypothesis that he might have been born in the Nineteenth rather than the Twentieth Century? Apart from the Smith who was actually born (or conceived) in the circumstances in which he was actually born (or conceived) there is no Smith at all. How could we identify someone born in the Nineteenth Century as our neighbor Smith? Falling into the Nineteenth Century, he would no longer be available to fall into the Twentieth; so there would be no neighbor Smith to serve as the basis of the identification. It may be objected that I am overlooking the possibility of a Nineteenth-Century Smith's being reincarnated in the Twentieth Century, thus being born or conceived twice. But to take this possibly seriously is precisely to regard Smith as an avatar. A non-avatar is a person who can be born or conceived only once. Hence it would be in principle impossible to identify a non-avatar with someone born or conceived at some other time or place. A non-avatar is defined by his place in the people rain.

The question that is beginning to emerge is, "What is the metaphysical status of the person?" It would seem that he has a different status under different circumstances. The ordinary person —the non-avatar—is regarded as a particular series of events. He is a complex and time-consuming member of the same category of which the passage of a jet aircraft through the sky is a simple and short-lived example. Just as it would be inconsistent to suppose that this particular passage could have occurred anywhere else or at any other time, so I cannot form the idea of my neighbor Smith as having had any biography except the biography he did have. But sometimes we regard persons as substances rather than as series of events. We think of their biographies, or at least of certain aspects of their biographies, as accidental, and feel that we can quite consistently imagine the same person as having undergone various possible biographies. Even someone refusing to accept Christian theology or contemporary genetics is bound to regard at least one person as a substance—namely, himself. I will expand this point later.

Question (3′) obviously applies to avatars only. The idea of a non-avatar who has not yet participated in the people rain is incoherent. The non-avatar does not begin to exist until he has landed. He defines himself by appearing. He is more like a bubble than a pellet. If all people were non-avatars, the pellet analogy would, in fact, be seriously defective, and ought then to be replaced by a bubble analogy. Like non-avatars, but like passages of jets through the sky, bubbles appear only once. It does not make sense to ask of this bubble, "Is that the same as the bubble that broke five minutes ago?" or if it does make sense to ask the question, we can answer it a priori.

The next question (3'a), applies to avatars and non-avatars alike, but cannot be answered with confidence except with respect to certain avatars and in terms of certain theologies. If Jesus had not been born at all, the world would still be immersed in Original Sin. But what if Napoleon had not been born? Would someone else have done what he did? This question is not straightforward nonsense like (2') and (3') when asked about non-avatars. It is instead very puzzling.

Questions (4')–(6') all presuppose a standard of value. In addition (4') and (5') presuppose that a person has an identity apart from the identity he acquires as the result of being conceived and born, i.e., those questions apply to avatars only. If I say to my friend, "Thanks for having been born in my time!" I am treating him like an avatar. But question (6') is not reserved for avatars only, for after his death a person continues to be identifiable. After Smith is gone we can still speak of the Smith that was, and hence we can speak of the value or disvalue of his death.

One feature common to all the questions so far is that they require answers from various points of view none of which can be identified as the point of view of the subject of any question itself. They are rather the points of view of people concerned with pellets or with other people. An important difference between the two sets of questions, however, is that (1) we can ask, "What is a pellet to those asking about it?"; but we cannot ask, "What is a pellet to itself?" On the other hand, (2) we can ask both, "What is a person to other people asking about him?" and, "What is a person to himself?" The second set of questions might be characterized as questions about members of a set P such that any x in P is capable of asking (and answering) any of the questions about x himself. Thus when a person says, "I am lucky to have been born in this country," he is in effect answering (4') about himself. To answer a question concerning himself, a person normally uses the first personal pronoun. A pellet, however, cannot use the first personal pronoun. But while the use of this pronoun would be inappropriate to the answers to any of (1')–(6')—since the questions are asked by persons other than the persons they are about—the persons they are about could, if called upon, use the first personal pronoun, while the pellets could not.

I turn to a third series of questions, all of which can be appropriately answered in terms of the first personal pronoun.

[131]

III

(1″) "Why was I born where and when I was?"

(2″) "What would I have been like if I had been born elsewhere?" [E.g., if my parents had never met?]

(3″) "What would I have been like if I had not been born at all?"

(4″) "Was it a good thing that I was born where and when I was?"

(5″) "Was it a good thing that I was born at all?"

(6″) "Would it be a good thing if I died?"

What sets these questions wholly apart from (1)–(6) is that what each question is about is precisely the asker of the question. The difference here is a difference in motivation. If the man who throws the pellets is inclined to ask questions about what has befallen them, such questions arise by virtue of an interest or curiosity on his part. Were it not for this man or some colleague, there would be no questions at all. Certainly, any of the pellets has a nature than can be defined without any reference to the fact that the questions have arisen. Similarly, I can identify another person without asking any of (1″)–(6″) about him. But I cannot identify myself without asking at least some of (1″)–(6″) about myself. For the way in which I identify physical things and other people is not a satisfactory way to identify myself. It may be a satisfactory way to identify myself to others, but not to myself. If all that I know about myself is my own biography, I know what person I am, just as I know what person Smith is, but I do not know what it is to be the person I am. I identify myself, but I do not recognize myself, i.e., my identification does not guarantee that I will feel that the person I identify is familiar. Victims of amnesia can be told what biographies they have lived, but such accounts do not entail recovery. The amnesiac must recognize himself. To recognize myself, I must know what it is to be the person I am, and hence what it is to be a person. To be a person is to consider the possibility of having had some other biography, or no biography at all; i.e., to recognize the person behind the biography. It is thus to ask (1″)–(6″) about oneself. That one asks the question is thus essential to one's identification of oneself as a person.

On my view, then, the fact that the questions can arise in the absence of any external spectator is essential to my nature. This is true in both a weaker and a stronger sense. As a person, I must be *capable* of asking questions, including questions about what has befallen me. But also, as a person I must *actually* ask at least some of these questions. One who did not ask any of them would be incapable of dealing with or evaluating himself. He would be a bubble. But he would not appear to himself at all, even as a bubble. As we shall see, anyone who appears to himself at all must regard himself as more than a bubble.

Turning now to (1″), we see that it *can* have the same kind of straightforward meaning that (1) and (1′) have. I *may* be curious about my own origins. But not necessarily, for the question may also express Weltschmerz. Why was I not born in a happier time? Interpreted in this way, the question presupposes that I could have been born in the happier time I have in mind. It presupposes, in other words, that I am an avatar. Each of us in fact is avatar to himself. This means that each of us supposes that he can recognize himself in some other way than the way in which he recognizes those of his friends whom he does not regard as avatars. In other words, he need not identify himself in terms of his own biography. My neighbor probably regards me as a person who could have had no existence at all except as having been born about fifty years ago, and thus would regard the task of recognizing me among those living at the happier time as logically impossible. But I, at least as I fantasize about a happier time, am assuming that I could recognize *myself* among those living at the happier time. This means that I do not necessarily identify myself as a person living here and now.

It may be objected that if I do *not* identify myself as a person living here and now, I contradict myself, for without my here-and-now memories of my name and origins, I cannot identify myself at all. One possible reply is that I am not claiming that my fantasizings are necessarily coherent. Perhaps there is a contradiction implicit in my supposing that if I were elsewhere and elsewhen, I would still identify myself. Indeed, if being elsewhere and elsewhen involves being stripped of all my present memories, there is a sense of "identify" in which I could *not* identify myself. But such an implicit contradiction must be contrasted with the explicit contradiction of supposing that my neighbor the non-avatar could have been elsewhere and elsewhen. This is simply a *contradictio in adjecto*, like a square circle. But although we cannot visualize square circles, it is psychologically possible incoherently to adopt premises leading to the conclusion that square circles exist.

But in making this reply, I am really conceding more than I

need to. If to identify myself means to be able to give my name and say something about my origins, then, if stripped of all my memories, it is true that as a denizen of the happier times I could not identify myself. But I could still recognize myself as a denizen of those times; I could see that I was there and then, even though I did not know who I was. I do not mean that I could see that I lived at times defined by their contrast with other times; for that too would require memory. I mean only that I could pick myself out as one of those alive. Indeed, this is something I can always do; my very use of the first personal pronoun is an act of self-reference or picking myself out. Hence the very hypothesis that I have been transported to happier times implies that I can recognize myself in my new surroundings. If I could not, it would not be I transported but someone else, transported or indigenous. On the other hand, the very hypothesis that my neighbor has been transported does not imply that I can pick *him* out.

Each of us is an avatar to himself simply because each of us can refer to himself. The password of the avatar club is simply the first personal pronoun "I," correctly used. If I use "I" merely to refer to someone whose biography is familiar to me, it is only an accident that I use it correctly. Someone else's biography may be totally unfamiliar to him, as in amnesia. But the victim of amnesia can still use "I" correctly. He does so when he uses it to achieve self-reference. What the self-referrer refers to is not a biography, but simply himself as a referrer.

If I can imagine myself in the happier time, why can't I imagine my neighbor as being there *with* me, having accompanied me there? Clearly I can—if I think of him as an avatar. If I do not think of him in this way, however, the task of picking him out in the happier times is logically impossible because he is *defined* as a person living in *these* times. Even if I do think of him as an avatar, I do not assume that I can pick him out in the happier times the way I pick myself out. In my fantasizings, what I am likely to assume is that he and I have journeyed into the happier times *together*, so that the problem of picking him out does not arise.

If I *can* think of my neighbor as an avatar, it may seem that the distinction between avatars and non-avatars is arbitrary. What is the point of the distinction? Why not simply consider everyone a non-avatar? Or simply consider everyone an avatar?

Not everyone can be a non-avatar, however, in view of the fact that each of us is an avatar to himself. Regardless of the contradictions that may or may not be implicit in our temporal fanta-

[134]

sizings, it is simply a fact that a person does not recognize himself exclusively in biographical terms. In making plans and decisions he identifies himself as relatively independent of the circumstances in which he actually finds himself. (He does this even though it may be the case that his plans and decisions are in fact entailed by his circumstances.) One who never transcended the circumstances in which he found himself, at least to the extent necessary to evaluate or comment on these circumstances, would not be a person at all, because he would not be self-conscious. At best he could be conscious in the sense of undergoing experience, but he could not criticize the experience undergone.

Not everyone, on the other hand, is ordinarily regarded as an avatar. Evidence for this can be seen in the strains to which the pellet analogy is subject. Such strains are expressed by the oddness of questions like (2') and (3') as applied to ordinary people. Ordinary people are defined by their biographies, and hence cannot be identified with people with different biographies. Further evidence is the conviction shared by many that a person's death terminates his role as a person on earth. If we did not regard death as final, we might regard life as cheaper than we do. In the Orient, life is cheap, but murder is still a crime.

Someone is certain to point out to me that despite all I have said there are Oriental philosophies and religions on which everyone *is* an avatar—indeed that there is an Occidental parallel in the Platonic Myth of Er. From such a point of view, the pellet analogy is sound through and through, and there is no strain in any of the questions I have so far considered. To this objection, it might be replied that there are also philosophies on which the bubble analogy is sound through and through; for example, the position expressed in Sartre's *Being and Nothingness.* Sartre's position seems to me to fail to do justice to our ability to transcend our projects: to fantasize and to plan. Similarly there are attitudes to which the Er-Oriental point of view seems not to do justice. We regard a life as fragile and as of infinite worth. We think of the individual as absolutely unique and irreplaceable. Such attitudes conflict with the belief that the individual cannot be destroyed and that his disappearance from history is never more than temporary. In fact, the Sartrean and Er-Oriental positions presuppose one another. Life is regarded as fragile and unique precisely because a man *can* transcend his projects to the extent of envisaging the end of his earthly existence; only as an avatar can he see that death is in the cards. But I transcend my projects, taking the position of an avatar, precisely because I attach a unique value to my own life. If I did not regard my life as worth preserving, there would be no motivation leading to the adoption of the view that I am an avatar.

The distinction I am trying to develop is not one that can be confidently and objectively applied, like the distinction between red and green or odd and even. It is rather a tension between two distinct ways of conceiving a person. Sometimes the pellet analogy is felicitous; we think of the person as having an existence that is not exhausted by the details of his biography. Sometimes, however, the bubble analogy is more felicitous, in that we find that we do not know how to think of the person apart from what he actually is. Thus we think of the person sometimes as a time-bound event and sometimes as a timeless congeries of characters in principle identifiable through a number of particular temporal appearances. In particular cases, we simply may not know how to think of someone confronting us, or we may be inclined to think of him in both ways.

I do not wish to leave the impression, however, that in my view whether we regard a person as an avatar or a non-avatar is always the outcome of an arbitrary metaphysical decision. In at least one case it is not. I must regard myself as more than a complex biographical event. This necessity is entailed by my capacity to refer to myself by using the first personal pronoun or in some other way. For I can refer to myself without referring to any of the details of my biography; if I am suffering from amnesia, I can refer to myself without even knowing any of these details. The use of "I" presupposes a commitment to a particular metaphysical view. It might be countered that an occasion on which "I" is used is itself a detail of a biographical event. But if "I" is used to achieve self-reference, this analysis cannot be correct. Perhaps events can refer—does the event of someone's shouting "Fire!" refer to a fire? —but part of an event (to wit, the person's use of "I") cannot refer to the total event of which it is a part.

When I ask (1″) in the sense of longing for a happier time (or of thanking my lucky stars that I did not live in some previous disagreeable time), I am in effect carrying out the speculation prescribed in (2″); I am imagining occupying various positions in the people rain. (3″), however, is puzzling. While I can identify myself under all circumstances, what would it mean for me to identify myself under no circumstances at all? Yet (3″) does arise as a presupposition of (5″). In order to decide whether it was a good thing that I was born at all, I must know what it would have been like not to have been born. And questions like (5″) do get asked. I can be glad or sorry that I was born. Such joy or sorrow, furthermore, can be the basis of specific action.

It is not necessary to consider in any detail the meanings of the remaining questions. Each presupposes that I am an avatar. Notice, however, that there are important differences between an avatar and a pellet. We can say with assurance that a pellet falling into the red dye will be stained red. But how can anyone, including me, be sure how I would have behaved in the Eighteenth Century? The avatar account asserts only that if I were alive in the Eighteenth Century, I could recognize myself; it does not prescribe my doings then. Of course, the account also holds that a Twentieth Century Mozart, created from Mozart's genes, would still be a musician. Once again, however, it is concerned only with the recognition of the individual; it does not prescribe what he is to do in the Twentieth Century other than to be a musical genius of the first order. As such a genius, he will in fact have to engage in creative activity of a kind that cannot be predicted. Similarly, I imagine myself as behaving with complete spontaneity elsewhere and elsewhen.

The person, then, is unpredictable in two ways. The non-avatar did not exist at all until he was born. Hence it does not even make sense to guess what he would have been or done under other circumstances. The avatar behaves spontaneously within his milieu. While we expect him to be to some extent shaped or colored by the environment into which he is born, we are never in a position to be able to say to what extent.

Both these versions of unpredictability interact and fuse as we assess the nature of other persons and of ourselves. The other—leaving aside the question whether he is an avatar or not—is unpredictable both as exercising spontaneity and as having no existence prior to his actual life. I see myself as partly the locus of an absolute spontaneity and partly a being who first came into being and then defined himself.

IV

What have I accomplished? My title was "On Being a Person." Under this title the reader might have expected some account of the distinction between what it is to be a person and what it is to be a stone or a corpse. What he got instead was a discussion of what it is to be me, i.e., what it is to be *the person I am*, a person living here and now but who might have been living elsewhere and elsewhen. This substitution may strike the reader as unsatisfactory, on the ground that its answer may seem to presuppose an answer to the question, "What is it like to be a person?" Can one discuss being the person one is without presupposing some view concerning what it is to be a person?

In reply, I will make two points. In the first place, one cannot completely answer the question, "What is it to be the person I am?," without contrasting the state of being the person one is with that of not being a person at all, e.g., a stone or a corpse. But presumably it was only the desire to know what it is to be other than a stone or corpse that led the critic to ask "What is it to be a person?" In the second place, the very question, "What is it to be a person?," can only mean "What is it *to the person* to be a person?," a question that can be answered only in terms of each person's knowledge of what it is like to be himself. One cannot be a person at all without being the person that one is. This necessity is peculiar to persons. A stone could be a stone without being the stone it is; it could have some other shape. But to be a person at all is to be *this* person.

The being of a person is reflexive in a way in which the being of an inert thing is not. One cannot be a person without knowing what it is like *to oneself* to be a person. It is entirely by virtue of this knowledge that persons place whatever value or disvalue they do on life. A stone neither fears nor embraces annihilation because it does *not* know what it is like *to itself—from its own point of view*—to be a stone. An animal fears and flees its enemies, but it does not fear or flee annihilation; for it does not know what it is like *to itself*—from its own piscine, avian, feline, or canine point of view—to be a fish, bird, cat, or dog. While it enacts the behavior of its species, it does so without taking a point of view. The fish behaves like a fish—not to itself, but to us.

RICHARD GOTSHALK

THOUGHTS ON GROWING UP*

I can remember, on a fall afternoon several years ago, driving
down a gravel road on the way to the river bottom land not far
from the farm house in southern Illinois in which my grandparents used to live. I had summered with my grandparents from
as early as I could remember until well into my college days. But so
rarely had I been in that part of the country at other times of
year, that summer, with its luxuriance of foliage and green, had
been unwittingly identified by me with the nature and character
of the place itself. So as I drove along slowly, with my eye on the
surroundings, the grays and browns and tans of late fall seemed
strange. But stranger still was the openness of the country: there
were no leaves to close off vision. And with openness came small-
ness: places that I had remembered as being quite a distance from
one another and connected only by circuitous routes, now were
visible side by side.

The impact of the difference in things from how I had remembered them was intensified by the changes that actually had
taken place. Along the gravel road was a house, large and once
well-kept, now uninhabited and untended. Across the road from
the house lay lowlands, openly visible now and showing an empty
mound of oil-permeated mud where once stood an oil well, the
excitement of whose drilling returned to me as I looked down the
dirt tracks that led out past the deserted location. Somewhat far-

[139]

ther down the road the house where my uncle had lived was gone, as was a barn into which we had unloaded hay on one hectic and intensely humid day many summers ago. Along the road and across from where my uncle had lived lay houses, familiar in their unpainted and grubby appearance. For the most part the people who now inhabited them were persons I had vaguely known, though in each of the houses death had taken a toll. Fleeting memories of those gone came back as I passed by the squalid houses of the living.

In a moment I came to a crossroad, at which the gravel road continued as a lane and then became a set of dirt tracks that led off into the bottom land. The lane led past the house of several brothers and a sister who still lived there together at the edge of the lowlands. Then suddenly it plunged downward, to level out quickly into tracks deeply rutted from vehicular traffic in muddy times of year. As the car bumped and swayed along and I entered the woods, the bleak colors of fall became replaced with the dark green of dense summer foliage, the swaying car replaced by a team of horses and a wagon creaking along.

For as I drove along I had suddenly been recalled into my childhood. I must have been about ten, not yet old enough to do much but get in the way, but eager to go along with my grandfather and uncle to work in the fields. It was an early summer day, the destination was unknown to me—someone mentioned something about the river—but since the horses were going I could ride along in the wagon and play around it for the afternoon if I wanted to. I remember the excitement of setting off, the creaking of the wagon and the plodding of the horses on the gravel, the musty smell of the sacks of corn seed, and the unyieldingness of the wagon bed. I sat toward the back, but "sat" is not really the word for it. *We* were going *to work!* The pride and innocent triumph at that fact are enough now to bring tears to my eyes. That pride mixed itself with my awareness of the fields we were passing by: was it to one of these that we were going? Then we came to the store and turned to the left toward a part of the world that was not familiar to me. Still, there was the same plodding, the same sound of harness and horse and gravel under wheelrim, the same jogging ride. It was some time before we got off that road onto a lane. As we passed by a house a man waved to my grandfather: evidently he was known in this distant and unfamiliar part of the country.

Soon I was completely lost, in another world whose connection with the farm house was unfathomable to me. It was a wilderness world. The wagon swayed and bumped as the horses plodded along. The wheelrims threw up a mixture of water and mud, so I moved toward the middle of the wagon at the back and watched the weeds pop up from underneath as we passed over and left them behind. It was a world of immense trees, and mosquitoes as well, and shade and heat and dampness. We wound our way along, passing a fork in the trail, finally coming to what seemed like a ditch. Across it we came out into an open field. There, on the rather small wilderness-crowded clearing of cultivated soil, sat a tractor and a corn planter.

Of the rest of that afternoon, I remember only fragments and snatches: brown earth and heat, the ground steaming in the sun as I watched the horses come to the end of a row; the narrow iron plate over part of the wooden tongue, making it difficult to keep my balance as I walked up and down it from ground to bed and back; the strange isolatedness of a small patch of land in an area of forest; the bite of mosquitoes, which were best escaped out in the sun; the sound of my grandfather's voice calling to the horses at the turn at the closer end of the field; the feel of grains of corn, the strange orange and yellow of their waxen bodies, the bits of cob and husk mixed in with the seed; the marvellous exhilaration of being part of a venture into the primeval, where no one was around and all had a sort of cast and hue and ring to it, an atmosphere that breathed of life and distance and vaguely felt richness and danger lurking in the interior of the woods.

Such was the day of my childhood into which I had been recalled by the swaying of the car, along with the suddenly familiar turn of the tracks and arch of the trees at the beginning of the woods I was entering. As I drove down the tracks I could see my grandfather's field, the one that abutted the river: that must have been the place. But it was hardly any distance at all from the beginning of the woods to there. Yet that was it, for there was the opening I remember; the wagon must have been over there to the left of the opening.

I took the tracks that skirted the field and led down its side to the bank of the river. At their end I got out to walk. I could not then, as I can not now, help marvelling at the contrast of what had been with what now was, what now is.

As on that occasion, so on others: I can at times become invaded by moments of my past, caught up in them so as to be there again. It is uncanny, this coming to relive something, to feel again alive in oneself the expectations and atmosphere and life of a time gone by. The sunlight, the earth, the trees, the horses, the wagon, my grandfather: these, as they were, are all gone now, yet they still remain, in me. And that young boy, those intimations of wilderness, that magic of life he innocently shared in: these also are gone, and yet not gone; that boy I am and for a moment can be with such strength and fullness that *that* time is now.

Yet not now. For however much my attention may become absorbed into a happening gone by, that absorption does not last, and afterwards it gives itself to me as what it was, as the awakening of the past in one who is therein recalled into what he was and in some way still is. I am the same, yet not the same.

That sameness, yet difference, is almost impossible to elicit accurately in thought, let alone to convey to others in words, however striking and evident it be in its character to me experientially. Yet in it lies what seems to me crucial for understanding the nature of the movement of growth in which human life is, by coming into its own.

It is that movement of growth which is to be the focus for the discussion which follows.

As a start I shall approach a rough characterization of such growth by considering something to which the experience I have just recounted attests. And that is this: that along the way of my life, I have recurrently come to find myself involved in an active relation to what is around me, such that in that relation is instituted a certain characteristic tonality and fullness, obtaining as well for a child of ten playing at the edge of a clearing in the woods as for a man of thirty walking along a river in country familiar yet strange to him. When I think upon such times and attempt to catch something of their character and import, I seem to be required to affirm a series of things. First, that whenever, wherever, and however I am in that recurrent fullness, I am to be found coming to stand with what is around me in such way that in the face of it I am enabled to find a place. Not just any place: it is *my* place into which I am entered. Second, that in this entry, what stands against me and helps me to find my place, releases and strengthens me, and does so as releasing and strengthening someone engaged in a movement. The movement in question seems best characterized as a venturing which, on those recurrent occasions when I find my place and find myself strengthened, comes to itself as an adventure within an unknown region. Finally, that in making that movement, I move on a path which is, among other things, the path of my growth. Those times of fullness which recur along that path are times when I am growing in distinctive and striking fashion.

Such times, then, are peculiarly pregnant with suggestion for a reflection seeking to understand the matter with which I am concerned here. Let me attempt now to indicate, briefly, schematically, and from the vantage point of the present, what my thought has been led to discern when it has sought to elicit from such times what they reveal about growing up.

First to be noticed are certain constants, factors which, however differently present at different times, are ever present in some fashion in the situation of my active relation to what is around me. These constancies provide a frame within which growth becomes possible and intelligible.

One is the factor of activity itself, that of myself as well as that of others. In myself, at least, that activity seems a more or less effective attending, which operates as that whereby I am primordially entered into the movement and growth in life. More particularly, in my playing as a child as well as in my walking and thinking as a man, I was venturing in such a way that my attending became drawn out and I become involved in an adventure.

A second factor, is a certain "I" which has persisted in identity throughout my life: a hidden presence, deeper than the active and particular side of myself, and the basis of all that I am in particular. Counterpart to this inward basis are kindred hidden presences inward to those persons with whom my path crosses, and to those things and places which I encounter. Whatever I may be doing, however effectively I may be doing it, with whomever and to whatever I may be related in my doing, there is a sameness in the fact of such presences to be found and reached to, a sameness in the fact of hidden sources that are needed and are able to provide support to my acting and being. This sameness in the fact of presence, however, does not signify sameness in the manner or mode or degree of presence.

A third and final factor is the presence of the convergent limits within which my activity bears me out into active relation to the limiting presence of others in the present. Those limits— birth and death, my beginning and end—are (as limits, and not as events) framing factors which ever become held together in my activity as the latter continually defines itself within their bounds.

[143]

In that ever current defining of itself, my activity fronts me on others, who are likewise active from out of themselves and who, so far as they front on me, are convergent upon me in their active existence. There is the sameness, then, of finitude, of future, past, and present limits, that persists throughout the variations and alterations that obtain in my active existence and experience.

In short, due to the presence of these three constants, those recurrent moments of fullness which seem to me crucial for growth are such that in them I ever find myself actively having to do with others within limits or bounds, my attending being drawn out so as to be operative within supporting bases effectively present in some fashion.

There is a fourth constant, as well; namely, I am continually human. Due to this humanity, however, I am human in a growing up, in a growth through childhood into adulthood, in a temporal and active working out of the humanly essential. Thus, intrinsic to the constancy of my being human, there are introduced the differences of growth.

Let me turn now to a suggestion of certain relevant differences which obtain in this growing in which I am involved in my active and particular side.

Least significant are the differences involved in the fact that I may be doing different things and that in these different things different powers are drawn into play. When I was walking and thinking, my body, my bodily powers, my mind, my mental powers, all came into play in a certain way; but the way and the kind of powers were both different from the way and kind involved in my playing and watching my grandfather and uncle at work.

More significant are such differences as revolve around the focus and mode of attention involved in my activity: as my attention differs in these respects, so my activity develops differently and my experiencing of myself and others is different. Thus, more so as a child than as a man, I came to stand in such a way, as, for the most part, to be unknowing of myself, scarcely knowing of the character of my experiencing. And this is fairly typical, for the focus and mode of attention normally mean that I am drawn out and held into what is at the focus of my attentiveness. For example, I am drawn out and held into the flight of the football attended to by me as player, the music attended to by me as listener, the work at hand attended to by me as someone engaged in certain affairs. Due to such differences in focus and in the ways of attending to what is at the focus, there emerges also a difference in the way in which the characteristic tonality in question is experienced to myself *in* my attentiveness at the time. For that tonality is one inclusive of attention, not itself to the fore or focus of attention, and thus is one experienced rather differently in the attending, even though retrospectively I can recognize that it is one and the same tonality.

All the differences I have mentioned so far *are* significant, and are significant with respect to my growing up. But their significance is that of differences in factors *in* and *through* which I grow. For "growing" is not to be identified with physical development, with development in bodily capacities and skills, with mental development, with any combination of the above, or with the accumulation of experience which these involve. Growing is something deeper, something inclusive of all these, something which accords them their place within itself as that through whose instrumentality growth takes place. And finally, growing is something which not only is not such forms of development and increase, but also is not simply a function of them.

What, then, is growth?

Let me answer this question by particular reference to the times of recurrent fullness. In them it seems to be suggested that when I grow I stretch forth and reach into a limit, I emerge onto a threshold and gain a foothold, I burst a shell, and thereby I become qualitatively altered as a human being: altered brokenly, sporadically, partially, compartmentally in a sense, yet essentially, in a way that goes to the core.

Thus when, from the vantage point of the present, I am recalled into such past moments as have distinctively instituted such growth, I find a peculiar combination. On the one hand, I am drawn out again, participant in an expansiveness, in a joy and love, in a potency. Something vital is somehow re-entered and relived. I find myself as I was in-the-making, in a crucial way growing. On the other hand, along with this, I find myself limited, saddened. Somehow what draws me out can not unfold far enough to contain me now. "If only I could then have been what I am now, have known and understood and been capable of what I am now" is one way crudely to express something of what is involved.

It is not simply that my attentiveness in that past was not all that it could have been, though perhaps that is also the case. It is not even that the fullness of those times was not all it could have been, though this also may be the case. It is rather that, recalled into that past experiencing in respect both of its patent and of its latent sides, I find myself in my active side, and yet, in that active side of myself, find something lacking, something which was not and could not have been there then. I find that entering into that expansiveness, I enter into something which, in one sense full, in another sense is not full. That is, entering into that expansiveness, I enter into my essential human power as it was once formed, and more particularly, as it was once brought to a fullness in potency appropriate to its time. But that sort of fullness was relative to that time in my life. As I grew, I entered further into that power, and on occasion found again a sort of fullness relative to that later time. This later fullness was a greater fullness, so that from out of it I found the earlier and lesser potency constrictive when I was recalled into and relived it.

Let me sum up my thoughts so far, by formulating in brief and still preliminary fashion what seems to me to characterize human growth. In growing up, we grow in respect of a power which, while in some sense always ours, is something which we must make our own by gradually entering into it in the course of a movement which carries onward through time and allows us to be instated in increasing measure in the potency that pertains to that power. Our growth, then, is in terms of a power, and is a growth into increasing potency in respect of that power; as we grow in the course of time, we grow more and more into our own power, and through such increasing potency, grow up.

At this point certain rather obvious questions press forward impatiently. For I have spoken of power and potency without having indicated the kind in question. And I have characterized growth as gradual accession in potency, yet have also spoken of growing as growing up, and that latter manner of speech normally implies a limit to the up, a maturity to be reached. The questions, then, which seem most pressing are these: "What sort of power and potency is it that is the essentially human?" "Does growth in such power and potency involve a *telos* into which one eventually enters, so as to terminate the movement upward?"

I would like to suggest answers to these questions, but to do so somewhat indirectly, by reference to a certain story which comes from the Puranic element of the Hindu tradition. First I would like to recount the story, reformulating the paraphrase of it offered by Heinrich Zimmer.[1] Then, in connection with this story, which I shall interpret as telling us something about our power, potency, and maturity, I will formulate such answers to these questions as I can.

The story in question begins with an account of the stage of creation within which the events are to take place. For the Hindu, creation has a cyclic character, moving through a series of four ages, which form one small pattern within larger patterns, all of which are repeated countlessly in the course of time.

In the case at hand, the world-order had come to the end of the last age, after which Vishnu, the Supreme Being, drew it back into himself, there to renew it before putting it forth again in the next cycle. Thus, we begin with Vishnu asleep, alone upon the primeval waters, a giant figure partly submerged and partly afloat. Inside the god is the world, like an unborn child within its mother; here, the world is restored to its primal perfection, ready to be born in the beginning of another cycle.

A holy man, Markandeya by name, is wandering inside the god, over the peaceful earth, as an aimless pilgrim. At shrines and holy places he pauses to worship, and his heart is gladdened by the piety of the people in the countries through which he roams. In the course of his aimless wandering, the old man slips, inadvertently, out through the mouth of the all-containing god. Vishnu is sleeping with his lips slightly parted, breathing with a deep, sonorous, rhythmical sound in the immense silence of the night. The astonished saint, falling from the sleeper's giant lip, plunges headlong into the primeval sea.

At first, due to Vishnu's *māyā*, Markandeya does not behold the sleeping giant, but only the ocean, utterly dark, stretching far into the all-embracing starless night. He is momentarily seized by despair, and fears for his life. Splashing about in the dark water, he becomes presently pensive, ponders and begins to doubt. "Is it a dream? Or am I under the spell of an illusion? Surely this circumstance, utterly strange, must be the product of my imagination! For the world as I know it, and as I observed it in its harmonious state, does not deserve such annihilation as it seems now suddenly to have suffered. There is no sun, no moon, no wind; the mountains have all vanished, the earth has disappeared. What manner of universe is this in which I discover myself?"

The saint, forlorn in the vast expanse of the waters and on

the very point of despair, at last became aware of the form of the sleeping god; and he was filled with amazement and joy. Partly submerged, the enormous shape resembled a mountain range breaking out of the waters. It glowed with a wonderful light from within. The saint swam nearer, to study the presence; and he had just opened his lips to ask who this was when the giant seized him, summarily swallowed him, and he was again in the familiar landscape of the interior. Thus abruptly restored to the harmonious world of Vishnu's dream, Markandeya was filled with confusion. He could only think of his brief yet striking experience as a kind of vision. Being back again, however, he resumed his former life, wandering over the wide earth and graciously pleased with the ideal state of affairs he observed. He wandered in safety for another hundred years.

But then, inadvertently once again, he slipped from the sleeper's mouth and tumbled into the pitch-black sea. This time, in the dreadful darkness and water-desert of silence, he beheld a luminous boy, a godlike boy beneath a fig tree, peaceful in slumber. Then again, by an effect of *māyā*, Markandeya saw the lonely little boy cheerfully at play, undismayed amidst the vast ocean. The saint was filled with curiosity, but his eyes could not stand the dazzling splendor of the child. So he remained at a comfortable distance, pondering as he kept himself afloat: "Something of this kind I seem to remember having beheld once before, long long ago." But then his mind became aware of the fathomless depth of the shoreless ocean and was overcome with fear.

The god, in the guise of the divine child, gently addressed him. "Welcome, Markandeya!" The voice had the soft deep tone of the melodious thundering of an auspicious rain cloud. The god reassured him: "Welcome, Markandeya! Do not be afraid, my child. Do not fear. Come hither." The ageless saint could not recall a time when anyone had presumed either to address him as "child" or to name him simply by his first name without any respectful appellation referring to his saintliness and birth. He was profoundly offended. "Who presumes to ignore my dignity, my saintly character, and to make light of the treasure of power stored in me through my ascetic austerities? Who is this who slights my venerable age, equal to a thousand years as the gods count years? I am not accustomed to this sort of insulting treatment. Even the highest gods regard me with exceptional respect. Not even Brahmā would dare to approach me in this irreverent manner. Brahmā addresses me courteously: 'O Long-Lived One,' he calls me. Who now courts disaster by naming me simply Markandeya?"

When the saint had thus expressed his wrath, the divine child resumed his discourse, unperturbed. "Child, I am thy parent, thy father and elder, the primeval being who bestows all life. Why do you not come to me? I knew your sire well. He practised severe austerities in bygone times in order to beget a son. Pleased with his perfect saintliness, I granted him a gift, and he requested that you, his son, should be endowed with inexhaustible life-strength and should never grow old. Your father knew the secret center of his own existence, and you stem from that center also. That is why you are now privileged to behold me, recumbent on the primal all-containing cosmic waters, and playing here as a child beneath the tree."

Markandeya's features brightened with delight, his eyes grew wide in humble surrender, he made as if to bow and he prayed: "Let me know the secret of your *māyā*, the secret of your appearance now as a child, lying and playing in the infinite sea. Lord of the Universe, by what name are you known?"

Vishnu replied: "I am the primeval One, manifesting myself in varied forms. I am the divine magician, who works the magic of the world and its ages, putting these forth, then drawing them back into myself. From me originates whatever has been, shall be, or is. And whatever you may see, hear, or know in the whole of the universe, know me as Him who abides therein. Consider that in your heart, obey the laws of my eternal order, and wander in happiness through the universe within my body. Know me as Him who manifests, yet whose manifesting magic remains unmanifested and not to be grasped."

With a swift motion, the Primeval Being brought the holy Markandeya to his mouth and swallowed him, so that he vanished again into the gigantic body. This time, the heart of the saint was so flooded with beatitude that instead of wandering further he sought rest in a solitary place. There he remained in lonely quietude and joyfully listened to the, at first, hardly audible, secret, yet universal melody of Vishnu's life breath, flowing in, flowing out. And this is the song that Markandeya hears: "Many forms do I assume. And when the sun and moon have disappeared I float and swim with slow movements on the boundless expanse of the waters. I am the Lord. I bring forth the universe from my essence, and I abide in the cycle of time that dissolves it."

Such is the story. It is rich with suggestion about many matters. Let me interpret it, and bring out its relevance to the questions I posed.

As I wish to interpret the story here, Markandeya is an image of ourselves in our active side. More particularly, the "Long-Lived One" is an image of ourselves in our immaturity, in our extended early life.

He is initially characterized as a holy man, who is wandering aimlessly over the earth, taking in the world and finding himself gladdened by it, apparently happy with himself and with what he finds. Let me begin my interpretation by considering this characterization.

I suggest that what is here portrayed is ourselves as active creatures whose life unfolds within a peculiar need to be related significantly to the real, to be aware of it and attentive to it and through that awareness and attention to be a significant part of it. But in life we begin and initially move by means of an active use and development of powers which involves a particular sort of attention and awareness. That initial kind of attention and awareness instates us in an openness to the real, but does so as bringing the real to focus in a limited sort of explicitness. More particularly, what becomes explicit in the focus of attention is the sensible aspect of the active side of things, which obtrudes itself for our attention due to the natural outward direction of our attention through the senses. Correlative with such focus, essential sides of the real, including the basic inactive side, are left implicit, unattended to. In the image of the story: Markandeya wanders on earth, his awareness and attentiveness exclusively focussed and drawn out in his relation to it; the void outside Vishnu, and Vishnu himself, do not come within his explicit cognizance.

Now not only does the focussing of attention in this particular direction and manner institute a correlative inattentiveness to much, but within the limited attentiveness that obtains we are entered into an unavoidable mistaking of the real. We unwittingly take that which is explicit of the real as if it were the real as such; that means, we take a part for the whole, the active side of things for things in their reality. Thus Markandeya wanders on an earth which, however perfect at this stage in creation, is a "dream world"; yet he relates to it as if it were the real world, the real in its fullness.

[150]

Due to the fact that his active relating to things is rooted in such inattentiveness and involves such mistaking, Markandeya is imaged as wandering aimlessly: wandering, because without the explicit presence of both sides of the real, that is, of the inactive source as well as of the active centers, his doings do not enter stably and evenly into the real; and aimlessly, for without explicit support in the inactive side of things, his doings are lacking in purpose and direction, which stem ultimately from that side of reality. Such a life may have its happiness, but it is that of the saying, "ignorance is bliss." Nevertheless, Markandeya *is* a *holy* man, and that means, a man who has, in the course of many lives, reached finally to a pinnacle of worldly perfection. Such perfection is worldly because it pertains to the powers of active existence as these are brought into play in the interplay of active centers without the explicit supporting presence of the inactive source of all such centers.

The suggestion, then, of the initial characterization of Markandeya, is that due to the one-sided awareness and attentiveness prevailing in the activity of our early life, the positive development of our powers and the attainment of a certain measure of growth are both held within a fundamental negativity. So long as there is the failure of awareness and attention to move within the explicit presence of both sides of the real, we are involved in an underlying mistaking of the real which makes life incomplete and gives to our condition the character of immaturity.

The events of the story provide some indication of how this initial and inescapable involvement in the illusion of *māyā* can be transcended, so that we attain that fullness wherein we are fullgrown. Such transcendence is initiated when, inadvertently, the one-sided direction of attention to the outward is broken. Then a side of reality which not only was previously merely implicit to attentive awareness, but also which can never come into the explicit focus of attention in the way in which the outward does, can become explicit and do so in its own way. In terms of the story: Markandeya falls out of Vishnu's mouth, and his attention and awareness come to be formed in a radically different region from that of the world inside Vishnu.

This trans-worldly awareness and attentiveness are also one-sided, in the reverse direction this time. Yet it is within such alternative one-sidedness that attention can come properly to be reformed, the mistaken presumption already to be cognizant of the real and to be living in fundamental accord with it can come to be removed, and the active use of powers can come finally to be entered into a service which is accordant with and supported in the fullness of the real. Such an outcome is possible because the one-sidedness in question here is directed toward what is basic in reality, the source of existence and of direction for activity.

If, now, I draw out the suggestion of the story in respect to my first question, I would say that the power which is involved in essential human growth is the power to be responsive: not simply to be aware, but to enter, within an awareness, into attentive and heedful activity. The awareness, attentiveness, and heedfulness intrinsic to human responsiveness are directed toward that which exists, and directed there so as to take whatever exists (inclusive of ourselves) into our activity as *needing* to *be realized* and need-ing the active contribution of others in order to be realized. Our activity, then, as one instrumentality through which that need can be met, is responsive because it is an attending which is funda-mentally drawn to be accordant with the real as needing (among other things) that activity for its realization, for its fulfillment in being.

Let me consider the story now with a view to my second question. Markandeya's wandering on earth eventually leads him to slip out of Vishnu's mouth. This slip, accomplished *through* his doing but not in a way which was *intended in* that doing or *foreseen* as *possible* issue of his doing, was inadvertent. The bot-tom suddenly dropped out of his world; what he had taken for the real (namely, the cosmos, things in their patterned and ordered intelligibility, things familiar) lost the capacity to sustain him, and he was plunged into an emptiness and darkness within which his awareness and attention gradually became explicitly opened to matters which had previously not been explicitly present.

In this slip and the succeeding events, we have imaged in par-ticular fashion both our initiation into a possible fullness of our responsive power and the course to be taken to develop this initia-tion toward its needed culmination. Let me note briefly certain of the major phases of the story which are suggestive in these respects.

In that slip, wherein we come to find ourselves at sea, we are fundamentally disoriented at first, the emptiness and darkness being marked for us in the beginning more by the absence of the familiar and reliable than by anything else. If we can remain afloat through our own efforts, we come to find the need for thought, and particularly for a reflection upon reality, for a fundamentally philosophical effort which brings to responsive formulation the strange problematicalness pervasive of our condition. As yet, how-ever, our awareness and attentiveness within this region are still colored predominantly by the negative elements which mark our estrangement; in a while, a positive side can make itself felt, that "sleeping god" which is inactive ground in creation or inactive side of the real. And with the presence of this factor to awareness, the emptiness can come mysteriously alive, our attention can be drawn to that presence itself, and we can be brought into further questioning. Thus, the initiation as Markandeya images it involves a radically altered awareness, altered attentiveness, and reflective questioning.

But such initiation is transient, passing: for a moment, awareness and attention are broadened, and the question of the real becomes a vital one. This is only a beginning, however, which needs to be developed, but is not developed without relapse back into the familiar. Far ahead in the future lies a possible final slip: within its happening and development can come an ultimate enlightenment concerning the basic and the active sides of the real, hence an ultimate breaking of delusion. This enlightenment and destruction of illusion occur as the outcome of a responsive dialogue with that inactive presence which speaks to one as including him and as asking: "Why do you not come to me?" That final recognition in which one "comes," that return to the source in an acknowledgment and submission, involves the extension of the effort to understand, the perpetuation of questioning; for without this, one cannot enter in full human fashion—and that means, in witting as well as willing fashion—into the fullness of life. What emerges from such questioning in the end is a recognition of a certain partial reticence of the real in the face of our efforts to comprehend. Nevertheless, what is needed for life has been discovered; for Markandeya is swallowed up again and returned to ordinary circumstances, there to live "listening" to things in their universality and divinity, finding them in their full reality. Thus, through the development of the awareness initially entered into in his first slip, Markandeya has been finally released into a life in which he is fully accordant with creation as it is, and this means, with the real as magical in essence, as mysterious.

From the course of events in the story, then, the suggestion emerges that the initiation involved when we first enter into explicit presence of the trans-worldly is a transient initiation into a possibility which must be entered into fully, and which must then in turn be relieved of its one-sidedness, if human life is to come to its fullness.

If now I relate these aspects of the story explicitly to my second question, the suggestion emerges that we do come of age, we do enter into a fullness in the human estate, but we do this in a complex manner. For the movement of life and growth leads us to a *telos* which, entered at first transiently, begins us in a possible way of life which reaches its culmination only when, in our responsive awareness and attentiveness to things worldly, things cosmic, things sensible and intelligible and moral, there is involved (at its basis) the steady awareness and attentiveness to the ground of creation itself. Then, attendant upon the source, we live in the world explicitly attuned to it as a "dream world," hence accordant with it in its full reality. The development of the initial and initiating slip occurs in the form of an education of our responsiveness, which is a schooling of ourselves in the responsibility that ultimately makes human life what it is. Not until we are equal to living responsively in the fullness of the real and constantly moving at rest among things and people come alive for us in their full reality, are we grown up.

To grow is to grow in responsive power and potency, to grow into that fullness in responsiveness which is embodied in a life of responsibility: such is the suggestion about growing up which I wish to draw from the story of Markandeya.

I have used that story to make this suggestion because the happenings and persons in it resonate for me from out of my experience and thought. But I would not want to have my thought identified with what the Hindu thinks. The latter is fraught with difficulties and with implications which seem not to be borne out in my experience. But rather than dwell upon the differences, I would like, in closing, to make one further use of the story; this will again indicate something in the story kindred to what I think, but will allow me to point in the direction of one significant difference.

At the outset I spoke of a day in the fall several years ago, a day on which I came to be recollected into an earlier and childhood day of many years previous. In speaking of that childhood day, I remarked on the magic of life I shared in then. In that phrase as I meant it, the term "magic" (which is cognate in root with the Sanskrit *māyā*) is to be thought as having its meaning primarily in the direction of enchantment. I entered into an enchanted world, a world which (as it stood over against me) so-to-speak secretly sang (chanted) to me, a world to whose singing I *unknowingly* listened, a world which drew me out as I listened, a world whose drawing power was an effective factor in my moving into such active relation to the things around me as brought me into a growth, into a responsive potency which was characterized by a certain appropriate fullness.

That magic, the magic of joy and marvellousness, the magic of child-like potency, was not as yet the magic or *māyā* which obtained in any of Markandeya's experiences. Nor, of course, were that singing and that listening hiddenly present in my experience, the singing and listening mentioned as Markandeya's at the end of the story. Yet, if I see this matter of magic from the perspective of my general discussion, it seems to me proper to say that growth is entry into the power of responsiveness to being in its magicalness. Thus, as one grows, one's gradual entry into his essential power deepens toward full explicitness in the presence of magic to one. One does not become aware suddenly, in mid-life, of something one had never been at all aware of before in any way. Rather, with the deepening in the mode and manner of responsive entry into life's magic goes a gradually transformed mode of effective presence of that magic in one's efforts. In my childhood time, there was as yet innocence, a sort of unknowing and incognizance which obtained within that effective presence. When I find such innocence now in children, a shudder is evoked in me: a shudder of recognition which becomes the urge to hold close—and the longing to see that child come to find that magic as I now find it—come to grow up and to find the sort of initiation into the emptiness wherein life begins in full earnest.

Whether, as the story suggests, there is a future after that initiation which holds a final enlightenment and rest, I do not know. But I do know something of that initiation. In our own philosophic tradition, it would have been spoken of by the Greeks as an initiation into wonder: wonder, which is not joy and marvellousness except as these emerge within the explicit presence of the emptiness that Markandeya entered and become thereby taken up into the urgency of reflective questioning which is therein engendered. With wonder, life begins in fullness. It has been the presumption of the Western philosophic tradition that this means that the only truly human life is the philosophic life. In this respect it seems to me that the story of Markandeya can provide us fuller insight: it matters not whether the life one enters is one of reflection, or one predominantly unreflective, it matters only that it be a life attuned in its full measure to the magic of creation.

[155]

With that suggestion, I draw this discussion to a close. What I have wanted to do by using my own experience and the story of Markandeya is merely to indicate certain thoughts which have come to be formed in me in my efforts to understand the matter of growing up. I am too well cognizant of my own limits in experience and in capacity, to think that what I have said on this occasion comes very close to truth itself. But I do hope that, despite the elliptical and allusive manner in which I have spoken my mind, I have been able to catch and to evoke in the reader something of what needs to be thought about in this matter, if not what needs to be said.

NOTES

* This paper is a slightly revised version of a talk given to the Undergraduate Philosophy Club at The Pennsylvania State University on May, 25, 1966. For the most part the revision has preserved the style of the talk as a talk, instead of trying to transform it into a style more characteristic of a written essay.

1. Heinrich Zimmer, *Myths and Symbols in Indian Art and Civilization* (New York, 1946). See pp. 35–53.

KAREL BERKA*

EXISTENCE IN MODERN LOGIC

The contemporary attempts to determine in a purely logical way the nature of existence, by constructing a *logic of existence*[1] or a *free logic* which makes "no assumptions about the existence of the purported designata of its terms, general or singular,"[2] seems to be still premature as long as the problem of existence in its philosophical implications is not adequately resolved. Historically, there are three main problems in logic involving a conception of existence, which clearly show that the logical problem of existence has a philosophical background influencing the "logic of existence" in its technical sense.

The first problem arose in the period of the algebra of logic, when G. Boole (implicitly) and E. Schroeder (explicitly) introduced the concept of the empty class. This innovation resulted in a criticism of the traditional square of opposites and Aristotelian syllogistics, and the conception of the existential import of categorical statements. A further consequence, already recognized in the period of G. Frege and B. Russell, was the interpretation of particular statements as existential statements and of universal statements as hypothetical ones. It was maintained that "all general propositions deny the existence of something or other,"[3] and for these reasons no valid inference of a statement with existential import from a statement without existential import was admitted.

The second problem comprises the "fanciful Russellian analyses of proper names in existential contexts,"[4] with its special theory of descriptions, directed against Meinong's conception that a grammatically correct denoting phrase stands for an object, even if it does not subsist, and a similar view of H. MacColl who assumed two sorts of individuals—real and unreal.[5] Russell's theory of descriptions is evidently a philosophical reflection of his views concerning the nature of existence as the fundamental problem of ontology, a technical term introduced for the first time by Chr. Wolff in his *Philosophia prima sive Ontologia . . .* (1730). For philosophical reasons, Russell attempts to refute the ontological argument of Anselm of Canterbury. In the course of his argument. he adopts both conclusions of Kant's refutation in his *Critique of Pure Reason* (B 620ff), namely that (1) "all existential propositions are synthetic" and that (2) *"Being* is obviously not a real predicate; that is, it is not a concept of something which could be added to the concept of a thing." His conviction that "existence is quite definitely not a predicate" is another reason for his introduction of the concept of the existential qualifier.

The third problem, introduced recently by W. V. Quine in his famous dictum, "To be is, purely and simply, to be the value of a variable,"[6] is connected with the contemporary discussion on universals and the attempts to reformulate the language of logic and mathematics in a nominalistic sense.[7]

I

Quasi-ontological assumptions. My discussion of some problems of existence in modern logic will begin with an introduction of certain minimal philosophical assumptions which I consider as sufficient for the elucidation of these problems. The standpoint that I am defending can be characterized as *realistic monism* in that it accepts the priority of reality, and as *methodological realistic dualism,* in that it admits besides the real world, a world of ideas which results from the practical and theoretical activities of mankind. More explicitly, I am basing a substantiated classification of semantical and hence of syntactical categories in logic, already anticipated by the theory of types, on a categorization of corresponding entities. This categorization will be called a *quasi-ontology* or prelogic in order to show its similarity and dissimilarity to the traditional conception of rationalism and the contemporary ontologies of N. Hartmann and M. Heidegger. With this modification, I fully agree with Rescher's statement "that the logical theory of *existence* must in the last analysis rest upon *ontological* and not purely logical considerations."[8]

The suggested quasi-ontology will be developed on two levels. The quasi-ontology of the first level, based on the common sense assumption of the priority of reality, comprises the following entities: facts (Sachverhalte), things, properties and connections (Beziehungen). All these entities are conceived as having an immediately or mediately observable temporal or spatiotemporal character. They are, so to speak, "really" existent.

One could argue that this conception does not make clear what is meant by a fact, by a thing and so on. It could be objected, as well, that it is not sufficient only to list these entities without analyzing their relations (e.g., between a thing and its properties), or discussing the question of their possible reductions. These and similar problems may be interesting for ontology, but are unnecessary for a philosophical analysis of the concept of existence in logic. In fact, I am not maintaining that there are, e.g., things as such, but only assume that there are things, without being interested in their special nature. This conception is not incompatible with the standpoint of common sense, which holds that there are in reality only special, concrete things and properties, but not things or properties in themselves.

The quasi-ontology of the second level assumes the following entities: truth-values (or other values, e.g. modal values), individuals, classes and relations. These entities are postulated as idealized entities. They are, so to speak, "ideally" existent. Being the result of human praxis, they are conceived as ideal constructions, related to entities of the quasi-ontology of the first level. In this sense, they are not wholly independent of the former, and stand thus in a mediated relationship to reality. The old philosophical question, "How do ideal entities exist?," with the implicit suggestion of the answer, "They exist *in* our minds," is unjustified and misleading. It is simply a mentalistic transposition or an anthropomorphic analogy with the existence of real entities *in* time and space.

The acceptance of the suggested stratification of reality reflected in the quasi-ontology of the first level as the basis of a further stratification of ideal entities is the expression of realistic monism. The supposition of the relative independence of the entities of the quasi-ontology of the second level is the expression of the methodological, realistic dualism. In both cases, no ontological or metaphysical implications are intended. I cannot, of course, deny that the quasi-ontologies themselves are idealizations, needed for the suggested philosophical analysis of existence in logic.

II

Existential commitments. The following analysis of existence resulting in a certain classification of different kinds of existence and its relativization in respect to different universes of discourse or theoretical frameworks will be distinct from the "ontological problem of existence" with its absolutistic claims. Being methodologically connected with a conception of relative existence, it stands in clear opposition to all absolutely conceived concepts of existence, found not only in metaphysics, but in the conception of some logicians, who, trying to avoid all philosophy, in fact adopt one-sided ontological standpoints. In this sense the suggested conception is influenced by Carnap's distinction between external and internal existential questions and statements.[9] If we further consider the controversial discussion of existence in mathematics between representatives of logicism, formalism and intuitionism,[10] rooted in the attempt to find just one criterion for mathematical existence, it becomes clear that existence is systematically ambiguous and cannot, even in one theoretical framework, be uniquely determined. It is therefore impossible to adopt just one criterion for existence. To maintain that we have to deal only with one kind of existence in all universes of discourse or in all theoretical frameworks is thus unjustified. For these reasons, I am adopting as another starting point of my analysis the well-known dictum of Aristotle that "there are several senses in which a thing may be said 'to be'."

First of all, it is important to differentiate clearly between logical existence (L-existence) and factual existence (F-existence), conceived as meaning "extra-logical" existence. L-existence, incorrectly identified by logicists and formalists with mathematical existence, can be identified with self-consistency. From the standpoint of logic all entities which are subjected to the *principium contradictionis* exist. Logic, or more explicitly, classical elementary logic, is in this sense applicable in all "possible worlds" (Leibniz) or, as we would say now, in all domains of things. These domains are in principle non-empty, because the assumption of L-existence rules out all internally inconsistent entities. From the standpoint of L-existence, only the "impossible world" is empty, and cannot therefore contain any entity. L-existence is assumed to stand for all consistent theoretical frameworks, which are in this regard similar to each other, whereas F-existence refers to a manifold of different universes of discourse, including in the first instance, natural systems of diverse entities.

The distinction between L-existence and F-existence, which underlies the difference between self-consistency and special criteria for existence in all other cases, is not sufficient for our purposes. A further classification of F-existence is required. It is clear that in regard to the assumption of both quasi-ontologies we must at least distinguish two kinds of F-existence, namely real existence (R-existence) and ideal existence (I-existence).

In both cases, special criteria must be established. R-existence is evidently determined, as we have indicated already, by temporal or spatio-temporal properties. For this reason any expressions like "x exists," "x's exist" or other similar formulations, insofar as "x" refers or has referred to entities of the quasi-ontology of the first level, is in principle incomplete. It must be understood as meaning: "x exists or existed at t," or more explicitly "x R-exists or R-existed at t," where "t" is a time parameter. The above mentioned alternative, "exists or has existed," is necessary; otherwise, we could not speak at tn of the R-existence of some entity which evisted a tm (prior to tn), but no longer exists at tn. In order to distinguish R-existence from I-existence, it is not required that an entity actually exist at some ti, but only that we can in principle—either directly or indirectly—establish that the criterion of R-existence is or was fulfilled. Because there are different ways to obtain idealized entities, not excluding the possibility of unwarranted or unsound idealizations and constructions, the establishment of the criteria for I-existence is more difficult. It is obvious, in any case, that there cannot be just one criterion.

The suggested classification can, in both cases, be still more refined. R-existence can be subclassified in accordance with different strata of reality, e.g., physical and biological existence, with possibly further subclassification. For a subclassification of I-existence, it is presumably most characteristic to assume that mathematical and mythical existence comprise its extreme cases. Now it might be objected that L-existence could equally well be understood as a proper subclass of I-existence and that, therefore, the suggested classification could be reduced to a dichotomy of R-existence and I-existence, or F-existence and L-existence. This standpoint is based only on a differentiation between idealized and non-idealized entities and neglects the specific nature of idealization in logic as well as its universalistic character, which clearly differs from the systems of I-existent entities, relativized to different frameworks with a limited range and specific criteria of existence.

To speak of F-existence without some explicitly or implicitly formulated criterion by which it could be decided, in respect to a certain universe of discourse, whether something exists or does not, is thus at least vague. For these reasons, all disputes about existence, without any determination of a corresponding universe of discourse, are simply idle. They cannot be settled by a purely logical argumentation.

This analysis of existence applies as well for "nonexistence," namely, for a similar differentiation between an L-empty class and F-empty classes. At the same time, it is important for a distinction between extensional and intensional contexts.

The L-empty class is determined by a self-inconsistent property which does not hold for any entity. This class can be considered as a representation of the "impossible world" of Leibniz. An F-empty class (viz., an R-empty class or an I-empty class) is determined by a property which does not hold for any entity of a fixed universe of discourse. The L-empty class is absolutely empty, but an F-empty class is only relatively empty. Its emptiness is relativized to a certain universe of discourse or to some subdomain of such a universe. There is, of course, no difference between an F-empty class and the L-empty class from a purely extensional point of view. There is, in both cases, no entity which is their element. But from the intensional point of view, they differ clearly. To neglect this difference in extensional contexts is not so harmless as it seems to be. But for a clear conception of L-existence, it is at least misleading to illustrate the concept of the empty class in logic by examples of F-empty classes.

It is clear that the question whether a given class is or is not L-empty, can be decided only by logical considerations. The existence of entities of the class of entities "not being identical with themselves," is impossible for logical reasons. But the question whether the class of "Men living on the Moon" is empty or nonempty, i.e., is or is not F-empty, cannot be answered so simply. This can be done only in respect to F-existence, and depends upon special criteria, characterizing different kinds of F-existence. The class of "men living on the moon" is at present R-empty, even though we are nearly certain that in the near future it will become R-nonempty.

This also holds for the famous arguments about the nonexistence of unicorns, centaurs and so on. When one speaks of their alleged non-existence, one has in mind entities of domains described by zoology, or entities with a supposed R-existence. But if we have in mind another context, e.g., the framework of Greek mythology, i.e., some kind of I-existence, we cannot speak of centaurs as nonexistent. The class of centaurs is evidently R-empty. However, it does not follow from this that it is equally I-empty or L-empty. This relativization does not hold solely in such extreme cases, often artificially constructed for the sake of argument, but quite commonly in regard to any entity usually considered as R-existent. Neglecting this relativization—unconsciously or consciously—by assuming some entity as R-existent which is only I-existent, is simply a fallacy.

We can speak of the nonexistence of entities in an absolute sense, only if these entities can be elements of the L-empty class. It follows from our conception of existential commitments that a decision whether an entity is an element of the L-empty class is primarily *intensionally* determined. Any existential assumption of such an entity implies a contradiction. On the contrary, all L-existential assumptions of universally valid logical systems, their components as well as the logical basis of other theoretical frameworks, imply a tautology. Only the assumption of L-existence is either tautologous or contradictory. The assumption of F-existence, being relative to a certain universe of discourse, is always contingent. This seems to be clear, at least in the case of entities related to the quasi-ontology of the first level, because no real entity necessarily exists. But it holds also in the case of I-existence. Any alleged necessary existence of an ideal entity is stipulated by definition and depends thus on a subjective decision of men.

The results of this discussion count against the old philosophical prejudgment concerning the nature of existential statements, namely, that all affirmative existential propositions are tautologies and all negative existential propositions contradictions.[11] It seems clear that all existential statements—with the exception of statements about L-existence—are synthetic statements (in the Kantian sense) or factual statements in the contemporary terminology.

I believe our conception of existential commitments settles the controversy about the ontological argument of Anselm. The existential statement "God exists" is from our standpoint significant only in the formulation "God I-exists." Because this proposition is a I-existential statement, it cannot be maintained that the property of existence is necessarily contained in the essence of God. Whether the opponents in this controversy will be satisfied by this suggested solution is, of course, hard to say.

[163]

III

Is "exists" a predicate? The emphatic rejection of the conception that "exists" is a predicate characterizes the attitude of many philosophers,[12] influenced by the ideas of B. Russell. In contemporary literature this negative standpoint is less predominant. This presumably is due to the impression that the opposite point of view does not necessarily involve the acceptance of the ontological argument, which is now only seldom defended.[13] It became also clear that a refutation of the thesis that "existence" is a predicate cannot be solely based on the desire to refute Anselm's a priori proof. It does not simply suffice to say, in order to avoid the supposed consequences of this proof, that "exists" in the statement "God exists" is not a predicate, or a "real predicate" in the Kantian sense. This negative attitude demands a positive solution: "What, then, is 'existence,' if it is not a predicate?"

We find in contemporary literature, at least, a more liberal standpoint. E.g., it is maintained that there is "no reason either for or against holding existence to be a predicate"[14] or that " 'exists' is a predicate which functions in some ways like a property-demarcating predicate."[15] In any case, existence is now considered as something that can be treated as a predicate of a special kind; but not being an irreducible predicate[16] it is in the language of logic, redundant. All these attempts, however, based on interesting technical procedures, do not settle the problem implicitly involved in the whole discussion: "Is existence an attribute or property?" The answer to this question seems to me prior to any possibility of treating existence as a predicate. Whether an expression is or can be a predicate is a syntactical or semantico-syntactical problem which can be decided by logic itself. But whether we consider some entity as a property or not lies generally outside the reach of logic alone.

I shall try to show that existence is a property which can be reasonably attributed to things. Being a property, it can evidently be expressed by a predicate.

Leaving aside existential statements used only for the sake of philosophical argumentation, it is obvious that we make existential statements as answers to existential questions. Because R-existence has a natural priority to I-existence, people raise existential questions only when they are not sure whether something does or does not exist, i.e., whether some entity is or is not R-existent. E.g., "Did Troy (really) exist?," "Has Atlantis (really) existed?," "Do atoms exist?," "Do fairies exist?." Hardly anyone would ask, e.g., "Does this house exist?," "Does life now exist on Earth?," "Do men exist today in Europe?." Similar questions, e.g., "Do men exist somewhere else in the Universe?" or "Does life exist on Mars?," are, of course, raised, because in these contexts they express a doubt concerning the R-existence of the mentioned entities. Analogously, scientists raise questions in regard to the I-existence of entities, if they are not quite certain whether some postulated entity is adequately idealized and fits into the theoretical framework in question or whether there is a method available enabling them to construct such an entity.

All these questions can be reasonably answered, and the corresponding existential statement conveys something new to us. After the archeological discoveries of H. Schliemann, the existential question "Did Troy (really) exist?" is answered in a different way than before. The existential question, "Do atoms exist?" implied for E. Mach a different existential statement than for a contemporary physicist. It is obviously very important for our knowledge if we discover that some entity previously assumed to be only I-existent, is or was actually R-existent, or when we can prove that an entity considered as R-existent, is in fact only I-existent, or when we can show that an entity which was assumed to be I-existent is internally inconsistent and therefore for logical reasons nonexistent.

From the conception that all entities are either existent or nonexistent in an absolute sense, it obviously follows that any negative existential statement is a contradiction and any affirmative existential statement is a tautology. We have already rejected this conception, yet in a certain sense it holds. By accepting a certain universe of discourse, we are making an existential assumption, namely that the domain of certain things is in regard to R-existence nonempty, or that the domain of individuals is in respect to I-existence nonempty. To maintain, then, that "x exists," where "x" is a thing or an individual of a fixed universe of discourse, is evidently misleading, because the admission of this universe involves the assumption of its nonemptiness. What is in regard to a certain previously determined domain of things or individuals really important and interesting, is only an existential question of a more restricted range. It makes sense only to raise an internal existential question, namely, does there R-exist a thing with special properties, e.g., "Is there a man who is older than 100 years?," or does there I-exist an individual fulfilling some conditions, e.g., "Is there a natural number that is even and prime?." This fact seems to explain the reason why Russell assigns existence to "described subjects," but not to "named subjects," and why he considers existence only as a property of propositional functions.[17]

If one admits only one kind of existence, or if we limit our considerations to one special universe of discourse, thus assuming implicitly that they contain either R-existent or I-existent entities, we obviously accept an important distinction between existence and any other property. The extension of such a property (e.g., of the property "breathing with lungs" in respect to the domain of living beings, or of the property "prime" in regard to the domain of natural numbers) is a *proper* subclass of the given domain. The extension of the property "exists" in respect to a domain of entities is, however, only an *unproper* subclass of this domain, i.e, it coincides with it.[18] This peculiarity seems to be decisive, when we are assuming only one kind of existence. If we, however, accept a relativization of existence, then the distinction, e.g., between R-existence and I-existence, is at least as relevant as the distinction between "even" and "odd." Whether the existence of a "named subject" is a trivial or a nontrivial property can thus be decided by a comparison of corresponding domains of things or individuals. In regard to different domains or subdomains of entities, especially when considering borderline cases involving an uncertainty as to the assigned kind of existence, it is a nontrivial property.

If it is granted that F-existence (with the mentioned restrictions) is, in fact, a nontrivial extralogical property either of named or of described entities of different universes of discourse, it can be expressed as a logical predicate. This holds as well for L-existence. There is, however, an important difference: L-existence as identified with consistency is a logical property, and for these reasons it must be understood as a metalogical predicate.

IV

Existential quantifier. In the period of the systematization of modern logic, the desire to settle "the historic controversy about existence in a way that definitely excludes misuses and pseudo-demonstrations manipulating the term"[19] was too strong. Because a predicative position for "exists" does not exclude the possibility of making unwarranted inferences from the grammatical form of the expressions "x exists" or "x's exist," it was considered an effective solution to find a suitable linguistic device in order to avoid such fallacies. For a shift from a predicative position of "exists" into a nonpredicative position, there are in English (also in French or in German, but not in all languages) favorable conditions. Instead of saying, e.g., "Men exist" or "Negative numbers exist," we can use in a rather more appropriate way expressions like: "There are men" (or "Some entities are men"), or "There are negative numbers" (or "Some numbers are negative"). This linguistic usage, applicable in the case of "described entities," cannot be correctly applied in the case of "named entities." To say, "There is Socrates," instead of "Socrates exists," seems even to a foreigner to be bad English. This linguistic fact, namely that the phrase "there is" requires a subject described, but not a subject named, is one reason for Russell's theory of descriptions. The introduction of the concept of the existential quantifier into logic was in any case influenced by two circumstances: Russell accepts the older conception of existential import of categorical propositions[20] and, in accordance with his logicist philosophy, identifies existence in mathematics with logical existence. Only now can it be proven by formal means that existence is not a predicate. This conception survives in a less dogmatic manner in the view that "existence is, if you want, a predicate, definable in terms of the existential quantifier."[21]

Now, the concept of the existential quantifier in logic is apparently not uncontroversial. It suffices to mention the problems connected with the extension of its role from finite domains of individuals, where it is a shorthand expression for a finite disjunction of singular propositions or propositional functions, to infinite domains. For our purposes, however, it is far more important to notice that in regard to the problem of existence, Russell's conception was from the very beginning burdened by three different intensions involving the meaning of the existential quantifier, namely, as

(1) asserting existence in the meaning of extralogical existence, i.e., F-existence;[22]

(2) asserting coherence of classes or functions, hence as expressing L-existence;[23] and

(3) in a neutral sense without any existential commitment, when correlated with the universal quantifier.[24]

From this third meaning, which, as I think, has to be considered as the fundamental and only reasonable one, it follows that the existential quantifier has, in fact, neither L-existential nor F-existential implications.

This conclusion is supported by Carnap's discussion[25] of the meaning of "existence" in statements with existential quantifiers. The statement, e.g., "There is an m between 7 and 13 which is prime" expressing the existence—Carnap makes here no further distinction—of a prime number "means just the same as 'it is not the case that for every m between 7 and 13, m is not prime," and otherwise it "has nothing to do with the ontological concept of existence."

The confusions in Russell's conception become still more clear, when we apply the above mentioned discussion of existential commitments. Let us first assume the validity of the first intended interpretation of the existential quantifier, i.e., as meaning L-existence. From this supposition the following unacceptable consequences can be inferred:

(1) the existential quantifier cannot have any implications for the existential import of factual propositions, and therefore, any logical transcription (of factual particular propositions) by means of this quantifier is incorrect;

(2) being identified with consistency, it becomes a metalogical term, therefore it cannot be correctly used in object language expressions;

(3) contrary to the view defended by Russell himself, just in order to refute the ontological argument, every existential statement has to be either a tautology or a contradiction.

Let us now assume the validity of the second interpretation, i.e., existence meaning F-existence. In this case the following unacceptable conclusions can be drawn:

(1) F-existence is a property of extralogical entities; it can evidently be expressed only as a descriptive predicate, as an F-constant; but the existential quantifier is an L-constant: hence an L-constant would function as an F-constant; and

(2) if the existential quantifier is a correct reformulation of F-existence, then a mere linguistic shift from a predicative position into a nonpredicative one would transform an F-constant into an L-constant.

All these objections, further supported by the following analysis of existential import, show already that existence and the existential quantifier (or rather, in order to avoid misleading associations, the particular quantifier) cannot be identified.

V

Existential import. The conception of existential import[26] was influenced in a twofold way by the concept of the empty class, disregarding, however, the distinction between the L-empty class and the F-empty classes.

In the first case, the empty class is used in an interpretation of categorical statements with the well-known result, namely $SP' = O, SP = O, SP \neq O, SP' \neq O$,[27] and the claim that only particular statements have existential import.

This transcription, to mention just one important objection, neglects the fact that the possible relations between S and P in a class-logical interpretation, namely inclusion, exclusion, and overlap, are primarily determined intensionally by a differentiation between dependent (essential) and independent (unessential) properties. Inclusion reflects one-sided dependent properties, exclusion exclusively dependent (incompatible) properties, and overlap independent properties. For independent properties, as the basis of particular statements, all possible products SP, $S'P$, SP' and $S'P'$ are in principle realizable, but for dependent properties, as the basis of universal statements, one of them is always excluded, and hence F-empty.

In the second case, the empty class is itself the subject of universal categorical statements. The formula O C X as a theorem of the logic of classes is obviously L-true. Therefore, any instance of this formula, e.g., "All immortals are smokers," has to be true, viz., L-true, in spite of the fact that—or, rather, just because—it contains an empty subject.

This supposed evidence for the nonexistential nature of universal statements became still more convincing, when Russell adopted with his existential interpretation of particular statements a conditionalization of universal categorical statements, based on an unclear, never appropriately elucidated, conception of formal implication, which was in practice understood in the same meaning as material implication, in spite of the claims to be different.[28]

I cannot discuss here the difficulties involved in Russell's conception, and it will be perhaps sufficient to notice that neither material nor formal implication can adequately express the intensionally determined relations between subjects and predicates in universal, categorical statements, which cannot be considered to be equivalent with hypothetical ones.[29] For an obvious implicit analogy of this conception between a true hypothetical statement (an implication) with a false antecedent and a true universal categorical statement with an empty subject an examination of existential import can unite both cases. That there is a confusion of the L-empty class with the F-empty classes seems to be quite clear, and must not therefore be repeated.

But how can we refute the thesis that statements with empty subjects are as instances of a logical theorem *eo ipso* true, viz., L-true? Is the assumption that the empty class is contained in every class, admitted at least for convenience, really useful? It was only MacColl who attempted—in order to avoid paradoxical consequences of such propositions as, "Every round square is a triangle," which from this standpoint must be L-true—to replace it by the assumption that the empty class is excluded from every class.[30] A logician or philosopher defending the existential import of particular propositions or the validity of the formula $O \subset X$, will usually use less counterintuitive examples, e.g., "Every American queen is a queen" or "Every American queen is a woman."

In order to discuss such examples the relationship between existence and the classification of propositions in L-propositions and F-propositions must be taken into account. It seems to be necessary to adopt a modification of Quine's refined classification,[31] including three instances, namely, F-propositions, L-propositions, and analytical propositions (propositions true for linguistic reasons). I suggest four instances:

(1) L-propositions, e.g., $XY \subset Y, O \subset X$;

(2) analytical propositions, e.g., "Every bachelor is an unmarried man";

(3) *illustrative* propositions, e.g., "Every English queen is a queen"; and

(4) F-propositions, e.g., "All men are mortal."

I consider this extension as sufficient to explain the alleged L-truth of statements with an empty subject. It is obviously irrelevant, whether we consider the proposition, "Every English queen is a queen" or "Every American queen is a queen," because the truth of such statements does not depend on their designations. Such statements contain extralogical constants, but they are not proper F-propositions. They cannot be L-propositions, containing extralogical constants, and differ even from analytical propositions, because they do not presuppose a knowledge of the meaning of terms given, e.g., by definition. They simply illustrate logical theorems. The ambiguity of these seemingly F-propositions lies in a confusion between L-existence and F-existence, viz., between L-empty and F-empty classes. The L-empty class cannot be used for any decisions concerning the existence or nonexistence of extralogical terms, i.e., it has no implications in respect to F-existence.

To defend the statement, "Every American queen is a woman," seems to be more promising. This is evidently an F-proposition with an F-empty subject. Is such a statement true or false? The one asserting that this statement is true usually argues as follows: one cannot doubt that if there really were an American queen, which in principle is not impossible, she would be a woman. He can also refer to the *dictum de omni et nullo*: if the class of "American queens" is included in the class of "queens," which is for logical reasons evident, and if the class of "queens" is included in the class of "women," which is verified by our experience, then the class of "American queens" must be included in the class of "women."

Against this argumentation, it can be objected that we must distinguish between what is logically possible and what can be realized in respect to given conditions. The existence of "American queens" is not inconsistent, but until now unrealized. Now, from L-existence F-existence does not follow. The truth of our example is inferred by analogy from similar statements. If we maintain that the relation between two classes is absolutely determined—without regard for possible modifications—we cannot consider corresponding propositions as factual. In other words, if one admits that the statement "Every American queen is a woman" is true, it is nonfactual. I.e., it is either true for logical or for linguistic reasons, which in our examples do not hold.

This standpoint will become more convincing, if I add some positive remarks. I presuppose the priority of singular propositions, i.e. propositions of the form Fx, Fxy, etc. All such propositions have something in common: existential import in the sense of F-existence. If we agree that singular propositions have F-existential import, because L-existential import would imply that they are tautologous, we must admit as well that it holds for generalized propositions. If the existential import of singular propositions is a necessary condition of their truth, this property must be hereditary not only for the particular but for universal propositions as well. I cannot imagine why, by the transition from singular propositions to generalized propositions, this property would be preserved only in the case of particular propositions, as is maintained under the influence of their identification with existential propositions. Not only is the interchangeability of both quantifiers directed against this asymmetry, but also the fact that a particular proposition does not exclude a universal one of the same quality.

Accepting this explanation, we have no more problems in deciding whether the universal statement "Every American queen is a woman" is true or not. For the subdomain of "American queens," the propositional form "x is a woman" is not fulfilled. Thus, if we cannot exhibit any true singular proposition of this kind, we cannot, *a fortiori*, consider as true its generalization, leading either to a particular or to a universal proposition. For these reasons, we cannot deny that universal statements have no F-existential import.

VI

Existence and ontological commitment. What conclusion can be drawn from our analysis of existence for the controversy between Platonism and nominalism? It now seems clear that the existence of idealized entities, i.e., of truth-values, individuals, classes, and so on, is distinct from the existence of entities of the quasi-ontology of the first level, especially in their concrete instances. To ask whether there are, e.g., classes, is in this form not exactly formulated and cannot be unambiguously answered. We can only ask whether they are or are not R-existent or I-existent. In the first case, our answer will be negative; in the second positive. To interpret I-existent entities as independent objects *sui generis* is to misinterpret their genesis, based as it is, historically and systematically on the entities of the quasi-ontology of the first level. To consider them in the traditional sense of Platonism as entities of a realm of Ideas is doubtless an unfounded metaphysical supposition, which is scientifically fruitless and misleading. This standpoint finds, of course, its support in nominalism by its one-sided, in principle empiricistic conception, of admitting only one kind of existence, namely R-existence.

The suggested differentiation and relativization of existence in respect to different frameworks leads to a modification and hence a trivialization of Quine's criterion of ontological commitment. We cannot simply say "to be is to be a value of a variable" without specifying the term "to be." By admitting in a formal language, e.g., class-variables, we only express the fact that the intended values of our variables are classes, without any possibility of deciding whether classes are R-existent or I-existent. This follows also from our conception of the particular quantifier. To make conclusions from the adopted vocabulary of a language to the existence of corresponding entities is from the standpoint of a realistic monism an idealistic conversion of the relationship between language and reality.

NOTES

* Mr. Berka was a visiting professor in our department during the Winter and Spring terms of 1969. He is now Professor of Philosophy at the Institute for the Methodology of Science, Prague, Czechoslovakia.

1. See esp. H. S. Leonard, "The Logic of Existence," *Philosophical Studies*, VII, 49–64.

2. K. Lambert, "Free Logic and the Concept of Existence," *Notre Dame Journal of Formal Logic*, VIII, 138. Comp. J. Hintikka, "Existential Presuppositions and Existential Commitments," *Journal of Philosophy*, LVI, 135.

3. B. Russell, "The Philosophy of Logical Atomism," *Monist*, XXIX, 191.

4. S. Candlish, "Existence and the Use of Proper Names," *Analysis*, XXVIII, 157.

5. Comp. B. Russell, "On Denoting," *Mind*, N. S., XIV, 479–493.

6. W. V. Quine, "On What There Is," *Review of Metaphysics*, II, 32.

7. See, e.g., N. Goodman and W. V. Quine, "Steps Toward a Constructive Nominalism," *Journal of Symbolic Logic*, XII, 105–22; I. M. Bochenski, A. Church, and N. Goodman, *The Problem of Universals*, (Notre Dame, 1956).

8. N. Rescher, "On the Logic of Existence and Denotation," *Philosophical Review*, LXVIII, 157.

9. R. Carnap, "Empiricism, Semantics, and Ontology," *Revue Internationale de Philosophie*, IV, 21ff.

10. See, e.g., O. Becker, "Mathematische Existenz, Untersuchungen zur Logik und Ontologie mathematischer Phänomene, Sonderdruck aus: *Jahrbuch für Philosophie und phänomenologische Forschung*, VIII, 441–809; E. W. Beth, *L'existence on mathématiques*, (Paris-Louvain, 1956); A. A. Fraenkel and J. Bar Hillel, *Foundations of Set Theory* (2nd ed.; Amsterdam, 1967).

11. See G. Nakhnikian and W. C. Salmon, "Exists as a Predicate," *Philosophical Review*, LXVI, 536.

12. E.g., J. Wisdom, *Interpretation and Analysis* (London, 1931), p. 62; W. Kneale, "Is Existence a Predicate?," *Arist. Society, Suppl.*, XV, 164; A. J. Ayer, *Language, Truth and Logic* (London, 1947), p. 43; C. D. Broad, *Religion, Philosophy and Physical Research* (London, 1953), p. 182f.

13. E.g., N. Malcolm, "Anselm's Ontological Argument," *Philosophical Review*, LXIX, 41–62.

14. N. Rescher, "On the Logic of Existence and Denotation," *Philosophical Review*, LXVIII, 180.

15. R. Routley, "Some Things Do Not Exist," *Notre Dame Journal of Formal Logic*, VII, 252.

16. J. Hintikka, "Studies in the Logic of Existence and Necessity," *Monist*, L, 66.

17. B. Russell, "The Philosophy of Logical Atomism," 195f.

18. R. Routley, "Some Things Do Not Exist," 251.

19. H. Reichenbach, *Elements of Symbolic Logic* (New York, 1948), p. 89.

20. B. Russell, "The Existential Import of Propositions," *Mind*, N. S., XIV, 400.

21. J. Hintikka, "Studies in the Logic of Existence and Necessity," *Monist*, L, 67.

22. B. Russell, "The Philosophy of Logical Atomism," 191; A. N. Whitehead and B. Russell, *Principia Mathematica* (Cambridge, 1910), Vol. I, pp. 174f.

23. B. Russell, "The Philosophy of Logical Atomism," 197. Comp. I. Thomas, "Existence and Coherence," *Methodos*, II, 78.

24. A. N. Whitehead and B. Russell, *Principia Mathematica*, p. 46.

25. R. Carnap, *Meaning and Necessity* (Chicago, 1947), pp. 43f.

26. See, e.g., J. N. Keynes, *Studies and Exercises in Formal Logic* (London and New York, 1906), pp. 210ff.

27. J. Venn, *Symbolic Logic* (London and New York, 1894), pp. 110ff.

28. See B. Russell, *The Principles of Mathematics* (Cambridge, 1903), p. 38; A. N. Whitehead and B. Russell, *Principia Mathematica*, pp. 20f, 139; B. Russell, *Introduction to Mathematical Philosophy* (London, 1919), pp. 158, 161, 163.

29. See J. Shaffer, "Existence, Predication and the Ontological Argument," *Mind*, N. S., LXXI, 312ff.

30. H. MacColl, "The Existential Import of Propositions," *Mind*, N. S., XIV, 401; cf. N. Rescher, "On the Logic of Existence and Denotation," 176ff.

31. W. V. Quine, "Carnap and Logical Truth," in *The Philosophy of Rudolf Carnap*, ed. P. A. Schilpp (La Salle and London, 1963), pp. 402f.

ROBERT PRICE

'EXISTENCE' AS A PREDICATE

I provide here a proposed analysis of 'Existence.' Since it has been fairly clear since Quine graciously gave the word to Wyman that for logical purposes, 'Existence' is largely redundant, motives are needed. They are as follows: (1) People who think they are asking philosophical questions about existence still seem sometimes not to be; I therefore append a series of unphilosophical questions together with unphilosophical answers which presuppose some such analysis as the one given. (2) Ordinary analyses which play on the redundant character of 'Existence' rarely permit discussion of the existence of entities other than individuals; the analysis offered will permit us to either affirm or deny that attributes exist. (3) Quine's gift, being somewhat Greek to begin with, needs careful inspection. I therefore attend to whether my analysis expresses Quine's notion.

I should perhaps add that 'Existence' is primarily useful, once confusions are set aside, in discussing analytical systems; it is obvious, I trust, that this is a limited use.

I first set out the definition. It involves, as did Tarski's definition of 'Truth,' the familiar passage from object to term. The need for the gambit is clear enough in Quine; ontic (or ontological) commitment arises when we commit ourselves to a language. Accordingly 'Existence' must be predicated of the name (or description) of a term. Our definiendum is provisionally:

'a' ε Existence

Under what conditions will we wish to make such an assertion? On Quine's view we will wish to do so when a (what is denoted by the term denoted by the term 'a') is a value of some set of variables of the language which has the term a (what is denoted by the term 'a') among its expressions. But we can easily say when this is so. We need only take some metatheorem which informs us that we may in general replace some variable, say 'x', by 'a' (and drop the prefix '(x)') in the course of constructing theorems of a prescribed sort. Thus:

$$\text{' (x) (..x..)} \supset \text{(..a..) ' } \varepsilon \text{ Theorem}$$

where this is understood as asserting that the sentence obtained by 'writing' '(..a..)' after '⊃', and that after '(x) (..x..)', where the first and third expressions are related as indicated above, and with the usual clauses on binding of variables, is a theorem. This, where derivable, is itself a metatheorem which guarantees that a is a value of the variables of the object-language. The above expression may then serve as provisional definiens yielding:

$$\text{'a'}\varepsilon \text{ Existence} = \text{df '(x) (..x..)} \supset \text{(..a..)' } \varepsilon \text{ Theorem}$$

But we may rewrite the definiens (using '⌢' for Tarski's concatenation) as:

$$\text{'(}{\frown}\text{'x'}{\frown}\text{)'}{\frown}\text{('}{\frown}\text{y}{\frown}\text{'x'}{\frown}\text{z}{\frown}\text{)'}{\frown}\text{'}\supset\text{'}$$
$$\frown\text{y}{\frown}\text{'a'}{\frown}\text{z ')' } \varepsilon \text{ Theorem}$$

with the added condition that it be such whenever y and z are such that '(x) (..x..)' is a well-formed formula. (This is to ensure that our metatheorem speaks of all sentences of the desired kind. As the reader will observe subsequently, we avoid in this way commitment to the existence of entities such that special cases are derivable, e.g., in some object languages, entities introduced via definite descriptions.) Our new definiens is now evidently a function of the expression 'a' as was our definiendum. We may accordingly write, where (- - 'a' --) is the metatheorem mentioned above:

$$\text{'a' } \varepsilon \text{ Existence} = \text{df (- - 'a' --)}$$

Clearly we are not faced with the difficulties that led Tarski to his treatment of 'True', and hence may write as a general definition (with respect to a given language):

$$\text{t } \varepsilon \text{ Existence} = \text{df (-- t --)}$$

[176]

But note that our definiens will not be true in any ordinary system unless the expression t is in fact the name of an expression of the object language and will be well-formed only if it is an expression of the meta-language. Accordingly, in the ensuing discussion I will refer to the provisional definition which better embodies the "point" of the definition.

We may now consider whether the definition offered above meets Quine's understanding of ontic commitment. Suppose the object-language in question is a nominalist language in which we quantify only over individuals. Clearly, if the language contains names of individuals, say a, b, c,..., and the usual rules of quantification, '(x) (..x..) ⊃ (..a..)' will be a theorem, and similarly for b, c, ... Hence we will be committed to ' 'a' ε Existence', ' 'b' ε Existence', and so forth. Equally clearly, where we have predicates, say F, '(x) (..x..) ⊃ (..F..)' will not be a theorem, regardless of choice of variables; hence we will be committed to ' 'F' ∉ Existence'. With respect to individual descriptions, say (ιx) (Fx), we may infer that '(ιx) (Fx)' ε Existence, in the usual systems, just when we have (Ex) (y) (Fy≡x=y) as a theorem. Thus we have ontic commitment where there is exactly one thing that F's; and if this is known not to be the case we have ' '(ιx) (Fx) ' ∉ Existence'.

But we have here our principal anomaly. Due to the incompleteness of even monadic predicate logic with respect to transformations of p into ∼p it will sometimes be the case that we will have the relevant metatheorem even where we do not know that the uniqueness clause is not satisfied. Thus where the clause is satisfiable, known not to be contradictory (even in relation to our "empirical" postulates) but not known to be valid, we must assert that '(ιx) (Fx)' ∉ Existence. Informally: We are committed to denying existence to such individuals introduced by description of which we would normally say (given present knowledge of our present linguistic commitment) that we cannot know that they do exist but we cannot know that they do not. But perhaps this is merely a strict formulation of Ockham's razor; the nominalist will deny existence even to entities of lowest type if he is not forced to accept their existence.

The situation with respect to languages which quantify over attributes is also as Quine would have it. In free-wheeling systems, such as that of Quine's Mathematical Logic, we have our theorem for all abstracts (*231), and hence all such classes or attributes exist. But in a system that used the theory of types without modification classes that correspond to abstracts which are unstratified, say x: ∼ (xεx), would not yield sentences, let alone theorems in the

[177]

desired case. But note that to say that a string of symbols is not a sentence, and hence not a theorem, is significant where the symbols are expressions of the meta language. Hence, in such a system our definition clearly yields what we want:

$$\text{'x: } \sim (x\epsilon x)' \notin \text{Existence}$$

The situation is then in general straightforward. Existence is predicated of expressions, and hence in this sense at least is a predicate and it is predicated of the expression of an object-language in a metalanguage precisely when the variables of the object-language range over what is "denoted" by those expressions.

But what happens when we in the ordinary way ask whether the expressions of the object language exist, i.e., whether we have an ontic commitment to 'a'. Clearly, if 'Existence' as defined above is a predicate in the meta-language, we can supply no answer; for our new question concerns the thesis:

$$\text{' 'a' ' } \epsilon \text{ Existence}$$

and our previous definiens would not be well-formed. But equally clearly we may define the new predicate 'Existence$_M$' such that:

$$\text{'A' } \epsilon \text{ Existence}_M =df \text{ '(X) (..X..) } \supset \text{ (..A..)' } \epsilon \text{ Theorem}_M$$

This is the analogue of our previous provisional definition and is framed in a meta-meta-language. What it asserts is that A, a term of the meta-language, denoted by 'A' in the meta-meta-language is a value of the variables of the meta-language. Thus if the meta-language quantifies over the expressions of the object language we will have as a meta-meta-theorem, where 'a' is the meta-language term which denotes the term in the object language which denotes a, our definiens, with 'a' replacing A. Thus we have in our meta-meta-language that ' 'a' ' ϵ Existence$_M$. Accordingly we may regard 'Existence' as a systematically ambiguous predicate, in the somewhat dubious sense of Russell, which may be defined for any language of the hierarchy.

Having defined 'Existence' in this manner, we may now consider the various questions which have been raised about existence and indicate the appropriate answers. These answers will of course frequently be conditional on the structure of the object- or metalanguage being considered. I make no particular claim to be offering solutions to the philosophical problem of existence, whatever that may be; but I do suspect that at least some of the people who thought they had philosophical problems did not have them. Furthermore, any analysis of the ordinary use of existence (if all uses are not extraordinary) will have, in its own way, to take account of the distinctions to be encountered. I use 'Existence$_O$' for that predicate of the meta-language which is applied to expressions of the meta-language which denote object-language expressions; 'Existence$_M$' is defined above; 'Existence$_{MM}$' is that predicate of the meta-meta-meta-language which is applied to names of expressions of the meta-meta-language; 'Existence$_n$' is that predicate of the $n + 1$st order language which is applied to names (or descriptions) of expressions of the nth order language.

Question I. Is existence a predicate?

Answer: (1) The expression 'Existence' is not among the list of predicates of any ordinary object language; nor is it clear how we could introduce it into such a list. 'Existence$_O$' ϵ Predicate$_O$ is not well-formed.

Answer: (2) 'Existence' may be defined as a predicate of higher order languages in the manner indicated above. 'Existence$_n$' ϵ Predicate$_{n+1}$

Question II: Is existence an attribute (or property)?

Answer: (1) 'Existence$_n$' as defined above is a predicate and not an attribute.

Compare: 'p' is a sentence and not a proposition.

Answer: (2) Existence$_n$ is an attribute, if and only if, 'Existence$_n$' ϵ Existence$_{n+1}$.

Compare: a is an individual, if and only if a exists.

　　　　　p is a proposition, if and only if p exists.

Question III: Does existence exist?

Answer: (1) The predicate 'Exists$_O$' is a term of the meta-language and hence among the values of the variables of the meta-meta-language.

' 'Existence$_O$' ' ϵ Existence$_{MM}$

Answer: (2) The question whether 'Existence$_O$' ϵ Existence$_M$ and hence the answer to II.2 will turn on whether the meta-language quantifies over its own predicates. If it does not: 'Existence$_O$' $\notin$ Existence$_M$. Hence Existence$_O$ is not an attribute.

Compare: 'F' $\notin$ Existence$_O$

If it does, we will have in general 'Existence$_O$' ϵ Existence$_M$. But this need not rule out the possibility of Existence$_O$ being identical with the null class (where, say, the object-language contains only primitive sentences and truth-functional compounds of

[179]

them). We may also construct systems that will yield the requisite meta-meta-theorem only where we meet special conditions concerning membership.

Answer: (3) As to 'Existence$_n$' ϵ Existence$_n$ we may note that it will not be well-formed given the usual language hierarchies. 'Existence$_n$ ϵ Existence$_n$' will on the other hand be well formed, but the relevant expression in the definiens

$$\text{'(x) (..x..)} \supset \text{(..'} \frown \text{Existence}_n \frown \text{'..)'}$$

will not be a sentence, let alone a theorem, so Existence$_n$ $\notin$ Existence$_n$. At least it will not be a sentence if the language obeys the theory of types. If it does not the relevant theorem may be obtainable, but only at great risk.

JOSEPH J. KOCKELMANS

SIGNS AND SYMBOLS

I

Introduction. It is doubtful whether signs and symbols have ever before been studied by so many persons and from so many points of view as they are today. Signs and symbols, in a very broad sense, are studied in such sciences as linguistics, logic, biology, archeology, cultural anthropology, psychology, sociology, history of religion, aesthetics, philosophy, and theology. In recent years a relatively independent discipline, dealing exclusively with signs and symbols as such has arisen; it is called *semiotic*. Semiotic may be conceived of as a descriptive discipline whose task is to analyze and accurately describe the most general structure and meaning of signs and languages and of the laws governing their use. It is divided into three parts: *pragmatics*, dealing with the way signs and languages are used; *semantics*, a study of the relations between the signs of a language and their meaning; and *syntax*, which considers signs aside from what they mean and is mainly concerned with the way signs are to be related to each other. Semiotic leaves further specification and determination of insights gained in this manner to the various sciences mentioned above. It is still a young science and in the first stages of its development.[1]

It cannot be denied that the numerous studies and investigations undertaken within the realm of these very different domains

[181]

have enriched our knowledge of signs and symbols considerably and that, in particular, they have clearly brought to the fore the predominant role played by signs and symbols in human life. On the other hand, in considering these investigations, one must come to the conclusion that we still do not have a satisfactory characterization of the mode of Being proper to signs and symbols and of the typical aspects distinguishing them from one another and from cognate categories such as index, ikon, signal, indication, image, metaphor, allegory, analogy, example, and the like. There are many reasons for this situation, the most important of which seem to consist in the following.

First of all, in determining the meaning and general structure of signs and symbols, many authors confine themselves to a mere enumeration of *some* general characteristics and then immediately pass on to a study of signs and symbols within the realm of a specific domain of application or of a particular human concern, without asking themselves whether these characteristics indeed specify signs and symbols, or only describe those aspects and properties which signs and symbols have in common with each other or with other cognate categories. G. Gurvitsch, for instance, in his depth sociology describes symbol as that sign which concealing reveals and revealing conceals and, at the same time, is an instrument of participation in values.[2] These characteristics are indeed distinguishing features of many symbols, but do not sufficiently distinguish the symbol from analogous categories.

Furthermore, the general philosophical climate which constitutes the framework within which different authors dealing with signs and symbols try to explain their points of view (varying as these do from author to author) is responsible for the differences in the conclusions. It is evident that investigations written from a neo-positivist point of view will lead to conclusions different from those obtained in reflections written from a critical, phenomenological, or existential standpoint, for the simple reason that in these philosophies different solutions are proposed for the basic ontological and epistemological problems, problems which seem to interfere with the determination of the essential characteristics of signs and symbols.

Even the thoroughgoing investigations within the realm of semiotic which purport to deal explicitly with the subject as such, have as yet been unable to put an end to the confusion and to solve the problems involved in a convincing way.[3]

According to the common use of language, a *sign* is a gesture serving to convey an intimation or to communicate some idea. A sign is also a mark or device having some special meaning or import attached to it, or serving to distinguish the thing on which it is placed. Sometimes it means a conventional mark, device, or symbol used technically in place of words or names written in ordinary letters.

Taken in a different context, a sign is a token or an indication, mostly visible or immediately perceptible, of some fact or quality, taken for the most part as either completely imperceivable or at least not immediately perceivable. Thus a sign is sometimes identical with a symptom. As derived from this meaning, a sign is also called a trace (of an animal, for instance) or an indication of something, a vestige. Sometimes the term 'sign' means the indication of some coming event or an act of miraculous nature, serving to demonstrate divine power or authority.[4]

According to the philosophical dictionary of Lalande,[5] in philosophy the different meanings of the term 'sign' are very often reduced to three basic ones. First, a sign is an externally perceptible activity serving to communicate a certain intention: e.g., to give a sign of willingness to depart. Also a sign is an actually perceptible phenomenon justifying (in a more or less certain way) an assertion about another phenomenon or thing: e.g., the frequency of the pulse as a sign of fever. Finally, a sign is a material thing, figure, or sound occupying the place of an absent thing or a thing that cannot be perceived, and serving either to remind someone of something, or to be combined with other signs of the same kind into a certain system: e.g., the signs representing the chemical elements, or the signs constituting a language.

Many authors are of the opinion that these distinctions are not convincing; first of all, most of them feel that it is possible to formulate a definition of 'sign' which covers the three cases which Lalande tries to distinguish.[6] And second, they say, if various kinds of signs are to be distinguished, then there are obviously many other classes to be added to the three mentioned by Lalande, even if one is not willing to go so far as Peirce in distinguishing 66 classes.[7]

In trying to define the sign in general, Ricoeur[8] argues that *in each sign* there is a perceptible vehicle which is the carrier of a signifying function which causes it 'to have value' in regard to something else. That is why in each sign one has to distinguish between *two* couples of factors which together constitute the unity of the sign's signification. There is first the duality consisting in the structure of the perceptible sign and the signification which it carries; de Saussure refers to these factors with the terms 'the

[183]

signifying' and 'the signified.' Furthermore there is the intentional duality of the sign (which itself implies already the signifying and the signified, the perceptible and the 'spiritual') and the thing designated. These two dualities, the structural and the intentional, are particularly manifest in linguistic signs; the words of a language express meaning and designate things; the signification of a word includes expression as well as designation.

Peirce has given many definitions of 'sign,' the simplest of which is perhaps the following: "a sign . . . is something that stands to somebody for something in some respect or capacity."[9] Elsewhere he says: "Now a sign has, as such, these references: first, it is a sign *to* some thought which interprets it; second, it is a sign *for* some object to which in that thought it is equivalent; third, it is a sign, *in* some respect or quality, which brings it into connection with its object."[10] And also: "I define a Sign as anything which is so determined by something else, called its Object, and so determines an effect upon a person, which effect I call its Interpretant, that the latter is thereby mediately determined by the former." And finally: "A sign, therefore is an object which is in relation to its object on the one hand and to an interpretant on the other in such a way as to bring the interpretant into a relation to the object, corresponding to its own relation to the object."[12]

In his *Foundations of the Theory of Signs* Morris[13] tries to determine the general structure and meaning of signs by taking his starting point in an analysis of *semiosis* as the complete process in which something functions as a sign. This process involves three different factors: that which functions as a sign, namely the *sign vehicle*; that which the sign refers to, namely the *designatum*; and the effect on some interpreter in virtue of which the sign vehicle functions as a sign, called the *interpretant*. The interpreter himself may be included as a fourth factor. According to Morris, it is clear that these new terms make explicit the factors left undesignated in the common statement that a sign refers to something for someone.

Indicating the sign vehicle with S, the designatum with D, and the interpretant of the interpreter with I, we may say, Morris posits, that the process of semiosis indicates that S is the sign of D with respect to I, to the degree that by the interpreter in I there is taken account of D in virtue of the presence of S. Thus semiosis is a mediated-taking-account-of. The mediators are the sign vehicles; the taking-account-of is an interpretant; the agents of the process are interpreters; and what is taken account of is a designatum. It is evident, Morris concludes, that the properties of being a sign, a designatum, an interpretant, or an interpreter are relational properties which things take on by participating in the functional process of semiosis.[14]

If one understands these authors properly they all agree that the essential character of a sign consists in the *referential structure* of something to something else for someone. If we compare this conclusion with the different meanings of the term 'sign' as used in our common language, and also with the different descriptions given by philosophers, we must come to the conclusion that this determination of a sign, indeed, describes the *formal* structure of every sign. However, we must ask ourselves whether this determination, which without a doubt is a description of an essential characteristic of every sign, suffices to determine a sign as such and to distinguish it from other analogous phenomena and categories. It is my opinion that the referential structure to which these authors point in their descriptions is to be found in every tool and piece of equipment as well. Since no one calls tools and pieces of equipment as such signs, one will have to look for further essential characteristics in order to determine sufficiently the formal structure of the sign. This is the task to be undertaken in the second part of this study.

If we now focus attention on the meaning of the term 'symbol,' we shall immediately find ourselves in an embarrassing situation because of the nearly perfect babel of tongue holding sway in the different investigations dealing with the subject.[15] Again, if for a first orientation, we take our point of departure in the common use of our language we shall see that several *different* conceptions are to be distinguished here. First of all, a symbol is a formal authoritative statement of religious belief, e.g., a belief of the Christian church, or a particular church or sect; in this case we often speak of a creed or a confession of faith. In addition, a symbol is something that stands for, represents, or denotes something else, not by exact resemblance, but by vague suggestion, or by some accidental or conventional relation; taken in this sense, the term 'symbol' seems to be synonymous with the term 'sign.' The word 'symbol,' however, is very often used to especially indicate a material object representing, or taken to represent, something immaterial or abstract; going in the same direction the term 'symbol' is used also to indicate an object representing something sacred. Finally, a symbol is a written character or mark used to represent something: a letter, a figure, or sign, *conventionally* standing for some object. In contradistinction to these meanings, all of which seem somehow to be closely bound up with the Greek word *sumbolon*, the term 'symbol' sometimes indicates a contribution, especially to a feast or picnic, a share or portion; in this case the term refers to the Greek word *sumbolē*.[16]

If we make abstraction here of the first and the last meanings, namely a symbol in the sense of a confession of faith, which is clearly a derivative meaning of the term, and a symbol in the sense of a contribution to a feast, which does not belong to the problem occupying us here, we still have two rather different meanings which have in common only the fact that a symbol is a sign used to represent something. In order to eliminate the confusion created by these two different meanings, several philosophers have proposed restricting the term 'symbol' to those signs which necessarily imply an analogous and 'natural' (in contradistinction to 'conventional') correspondence between the sign and the 'object' which is symbolized in the sign (Delacroix). The consequence of this would be that numbers cannot be called 'symbols' (Hémon). Brunschvicg even believes that the difference between signs and symbols consists precisely in that a sign is something artificial while a symbol always possesses 'an internal power of representation'; for instance, the snake which bites its tail as a symbol of eternity.[17] Other philosophers want to suppress the meaning described by the philosophers just mentioned and affiliate themselves with the generally accepted use in the logical and mathematical sciences and maintain only the semiotic conception of symbol. Not only do neopositivist authors tend to go in this direction, but the view is defended also by such thinkers as Newman, who seems in this to represent a very old tradition in English philosophy. Newman writes, for instance: "Now, without external symbols to mark out and to steady its course, the intellect runs wild: but with the aid of symbols, as in algebra, it advances with precision and effect. Let then our symbols be words: let all thought be arrested and embodied in words. Let language have a monopoly of thought; and thought go for only so much as it can show itself to be worth in language. . . ."[18] However, these authors, too, wish most of the time to maintain a certain difference between signs in general and symbols. For example, Morris who seems to accept this point of view in general, explicitly makes a distinction between indexical signs, icons, and symbols. An *indexical* sign at any instant designates what is pointed at and need not be similar to what it denotes. A *characterizing sign* characterizes what it denotes; if it does so by exhibiting in itself the properties an object must have to be denoted by it, the characterizing sign is an *icon*;

if it does not exhibit the properties such an object must possess, the characterizing sign is called a *symbol*.[19]

Most of the philosophers, however, hold that it is not right to suppress one of the *basic* meanings of the term 'symbol' and that the common use of our language is to be respected. They point, furthermore, to the fact that suppressing the one or the other meaning very often leads to one-sidedness and frequently is a sign of prejudices of some kind or other.[20] Notwithstanding this fundamental agreement, these authors have quite different conceptions in regard to what precisely is to be understood by 'symbol' in the second and narrower sense of the term. A few interpretations of the concept of 'symbol' will be mentioned here to illustrate this point.

We have seen already that Ricoeur is of the opinion that in each *sign* there is to be distinguished a structural as well as intentional duality. As far as symbols are concerned, Ricoeur argues that here there is still another duality, one of higher degree, which is to be added to those characteristic of the sign as such. This duality is a relation of meaning in regard to meaning. A symbol is a sign which already has a first, literal, and manifest meaning, but a meaning which now (in the symbol) refers to another *hidden* meaning. Thus symbols are expressions with *multiple meanings* which, for that reason, must be *interpreted*.

In Ricoeur's view the problem of the symbol is equal to the problem of language in general. There is no symbolism before man speaks, even if it is and remains true that the very root of the symbol is to be found much deeper, be this the fundamental expressivity of the cosmos, the fact that desires want to say something, or the imaginative variety of the subjects. There are symbols because language produces signs with a double, and even a multiple, meaning.[21] Thus a symbol is to be found where the linguistic expression lends itself to interpretation because of its double or multiple meaning. The interpretation is necessitated mainly by the intentional structure which does not consist in the relation between meaning and thing, but in an architecture of meaning, in a relation of meaning to meaning, of the second to the first meaning, regardless of whether the first meaning conceals or reveals the second meaning.[22]

Susanne Langer suggested that, in addition to the merely semiotic conception of the symbol found in logical and mathematical treatises, another conception is to be added which cannot be defined in terms of denotation, signification, formal assignment, or reference. She believes that Cassirer's *Philosophy of Symbolic Forms* can be of the greatest importance in this connection.[23] Although I concur with Langer's thesis and share her high esteem of Cassirer's work, I nevertheless agree with Ricoeur that Cassirer's conception of the symbol is too broad to solve the most important problems which have arisen in this context. For Cassirer is of the opinion that the 'symbolic function' is the general mediating function by means of which the mind constitutes all its 'worlds of meaning.' In other words, the symbolic function is at the very root of all acts of synthesis and all the realms of objectivation which correspond to them. All mediating functions refer to one unique function, the symbolic function so that 'the Symbolic' (*das Symbolische*) is the common denominator for all modes of objectivation, of all modes of giving meaning to reality.[24]

It will be clear that in this view the expression 'the Symbolic' becomes equivalent to the concept 'world' or 'culture.' Ricoeur has rightly pointed to the fact that in this way the distinction between the univocal and the 'multivocal,' the semantical and the hermeneutical (which, in his view as well as in the view of many other authors, is *essential* for the symbol) vanishes.[25] The symbolic function seems precisely to consist in this: that one wants and intends to say something different from what one says literally.[26]

On the other hand, some people believe that symbol is identical to analogy. However, identifying the symbol with analogy is tantamount to having too narrow a conception of the symbol. One cannot deny that there is a great similarity between symbolism and analogy; one can say that many symbols imply analogy. But whereas analogies can be developed into analogy arguments, a symbol cannot be employed in that way because in the symbol one is unable *intellectually* to dominate the similarity which, indeed, is present there.[27]

Be this as it may, the central questions to be considered in regard to the term 'symbol' are the following: what is the precise difference between the two basic meanings of the term mentioned, and what are the necessary and sufficient conditions which must be fulfilled in order that we may indicate something with the term 'symbol' in either of the two conceptions cited? Investigating these questions will be the task of the third part of this study.

II

Equipment and Sign. In the introduction we noted that, in the opinion of many authors, the *essential* characteristic of a sign consists in the *referential structure* of something to something else for someone. Although it is clear that in this way at least *one* essential characteristic of the formal structure of a sign is indicated, we must ask, nevertheless, whether this determination suffices to sufficiently characterize the sign as such and to distinguish it from other analogous categories. For it seems that this referential structure is found also in every tool and piece of equipment. With this the case, one has to look for further characteristics in order to determine sufficiently the formal structure of the sign. This is the topic for the second part of this essay in which I wish to draw attention to some insights proposed by Heidegger in *Being and Time*.[28]

In his everyday life man's dealing with intramundane things can assume many concrete forms: "having something to do with something, producing something, consuming something, abandoning something or letting it get lost, undertaking, accomplishing, inquiring, questioning, considering, talking over, determining . . ."[29] All these activities show man's interest in things, his concern for them. Man's everyday life must even be characterized as 'concern,' for his concern for things is not just an occasional feature of his Being, but rather a feature which essentially belongs to him. Even when man stops manipulating things, abandons them, or is careless about them, even then his activities presuppose that man is essentially a concernful being.

In other words, concern is the very basis of man's relation to the world, and in no way does this basis consist in the reference of man as a subject to the world as an object. In other words, man's dealing with intramundane things does not first and foremost consist in theoretical knowledge (as many philosophers since Descartes have claimed), but rather in the kind of concern which 'handles' and 'manipulates' things and puts them to use. True, theoretical knowledge is one of the ways in which a human being can be related to things, but theoretical knowledge is merely a derivative mode of man's primordial concernful dealing with things. It is true also that every concrete mode of concern is guided by knowledge, but this knowledge is primarily not man's theoretical knowledge, but rather a kind of 'practognosy.' This kind of knowledge is not opposed to theoretical knowledge simply as a-theoretical, nor is it an inferior kind of knowledge. Practognosy is prior to theoretical, as well as practical, knowledge as both are conventionally understood. Heidegger calls this kind of knowledge 'circumspection.'[30]

We must now first try to answer the question about the way

in which intramundane things are present to man in his concernful dealing with them. For this purpose we must carefully analyze and describe some concrete forms of concernful dealing with intramundane things. We have seen that man's primordial encounter with things is never such that he finds them in the world as 'mere objects.' Objects are things in a purely theoretical relation to a subject. In his concernful dealing with things man meets them as tools, implements, pieces of equipment. Thus our original question becomes: what is typical and characteristic of equipment as such, what makes equipment equipment?

First we must realize that there is no such thing as an isolated piece of equipment. To the mode of Being characteristic of any 'equipment' there always belongs an equipment-totality in which this piece of equipment can be what it is, because equipment is essentially something in-order-to. A piece of equipment is what it is through its belonging to other pieces of equipment with which it constitutes a totality: forks, spoons, knives, dishes, chairs, table, other furniture, windows, doors, room. These things never show themselves proximally as they are for themselves so as to add up to a sum of 'real things' and furnish a room. What we encounter as closest to us, although not as something explicitly taken as a theme, is the room; and we encounter it not as an empty or a filled space between four walls in a geometrical sense, but as equipment for eating or residing. From this totality the 'arrangement' arises and emerges. And it is in this fashion that any piece of equipment shows itself as that which it is. But before it is able to do so, a totality of equipment must already have been discovered in advance.

In our practical dealing with a piece of equipment such as a hammer for instance, the equipment is not grasped thematically as 'something objectively present at hand.' By using the hammer I do not increase my theoretical knowledge of the hammer's character, but I certainly appropriate it in a way which could not possibly be more suitable. In using the hammer I subordinate my concern to the 'in-order-to' which is constitutive for the tool I am utilizing. The more I employ the hammer properly, the more I discover its manipulability (*Handlichkeit*); this term clearly indicates the hammer's relation to the hand. A piece of equipment is a thing that is 'ready to hand.' Heidegger suggests that we call the kind of Being characteristic of the equipment as such its 'readiness-to-hand.'

If we look at things in a merely theoretical way, we can do quite well without understanding their readiness-to-hand. But when we deal with them by manipulating them, our manipulation possesses its own kind of 'seeing' which shows us the piece of equipment in its readiness-to-hand and immediately discovers the fundamental assignment of each piece of equipment, its peculiar reference to its 'in-order-to.' It is this kind of 'seeing' which Heidegger calls *circumspection*, in contradistinction to the 'seeing' proper to our theoretical knowledge.

However, the readiness-to-hand of a piece of equipment is not *explicitly* evident in our concernful dealing with it. For in his concern man is not primarily occupied with his equipment as such, but with the piece of work to be done. That with which man concerns himself primarily is the work to be done; and this is somehow ready-to-hand, too. And it is just the work to be done which carries with it the referential totality within which the equipment is encountered as such.

The work to be done, as the 'toward-which' of the pieces of equipment employed in its production, also has the kind of Being characteristic of equipment; it too is 'meant for . . .' or 'serves to . . .' But in the work to be done we not only discover a constitutive reference to its 'towards-which,' its usability, but also a reference to the materials man uses, a reference to its 'where-of.' Furthermore, in the work to be done we find, in addition to the 'toward-which' of its usability and the 'where-of' of the materials of which it consists, a reference to the person who is to use or to wear it. Thus, side-by-side with the work to be done, we encounter not only things which are ready-to-hand, but also beings which have the kind of Being proper to man himself, beings for which, in their own concern, the product becomes ready-to-hand. And in company with these beings we encounter the world in which wearers and users live.

The structure of the Being of what is ready-to-hand as equipment is determined by references and assignments; this is the general conclusion of the foregoing descriptive analysis. For the most part, however, we are not *explicitly* aware of all these references and assignments in our everyday concern. The reference-structure of an item of equipment comes to the fore explicitly under special circumstances. When man concerns himself with something, the things which are most closely ready-to-hand might be met as something unusable, or as not properly adapted for the use he has decided upon. The tool may turn out to be damaged, or the material inappropriate. In each of these cases *equipment* remains, and it is still somehow ready-to-hand. We discover its unusability not by looking at it and establishing its properties as we do in our theoretical knowledge, but rather by the circumspection of the dealings in which we use it. When its unusability is subsequently discovered, equipment becomes conspicuous. This conspicuousness presents the ready-to-hand equipment as a certain unreadiness-to-hand. And this implies that what cannot be used just lies there; it shows itself as an equipmental thing which looks in such and such a way and which (in its readiness-to-hand as looking that way) has constantly been present-to-hand, too.

In our concernful dealings, however, we encounter not only unusable things within what is already ready-to-hand: we also discover that things are missing, and thus are not at-hand at all. Again, for something to be missing in this way amounts to coming across something unready-to-hand. When we notice what is unready-to-hand, what *is* ready-to-hand enters in the mode of obtrusiveness. The more pressing our need for what is missing, and consequently the more authentically it is encountered in its unreadiness-to-hand, all the more obtrusive does that which *is* ready-to-hand become—so much so, in fact, that it seems even to lose its character of readiness-to-hand.

In our everyday concern the unready-to-hand can be encountered not only in terms of what is unusable or simply missing, but as something which, not missing at all and not even unusable, 'just stands in the way.' Then it appears as something to which our concern refuses to turn, that for which we have no time. Anything which is unready-to-hand in this way is disturbing to us, and lets us see the obstinacy of what we must concern ourselves with in the first place.

The conspicuousness, obtrusiveness, and obstinacy which make themselves felt when equipment for some reason cannot be used at the moment imply that the constitutive assignment of the 'in order to' to a 'towards this' has been disturbed. In our everyday concern these assignments are not observed explicitly; but when an assignment has been disturbed, it becomes immediately explicit. When an assignment to some particular towards-this has been thus circumspectively aroused, we catch sight of this towards-this itself, and along with it of everything connected with the work, and the whole workshop as that wherein concern always dwells. Thus the equipment context is illuminated, not as something never seen before, but as a totality constantly sighted beforehand in circumspection.

When something ready-to-hand is found to be missing, though its everyday presence has been so obvious that we have never really noticed it, this makes a break in those referential contexts which

circumspection discovers. Our circumspection encounters emptiness, and now sees for the first time *what* the missing article was
ready-to-hand *with*, and *what* it was ready-to-hand *for*. The environment proclaims itself anew, and in it the world of everyday
concern itself.[31]

Now in our descriptive interpretation of the ontological structure which is characteristic of equipment as such, the phenomenon
of reference occupied a central position. We must now try to grasp
this phenomenon more precisely. And this can be done by means
of an ontological analysis of a kind of equipment in which one
encounters *different types* of references, as for instance in signs.

The word 'sign' can designate many kinds of things, as we
have seen, but in the first instance, signs are pieces of equipment
whose specific character as equipment consists in *indicating*. In
our everyday life we find such signs in traffic signs, signposts,
boundary-markers, water buoys, signals, banners, and the like.
Showing or indicating can be defined as a kind of referring; and
referring itself, if taken as formally as possible, is a form of relating.
But relation cannot be conceived of here as the genus for the
kinds of references which may become differentiated as sign, icon,
symbol, expression, signification, and so on. A relation is something formal which is constituted by a process of formalization
which may take its point of departure from any concrete kind of
context. The formally general character of relation can be brought
to the fore if we realize that every reference is a relation, but not
every relation is a reference; that every indication is a reference,
but not every reference an indication; and finally that every indication is a relation, but not every relation an indication. This being
true, it becomes evident that, if we are to investigate such phenomena as references, signs, or even significations, there is nothing to be
gained by characterizing them as relations. One may even ask
whether relations, because of their formally general character, do
not have their ontological root in the phenomenon of reference.

Therefore, even if the present analysis is to be confined to
the interpretation of signs as distinct from the phenomenon of
reference, even within this limitation we cannot properly investigate the full multiplicity of possible signs. For among them there
are indices, numbers, pointer-readings, warning signals, symp-
toms, signs which refer to something in the past, signs to mark
something, signs by which things can be recognized, all having
different ways of indicating, regardless of what may be serving as
such a sign. Furthermore, from such 'signs' we must distinguish
traces, residues, memorials, documents, testimonies, significations,

[193]

appearances, expressions, symbols. Obviously these phenomena can be formalized quite easily because of their relational character. But what we shall find in this way in the end says nothing that is more than the easy schema of content and form. It is for this reason that we intend to restrict ourselves to an analysis and description of signs which—from the viewpoint of our common language—are signs in an authentic and, moreover, original way, in order to focus not on their reference-structure as such, which they—as we have seen—have in common with every item of equipment, but on the characteristic traits of the reference-structure of the sign as such.

Let us, therefore, take as an example the turn-signal arrow a bus uses to indicate the direction it will take at an intersection. This sign is an item of equipment which is ready-to-hand for the driver in his concern with driving, and for those who are not travelling with him and make use of it either by yielding the right of way on the proper side or by stopping. This sign is ready-to-hand within the world in the whole equipment-context of vehicles and traffic regulations. It is *equipment for indicating*, and *as equipment* it is constituted by reference. It has the character of the in-order-to of every equipment. But in addition to this it has its own definite serviceability: it is for indicating. This indicating which is characteristic of the sign can be determined as a kind of referring-to, but then *this* referring is different from the ontological structure of the sign *as equipment*.

Referring taken as indicating is founded on the ontological structure of equipment: thus, on the serviceability, which is characteristic of equipment as such. But a thing may be serviceable without, for that matter, being a sign. As equipment, a hammer too has a certain serviceability, but this does not make it a sign. Indicating, as a form of referring, is a way in which the toward-which of a serviceable thing becomes concrete: it determines an item of equipment as for this concrete toward-which. On the other hand, the kind of reference we have in serviceability-for is a characteristic trait of equipment as equipment. That the toward-which of a serviceable thing is made concrete here in the form of 'indicating' is accidental for the constitution of a piece of equipment as such. In this example the difference between the reference of serviceability and the reference of indicating is already roughly indicated. These two certainly do not coincide; and only when they are united does the concreteness of a definite kind of equipment manifest itself. It is certain that indicating differs in principle from referring taken as a constitutive characteristic of equipment as such; but it is certain also that the sign is related in a distinctive way to the kind of Being characteristic of whatever equipmental totality may be ready-to-hand in the environment. Thus we may conclude that in our concernful dealings equipment-for-indicating is utilized in a very special manner. The root and the meaning of this special manner must now be clarified.

A sign indicates; what precisely is meant by this? In answering this question one must focus on man's typical kind of dealing which is appropriate to equipment for indicating, and see what this teaches us about the readiness-to-hand characteristic of that kind of equipment. The appropriate way of dealing with a sign, such as a turn-signal, certainly does not consist in staring at it, or explicitly identifying it as an indicator. Nor is such a sign authentically encountered if we turn our glance in the direction which the signal indicates and focus on something present-at-hand which is found in the region indicated. Such a sign seems rather to address itself immediately to man's circumspection which is characteristic of his concernful dealing with things, impelling it to bring into an explicit survey whatever the environment may contain at that moment. Such a survey obviously does not grasp the sign's readiness-to-hand, but tries to bring about an orientation in the environment.

But if it is true that signs of this kind make some environment accessible to us so that our concerned dealings receive an orientation, then it is evident that a sign does not stand in the relationship of indicating to just *one* other thing or *some* other things *in concreto*; it is rather a piece of equipment which explicitly brings an *equipment totality* within the range of our circumspection. In other words, signs indicate two things: first the environment wherein one lives and where one's concern dwells, and then the typical way in which man is involved there with something.[32]

We can obviously carry on this analysis in many directions, as Heidegger explicitly does. For our purpose, however, this seems not to be necessary, because the preceding interpretation of the sign permits us to infer already the following general conclusion which seems to be of prime importance for our investigation: signs are pieces of equipment which *in addition to* referring to a possible equipment-totality, *indicate* something. This indicating is founded upon the equipment-structure, that is the in-order-to of the equipment as such, and *concretizes* the towards-which of its serviceability. Furthermore, the sign's indicating (just as the equipmental character of anything which is ready-to-hand) functions in an equipment totality, that is, in a whole context of references.

[195]

Finally, a sign is not merely ready-to-hand together with other pieces of equipment. Its readiness-to-hand makes the environment in each concrete case explicitly accessible for circumspection. In other words, a sign is something ontic which is ready-to-hand and which (in addition to being this definite equipment) explicitly *indicates* the ontological structure of what is ready-to-hand, of referential totalities, of 'worlds,' and in the final analysis of 'the' world.

Concluding this part of our investigation we may say that the so-called reference-structure as such is a necessary but nonsufficient characteristic for a sign as sign, because this structure is characteristic for every item of equipment. The distinguishing characteristic of a sign is that it, via this general reference structure, *indicates* something, points to something within a concrete context of references. In indicating something concrete the sign also points to this referential totality and finally even to the world, or at least to a certain world in which the sign is meaningful. The final meaning of this indicating and pointing-at consists in the fact that it makes a certain environment, a referential totality, explicitly accessible for circumspection by pointing in a direction, indicating an orientation, making possible a differentiation, making understandable a structure, and so on.

III

Signs and Symbols. Now as was stated in the first part of this essay, most of the scientists and philosophers believe that it is impossible to identify signs and symbols completely. Indeed, all symbols are signs, but not all signs are symbols. The basic structure of a symbol implies the essential characteristics of a sign, but the symbol itself possesses some typical aspects which in the notion of the sign as such are missing.[33]

Furthermore, it seems to be necessary to distinguish between at least two irreducible and basic meanings of the term 'symbol.' The first, generally accepted among scientists, consists in this: that a symbol is a conventional sign within a certain referential context, indicating something in such a way that it characterizes what it denotes without exhibiting the properties such an entity must possess. In this way symbols are spoken of in logic, mathematics, physics, chemistry, biology, and economy. Most of the psychologists, sociologists, cultural anthropologists, and philosophers admit the validity of this meaning of the term 'symbol' and very often speak of it in this way, although they normally use the term in another sense.

In referring to the historical investigations of Calepino and especially to those of de Campos Leyza, Alleau proposes to avoid confusion and to eliminate unnecessary problems by indicating this group of signs with the term 'synthema.' In his opinion, it would be important also, to distinguish within this class of signs the following subclasses of synthems: logical synthems (comprising logical, mathematical, and linguistic signs constituting different languages), abbreviating synthems, mnemonic synthems, distinguishing synthems, monistic synthems (my signature, my 'number' in the mill, a.s.o.), technical synthems, strategical synthems, chronological, topological, didactical, numismatic, cryptographic, semeiologic, curiologic, metabolic synthems, etc.[34] Even if one does not want to follow Alleau in his introduction of the new term 'synthem' and in his making of all these distinctions, it seems at least to be of some importance to accept certain major subclasses in this class of signs, because the way in which these signs indicate and characterize what they denote is clearly different in different cases.

At any rate, none of this, as far as I know, creates serious problems. Serious problems arise only when the second meaning of the term 'symbol' is brought into the discussion. For many philosophers as well as scientists definitely refuse to admit the validity of the second meaning and claim that this use of the word 'symbol' is illicit. Others want to suppress the first meaning in order to avoid confusion.[35] These problems arose when scientists dealing with the history of religion, cultural anthropology, and depth psychology came to the conclusion that it is impossible to adopt the positivist point of view in which myths and symbols are only fables, and dreams have merely a purely subjective meaning, if they have meaning at all. These scientists, and many philosophers with them, believe that it is impossible to approach dreams, myths, and poetic symbols in terms of scientific truth or error: dreams, myths, and poetic symbols have meaning that can be understood. These authors thus refuse to identify the 'symbol' with what Alleau calls 'synthem.'[36]

Seen from this point of view it becomes clear that the root of the problems raised is to be found in the philosophical standpoints which the various authors have implicitly or explicitly adopted: those who in one form or another are inclined to positivism or scientism wish to exclude the second meaning of the term 'symbol,' since it does not have a 'scientific' signification and interest; the other group of authors, belonging to different trends in philosophy, want to make a clear distinction between symbols and signs and for that reason are very often inclined to exclude the first meaning of the term 'symbol,' indicating the phenomena covered by it with the term 'sign' or 'synthem.'

In comparing the different publications dealing with the subject one sees immediately many questions in addition to those which are necessarily connected with the difference in philosophical standpoints just suggested: if the term 'symbol' has a second meaning, what then is precisely to be understood by it? What are the characteristic aspects of symbols taken in this sense? How are those symbols to be distinguished from other signs and especially from 'synthems'? In what does the typical reference-structure consist in cases where we are dealing with mythological and oneirotic symbols? Are symbols to be analyzed, or are they to be interpreted? How and by what means are their meanings to be understood? In the latter case we would need in semiotic, in addition to syntactics, semantics, and pragmatics, a hermeneutic of symbols.[37] There are evidently more questions which could be legitimately asked, but let us restrict ourselves to these, since they seem to be the most important. However, before dealing with these problems we must first make a few remarks about their historical origin.

One of the first works which brought these problems to the attention of philosophers was Freud's *Interpretation of Dreams,* which appeared in 1900. In this book dreams are interpreted in terms of symbolic manifestations of the unconscious. In dealing with a dream one must make a distinction between the apparent meaning of the dream as dream (which is incoherent and absurd), and the *hidden* meaning which is full of meaning. The latent meaning, disguising itself by employing certain 'mechanisms' takes on the form of the absurd, apparent meaning. This is why the latent meaning can be understood only by means of an *interpretation* of the apparent meaning, and why Freud speaks of *Traumdeutung.*[38] Freud's original ideas have been further elaborated by many modern psychiatrists and psychologists. In this context the publications of Jung, Verneaux, Binswanger, Piaget, and Lacan are (among others) to be mentioned.[39]

Later it became clear that symbolism does not belong exclusively to the domain of the psychologist. Symbolism is found not only in dreams, but in many other modalities of man's Being as well. It seemed that a more careful study of these modalities, in which art and religion occupy a predominant place, could lead to a better understanding of man himself. This explains why in addition to psychological studies on the subject of symbolism, there are many contemporary investigations into the meaning of poetic imagination in its symbolic function.[40] It explains also why the fields of theology, history of religion, cultural anthropology, and sociology have begun to pay more attention to the phenomenon of symbolism in its various aspects. In this connection the works of G. Bachelard, Medicus, Plachte, Leese, M. Eliade, E. Ortigues, and the later publications of Lévy-Brühl may be mentioned.[41]

For most of these authors it is clear that symbols cannot be simply identified with 'synthems,' but they do not agree with one another when it comes to circumscribing the precise meaning of the concept 'symbol.' Some authors still follow de Saussure who in *Traité de linguistique général* defends the point of view that only those signs are symbols which maintain a natural tie with that which is signified. According to de Saussure, that which in fact is characteristic for the function of *signs* is the arbitrary convention which relates the sign to its designatum. Although all languages are built up in a systematic way so that the meaning of one element is defined in relation to the meaning of the other elements, this systematic character of a language does not contradict the arbitrary character of the individual words. The *symbol*, on the other hand, is never *completely* arbitrary: it is not 'empty,' and there is always at least a rudiment of a natural relationship between that which functions as a sign and its designatum.[42] Although this point of view is still defended by many authors, such as Brunschvicg, Delacroix, Hémon, and many others, most of the authors share the opinion that there is no doubt that there are many symbols which have a strictly conventional character. Furthermore, they point up the fact that it is not very clear what precisely is meant by a 'natural relationship.' The reference to a 'certain analogy' between the sign and its designatum does not suffice to explain the final meaning of this relationship.[43]

Most authors see the *essential* characteristic of the symbol, in contradistinction to what we called a 'synthem,' in the fact that symbols refer to a referential totality, an order of things, a 'world' which as such is *not present* or even *hidden*. The symbol implies the presence of a perceptible figure which refers to a 'world' which itself is not perceptible.[44] According to Dumas, man betakes himself to symbols because of the great difficulties often connected with an immediate knowledge and the psychological and ethical difficulties connected with an immediate expression and manifestation. This is why symbols are indispensable in religion, although we use them in nearly all realms of our life.[45] Jung, who implicitly rejects the semiotic conception of the symbol, calls the symbol the best possible expression of a relatively unknown fact. Man uses symbols when there is no other formulation available which can represent the meaning of a fact as clearly and as characteristically as the symbol can. In other words, symbols disclose something which is not known independently of the symbol. That is why symbols can be recognized only by people who are open to *hidden* meanings. This is finally why symbols demand interpretation.[46] In the view of Bonsirven, who follows Bergson in this respect, the symbolic way of thinking and, accordingly, our symbolic way of speaking is even irreducible to logical thought and conceptual discourse. The typical characteristic of the symbol is that it points to a world which is impervious for logical thought and science.[47] Mircea Eliade defends a similar point of view when he says that symbolic thought precedes our discursive reason and our logical discourse. As we have seen already, he holds that a symbol reveals certain aspects of reality to us, and even the most profound ones, to which our scientific knowledge does not have any access.[48] An analogous view is defended by Ricoeur, as we have seen, also.[49] And Alleau goes so far as to posit that every symbol is a sacral sign, referring man from the intramundane to the sacred. The symbol is the represented sacred.[50] Although most of the authors admit that the religious symbols constitute a very important realm in the domain of symbols, they do not choose to follow Alleau for the simple but good reason that there are so many other aspects of man's life to which science does not have immediate access and which can be expressed by means of symbols, as is convincingly clear in psychology, psychoanalysis, literature, art, etc.[51]

Concluding this survey we may say that in the opinion of most of these authors, in and through symbols an 'invisible world' takes shape within our perceptible and understandable world and invests this latter with 'trans-real' values which constitute the profoundly significative character of perceptible reality. It is this revelational function which really defines the symbol and which distinguishes it from allegory and sign, because both the allegory and the sign evoke for man only objects already known.[52]

If one adopts this point of view, he evidently must explain how and by what means man in his symbolic function has access to this 'invisible world.' Most of the authors make an appeal here to a 'certain intuition' or a 'certain kind of symbolic attitude' (Jung), which manifests itself in man's affectivity and emotionality, as this is for instance explained by Scheler who was able to show that sentiments and emotions are not 'states of the soul' or purely subjective events occurring in the 'sealed vase' of man's interiority, but intentional acts and modes of 'understanding the world.'[53] That a so-called 'magical affectivity' plays an important role in symbolization is shown in a convincing way by investigations of Piaget and in certain early publications Sartre has pointed in the same direction.[54] In a remarkable study Vergote has shown that our affectivity in its symbolic function necessarily depends on schemes borrowed from our imagination, because of which every symbol has a typical imaginary dimension. For this point of view Vergote is able to refer to several publications in which it becomes clear that not only psychology and psychoanalysis, but also cultural anthropology, and history of religion support this thesis.[55] In the same study Vergote refers to another aspect which seems to be of great importance in this context. Since there is an imaginary dimension in every symbol, because the invisible is proposed in it in a visible form and, furthermore, because every symbol refers not so much to a concrete entity, value, or meaning, but rather to a 'world,' it is evident that every symbol is polysynthetic and ambiguous. This is why symbols cannot be simply understood, but are to be interpreted, and why (most of the time) they can be interpreted in different ways.[56]

In adopting Vergote's central point of view I would pose the following questions: is it possible to clarify further the role played by man's affectivity in the process of symbolization? And, furthermore, if in a symbol a visible sign refers to an invisible world, is it possible to describe the formal structure of this reference in a clearer way? Regarding the first question Vergote refers to Heidegger's investigations concerning man's fundamental mood.[57] Let us, see, therefore, how much more light these investigations may be able to shed upon the way in which symbols give us insight into an 'invisible' world.

In *Being and Time* Heidegger denotes man by the term 'There-Being' (*Dasein*). According to his view There-Being is a being which does not just occur among other beings. Rather, it is distinguished ontologically by the fact that in its very Being, that Being itself is an issue for it. This implies that There-Being, in its very Being, has a relationship towards its own Being and that this Being is disclosed to it. That is why understanding of Being is itself a definite characteristic of There-Being's Being. That Being towards which There-Being can comport itself in one way or another, and always does comport itself somehow, is called 'ek-sistence.' Man ek-sists; he is essentially 'standing-out-towards,' and that towards which man as There-Being is standing out is, generally speaking, the world. There-Being is therefore essentially Being-in-the-world.[58] This compound expression 'Being-in-the-world' stands for a unitary phenomenon. But although Being-in-the-world constitutes a whole, this does not prevent it from having several constitutive aspects in its structure. And indeed the following aspects might be brought to the fore: the 'in-the-world,' the *being which* is in-the-world, and finally, the *In-Being* of this being which is in-the-world.

By *Being-in* is not meant 'Being in something.' This term normally indicates that kind of Being which a being has when it is 'in' another being, as water is 'in' the glass and my coat is 'in' the cupboard. By this 'in' is meant the relationship which two beings extended 'in' space have to one another with regard to their location in that space. In-Being, on the other hand, is a state of There-Being's Being. Heidegger calls it an 'ek-sistentiale.' In-Being does not indicate a spatial 'in-one-another-ness.' 'In' is derived from '*innan*,' and this means 'to dwell.' '*An*' means 'I am familiar with.' In-Being, therefore, means 'to reside alongside . . . ,' 'to be familiar with . . . .' 'In-Being' is thus the formal ek-sistential expression for the Being of There-Being which has Being-in-the-world as its essential state.[59]

Thus, a further clarification of 'In-Being' will bring to the fore in a clearer way precisely what is meant by the 'There' of man's There-Being. For the being which as ek-sistence is essentially constituted by Being-in-the-world *is* itself, in every case, its 'There.' Man as ek-sistence carries in his ownmost Being the character of not being closed-off. The expression 'There' indicates this essential disclosedness by means of which man is 'there' for himself and by reason of which the world is 'there,' and the beings become manifest as beings. When we speak of a *lumen naturale* in man we have in mind nothing other than this structure of man—that he is in such a way as to be his own 'there.' He brings his own 'there' along with him and gives the world and the intramundane things their 'Being-there.'

According to Heidegger the 'There' of 'There-Being' implies three fundamental constituent elements: original mood (*Befindlichkeit*), primordial understanding *(Verstehen)*, and logos *(Rede)*. In the pages to follow we shall restrict ourselves to a brief survey of Heidegger's view on mood.[60]

The fundamental characteristic of man's Being which Heidegger calls '*Befindlichkeit*' corresponds to what we in our everyday life call 'mood,' or "being-attuned"; *Befindlichkeit* is the ontological condition of the mood's possibility. Man is always in a certain mood. Even the pallid, evenly balanced lack of mood is far from being nothing at all; it rather consists in the fact that man becomes satiated with himself; his own Being has become manifest as a burden and why it should be, one does not know. And man cannot know this because the possibilities of disclosure which belong to our theoretical knowledge reach too short a way compared with the primordial disclosure characteristic of moods in which man is brought before his Being as 'there.' A mood discloses 'how one is'; in this 'how one is' man's being-tuned brings Being to its 'there.'

In having a mood man is always disclosed moodwise as that being to which he has been delivered over in his own Being; in this way he has been delivered over to the Being which in ek-sisting, he has to be. In the most indifferent everydayness the Being of man can burst forth as a naked 'that it is and has to be.' This pure 'that it is' manifestly shows itself, but its 'whence' and 'whither' remain in darkness. The 'that it is' which itself is veiled in its 'whence' and 'whither', is nevertheless a characteristic of man's Being. Heidegger calls this characteristic man's *thrownness*, an expression which is meant to suggest the facticity of man's being delivered over to his own Being.

We would wholly fail to recognize both *what* mood discloses and *how* it discloses, if that which is disclosed were to be compared with what man is acquainted with, knows, and believes at the same time he has such a mood. Even if man is assured in his belief about his 'whither', or if, in reflexive and theoretical knowledge, he thinks he knows about his 'whence', all this counts for nothing against the phenomenal fact of the case: the mood brings man before the 'that he is' of his 'there' which, as such, forces itself upon him with the inexorability of an enigma. There is not the slightest justification for minimizing what is 'evident' in moods, by measuring it against the apodictic certainty of our theoretical knowledge of intramundane things in their being present-at-hand. However, the phenomena indicated are no less falsified when they are relegated to the sanctuary of the 'irrational.' It is often said that man can, should, and must, through knowledge and will, become master of his moods. This suggests a priority of cognition and volition above mood. And yet one must not be misled here into denying that mood is a primordial kind of Being for man, in which man is disclosed to himself prior to all cognition and volition, and even far beyond their range of disclosure.

Thus the first essential characteristic of moods consists in this: that they disclose man in his thrownness and (proximally

[203]

and for the most part) as someone who tries to evade this by turning away from it.

But not only do moods shed light upon our thrownness; each
mood has already disclosed, in each case, our Being-in-the-world
as a whole and, thus, makes it possible first of all to direct ourselves
toward something concrete.

But in addition to these two essential characteristics of moods,
namely the disclosing of thrownness and the disclosing of our own
Being-in-the-world *as a whole*, we must now note a third. We have
seen already that in his everyday concern man encounters intramundane things within the context of a horizon, that is within
the world taken as a referential totality. Thus the world must be
disclosed as such beforehand. Precisely because the world is given
to man beforehand, it is possible for man to encounter intramundane things. Now this prior disclosedness of the world is co-
constituted by one's mood. Man's openness to the world is constituted ek-sistentially by the attunement of a mood. Ek-sistentially,
a mood implies a disclosive submission to the world out of which
we can encounter something which matters to us. That is why
from the ontological point of view we must as a general principle
leave the primary discovery of the world to 'bare moods.' All
theoretical and scientific knowledge, even if it were able to pene-
trate to the innermost core of the Being characteristic of something that is present-at-hand, always presupposes a certain disclosedness of the world in which the being can appear as intramundane thing.[61]

Applying these few remarks to the subject under investigation
it becomes understandable that, if it is true that only moods and
emotions can 'open' man towards the world *as a whole*, which as
such in all 'theoretical and scientific' activities is already presupposed and pre-understood, and if, furthermore, it is true that
every symbol (taken in the narrower sense of the term) refers to a
'world,' then man's mood must play a very important role in the
process of symbolization. Psychoanalysis, cultural anthropology,
history of art and of religion have been able to point to numerous
cases which substantiate and concretely exemplify the importance
of this general thesis.[62]

With respect to the second question posed in the preceding
discussion, namely whether it is possible to describe the formal
structure of the reference of the visible sign to an 'invisible world'
in a clearer way, some authors admit implicitly at least that *every
possible sign* (and, therefore, symbols too) must have the same
basic structure, and that for this reason every possible sign must

refer to something which is signified, and thus that the formal structure of the reference essentially inherent in every sign must be described in terms of a semantical relation between the sign vehicle and the object it denotes. If we take a dream, however, it is immediately evident that its reference-structure cannot be described adequately in terms of a semantical relation between sign vehicle and designatum. For it is not the case that images refer to a certain meaning or a 'world of things' which constitutes the symbol character of a dream, but rather it is the fact that this meaning or this 'world of things' refers to another *meaning* or another *'world of things.'* The images of the dream refer to an apparent world, and it is this apparent world which in some way or other refers to a hidden world. Now it is precisely this latter relation which seems to be constitutive for the symbol as such.[63] In a poem certain words refer to certain things, a phrase refers to a certain state of affairs, a strophe can refer to a certain 'world of things'; in a case of poetic imagination these words or word-groups become symbols when the poet by means of the literal meaning of the words refers to an 'invisible' world. Here again it is the reference of the first signified to this 'invisible world' which constitutes the symbol.[64] If in a primitive religion people speak about the 'Heavens,' the word 'Heavens' first refers to an aspect of the cosmos which we immediately experience in our everyday life, but this aspect of the cosmos refers those people to a God who, for instance, is thought of as 'far away.'[65] Also, in this case the symbolic meaning is superimposed on the literal meaning of a word which is already the result of a semiological process. That is also why it takes a special science to elucidate symbols, a science of interpretation (hermeneutics) which is not interested in the relation between the signifying sign and the signified entity, between sign vehicle and designatum (semantics), but in the relation between the literal meaning and the 'hidden' meaning which the first only 'symbolizes.'[66] The literal meaning in an 'analogous' way intends a second meaning which is given in no other way, and most of the time, cannot be given in another way. This analogy does not operate on the level of the relation between the signifying sign and the signified entity, but on the level of the relation between the immediately signified and the secondly signified.[67]

In a symbol we thus find a procedure which is diametrically opposed to that which we encounter in the constitution of a synthem. A synthem refers to a certain entity in such a way that that which is signified is reduced to its 'definition' so that a group of characteristic properties and a certain complex of 'notes' belonging to the comprehension of the notion of such a thing or entity are 'cut out' and are not to be taken into consideration. It is evident that such an entity itself as such for the most part is much more than what the definition tells us about it. In the case of a symbol, however, the immediately signified is taken without any restriction or abstraction as the necessary consequence of an idealizing functionalization. And furthermore a 'new world' of meanings is taken into account because of a certain 'analogy' of the immediately signified with this 'new world.'[68]

We have said previously that the relation between the literal meaning of a symbol and the hidden meaning is not to be located on the same level with the semiological relation which is constitutive for every symbol in the broader sense of the term (synthem). Furthermore, we drew attention to the fact that, seen from the point of view of the semantical relation proper to every word of a 'natural' language, the relation characteristic of the symbol is opposite to that between sign and designatum as studied by semantics. The relation characteristic of a symbol, finally, is not to be *understood* as is the semantical relation, but is to be *deciphered*[69] and *interpreted*, because of the polysynthetic and ambiguous character which is essential to the symbol.[70] What is meant here can be made clear with Vergote's analysis of the symbolism of the serpent: the serpent can refer to opposite and even contrary 'worlds.' Vergote rightly concludes from this fact that every symbol is a *coincidentia oppositorum*.[71] Since the relation proper to the symbol is not to be *understood*, but must be *interpreted*, some authors call this relation a 'hermeneutical relation,' since it is to be studied, not in semantics, but in hermeneutics.[72] But there is still another reason why we must refer to the science of 'hermeneutics' here. If it is true that man's affectivity and emotionality play an important part in the constitution of symbols, then it should be apparent that symbols cannot be simply 'understood,' but that they are to be interpreted according to the basic rules of hermeneutics.[73]

Analysis of the analogy which joins the literal meaning to the symbolic meaning is made difficult by the fact that the symbolic meaning is only given by means of an event in the immediately signified, *and nowhere else*.[74] This is particularly clear in the case of religious symbols. Certain words and expressions, immediately referring to things and states of affairs of our everyday life, point towards a world which—as such—is inexpressible and indescribable. The evocative power of religious 'images' resides entirely in the cultural and ritual words themselves as given in a certain context.

[206]

The analogy is like an intention contained in what is immediately signified by the cultural or ritual words. So the analogical relation that binds the symbolic meaning to the literal meaning cannot be 'objectified' and 'translated' by other words or expressions. Living in the literal meaning one is drawn by it beyond itself to a second meaning, because the symbolic meaning is constituted in and by the literal meaning and because the literal meaning brings the analogy about by giving me the analogue within a determinate context.[75]

Analogy between the literal meaning and the figurative meaning can be more or less close and more or less contingent. We must therefore oppose symbol and allegory. According to Ricoeur, in allegory there is a simple relationship between two independent 'texts.' The authentic symbol, on the other hand, gives its symbolic meaning in such a way that the apparent meaning evokes the latent meaning, which it necessarily conceals at the same time that it indicates it. That is why a symbol always remains enigmatic.[76]

IV

Conclusion. In concluding this essay we may say that the semantical relation characteristic of every sign is not sufficiently described by pointing to the relation between the sign vehicle and its designatum, as long as the nature of this relation is not adequately determined. In my opinion the distinguishing characteristic of a sign is that in and through this general reference-structure it *indicates* something within a certain *context of references* and that, at the same time, it points to a *referential totality* or 'world' in which the sign functions meaningfully. The final meaning of this complex pointing-to consists in the fact that a sign makes a certain referential totality accessible for our circumspection by indicating a direction, bringing about an orientation, constituting a differentiation, making understandable a certain structure, and the like.

Another result of this investigation is that it appears to be desirable to make an explicit distinction between symbols taken as 'synthems' and symbols in a narrower sense of the term. Characteristic of 'synthems' is that they designate what is pointed to, characterizing what they denote, but not exhibiting the properties such an object must possess. Characteristic of a symbol in the narrower sense of the term is that in addition to the semantical relation mentioned, there is a hermeneutical relation between a first signified and a second signified which cannot be simply understood, but must be interpreted within a certain totality of meaning or 'world.' Such an interpretation cannot be given by semantics, but belongs to the science of hermeneutics.

I wish to draw a practical conclusion from these two 'theoretical' remarks. In the generally accepted description of 'semiotic,' this science has a double goal: to explain the *nature* of signs as such and to explain the *relations* between signs in sign-systems or languages. However, if the science really hopes to materialize both these goals, the necessary consequence is that the science must be augmented with a new chapter dealing with the very nature of symbols taken in the sense in which history of religion, psychoanalysis, and the study of art and literature speak about symbols. Furthermore, consideration of these kinds of symbols would require in addition to syntactics, semantics, and pragmatics, a certain type of hermeneutics necessary for indicating and describing the general rules according to which symbols in the narrower sense of the term are to be interpreted.

NOTES

1. Charles W. Morris, *Foundations of the Theory of Signs (International Encyclopedia of Unified Science*, Vol. I, Number 2). (Chicago, 1960), pp. 1–3.

2. G. Gurvitch, *La vocation actuelle de la sociology* (Paris, 1950), pp. 74–81.

3. A. Van Leeuwen, "Enige aantekeningen over het symbol," in *Bijdragen* 20(1959) 1–14, pp. 1–2.
Among the numerous studies on this subject I would refer the reader to the following: R. Alleau, *De la nature des symboles* (Paris, 1959); E. Cassirer, *The Philosophy of Symbolic Forms,* 3 vols. (New Haven, 1965); C.H. Hamburg, *Symbol and Reality Studies in the Philosophy of Ernst Cassirer* (The Hague, 1956); C.S. Peirce, *Collected Papers,* Vols. I–VI, ed. C. Hartshorne and P. Weiss, Vols. VII–VIII, ed. A. Burks (Cambridge, Mass., 1931–1958), Vol. II, passim; *Selected Writings,* ed. Philip P. Wiener (New York, 1958); Charles W. Morris, *Foundations of the Theory of Signs* (Chicago, 1960); *Signs, Language, and Behavior* (New York, 1955); *Logical Positivism, Pragmatism, and Scientific Empiricism* (New York, 1947); Charles Osgood, *Method and Theory in Experimental Psychology* (New York, 1956), Chapter 16; Susanne K. Langer: *Philosophy in a New Key: A Study in the Symbolism of Reason, Rite, and Art* (Cambridge, Mass., 1942); "On a new Definition of Symbol," in *Philosophical Sketches* (New York, 1964), pp. 53–61; Paul Ricoeur, *De l'interprétation. Essai sur Freud* (Paris, 1965); *Le symbolisme du mal* (Paris, 1962); "Symbolique et temporalité," in *Archivio di Filosofia* 33(1963) 5–31, 32–41; "Le symbole et le mythe," in *Le Sémeur* 61(1963) 81–96; "Langage religieux, mythe et symbole," in *Le Langage,* Vol. II. Actes du XIIIe Congrès des Sociétés de philosophie de langue française

(Neuchâtel, 1967), pp. 129–37 and 138–45; "Le symbole donne à penser," in *Esprit* 27(1959) 60–76; Karl Jaspers, *Truth and Symbol*, trans. Jean T. Wilde, William Kluback, and William Kimmel (New Haven, 1959); W.M. Urban, *Language and Reality* (New York, 1939); Philip Wheelwright, *The Burning Fountain* (Bloomington, 1954); H.H. Price, *Thinking and Experience* (Cambridge, Mass., 1953), Chapters 4, 5, and 6; C.G. Jung, *Psychological Types*, trans. H. Godwin Baynes (New York, 1923); A.C. Benjamin, *The Logical Structure of Science* (London, 1936), Chapters 7, 8, and 9; R.M. Eaton, *Symbolism and Truth* (Cambridge, Mass., 1925); Carl R. Hausman, "Art and Symbol," *The Review of Metaphysics*, 15(1961) 256–70; R. Gätschenberger, *Zeichen* (Stuttgart, 1932); E. Husserl, *Logische Untersuchungen*, 3 vols. (Halle a.d.s., 1921–1922), Vol. II, Part I; C.K. Ogden and I. Richards, *The Meaning of Meaning* (New York, 1927); F. Medicus, *Das Mythologische in der Religion* (Zürich, 1944); K. Plachte, *Symbol und Idol* (Berlin, 1931); H. Loof, "Der Symbolbegriff in der neuren Religionsphilosophie", in *Kanstudien*, 69(1955); Mircea Eliade, *The Sacred and the Profane: The Nature of Religion*, trans. W. Trask (New York, 1959); *Myths, Dreams, and Mysteries*, trans. Ph. Mairet (London, 1960); *Myth and Reality*, trans. W. Trask (New York, 1963); *Images and Symbols*, trans. Ph. Mairet (New York, 1961); *Traité de l'histoire des religions* (Paris, 1949); L. Binswanger, "Traum und Existenz", in *Ausgewählte Vorträge*, 2 vols. (Bern, 1947), Vol. I, pp. 74–97; J. Piaget, *La formation du symbole chez l'enfant. Imitation, jeu et rêve. Image et représentation* (Neuchâtel, 1945); J.-P. Sartre, *The Emotions: Outline of a Theory*, trans. Bernard Frechtman (New York, 1948); R. Hostie, *Du mythe à la religion. La psychologie analytique de C.G. Jung* (Paris, 1955); J. Lacan, "Fonction et champs de la parole et du langage en psychanalyse," in *Psychanalyse*, 1(1956) 81–166; A. Vergote, "Le Symbole," in *Revue Philosophique de Louvin*, 57(1959) 197–224; M. Merleau-Ponty, *Signs*, trans. R.C. McCleary (Evanston, 1964) pp. 39–45, 80-3, 86–92.

4. *The Shorter Oxford English Dictionary*, rev. and ed. by C.T. Onions (Oxford, 1955), pp. 1891–2.

5. A. Lalande, *Vocabulaire technique et critique de la philosophie* (Paris, 1956), pp. 991–2.

6. Cf. however Edmund Husserl (*Logische Untersuchungen*, 3 vols. (Halle a.d.s., 1921–1922), Vol. II, 1, *I. Untersuchung*) who is of the opinion that it is of importance to carefully distinguish between significant signs and marks. In his view the term 'sign' is essentially ambiguous. Although it is true that each sign is a sign of something, this does not mean that every sign has a signification (*Bedeutung*) or meaning (*Sinn*), which is expressed by the sign. Signs in the sense of *marks* (*Anzeichen*), taken as such, do not express anything. A mark *indicates* and the relation obtained here is called indication (*Anzeige*). If a fact *A* is considered as a mark of another fact *B*, then the mark *A* refers to the fact *B*; but this does not necessarily mean that there is an objective, necessary connection between *A* and *B*.

Significant signs, on the other hand, do not merely refer to something else, but in addition to referring to something they also *express* meaning. Since the concept of a mark is certainly not the genus of

[209]

that of expression, Husserl argues, it is thus not right to conceive of signs in the strict sense as a subclass of the class of marks.

7. C. S. Peirce, *Selected Writings*, p. 407.

8. P. Ricoeur, *De l'interprétation*, pp. 21–2.

9. C. S. Peirce, *Collected Papers*, Vol. II, p. 228.

10. C. S. Peirce, *Selected Writings*, pp. 51–2.

11. *Ibid.*, p. 404.

12. *Ibid.*, p. 390.

13. Charles W. Morris, *Foundations of the Theory of Signs*, p. 3.

14. *Ibid.*, pp. 3–4.

15. Susanne K. Langer, "On a New Definition of Symbol," pp. 55–6.

16. *The Shorter English Dictionary*, pp. 2108–2109.

17. Lalande, *op. cit.*, pp. 1079–81.

18. J. H. Newman, *An Essay in Aid of a Grammar of Assent* (London, 1930), p. 263 (quoted in A. Vergote, "Le symbole," p. 199).

19. Charles W. Morris, *op. cit.*, p. 24; cf. for a similar distinction: C.S. Peirce, *Selected Writings*, pp. 390–2.

20. P. Ricoeur, *De l'interprétation*, pp. 55–61; S. Langer, "On a New Definition of Symbol," pp. 55–7.

21. P. Ricoeur, *op. cit.*, p. 25.

22. *Ibid.*, pp. 25–6.

23. S. Langer, *loc. cit.*, pp. 56–61.

24. P. Ricoeur, *op. cit.*, pp. 19–20.

25. P. Ricoeur, *op. cit.*, p. 21; Mircea Eliade, *Images et Symboles. Essais sur le symbolisme magico-religieux* (Paris, 1952), pp. 9–31 (passim).

26. P. Ricoeur, *op. cit.*, p. 21.

27. *Ibid.*, pp. 25–6; C.G. Jung, *op. cit.*, pp. 601–10.

28. M. Heidegger, *Being and Time*, trans. John Macquarrie and Edward Robinson (New York, 1962), pp. 95–122 (passim).
Although in the next section I follow closely upon Heidegger's text, I do not intend to deliver a *complete* survey of this part of *Being and Time*. I restrict myself to what seems to be indispensable for our problem and try to avoid every technical term which is not essential to the topic in question. Most of the time I follow the translation proposed by William J. Richardson (*Heidegger: Through Phenomenology to Thought*, The Hague, 1963, Glossary, pp. 689–704).
Heidegger's term 'Sein' is always translated by 'Being', whereas 'Seiendes' is translated by 'being'. This rule is followed in compositions such as 'There-Being' for 'Da-Sein', also.

29. *Ibid.*, p. 83.

30. *Ibid.*, pp. 86–90.

31. *Ibid.*, pp. 95–107.

32. *Ibid.*, pp. 107–14.

33. *Ibid.*, pp. 114–22.

34. P. Ricoeur, "Le symbole donne à penser," p. 64.

35. R. Alleau, *De la nature des symboles*, pp. 15–17, 18–27, 35–46.

36. Cf. Charles W. Morris, *op. cit.*, p. 24, and C.G. Jung, *op. cit.*, pp. 601–10.

37. Karl Jaspers, "Myth and Religion," pp. 15–21, in *Myth and Christianity. An Inquiry into the Possibility of Religion without Myth* (New York, 1958), pp. 1–56; P. Ricoeur, *De l'interprétation*, pp. 55–61.

38. Ricoeur, "Le symbole donne à penser," pp. 62–7; *De l'interprétation*, pp. 13–64, 476–94.

39. J. C. Flugel, *A Hundred Years of Psychology* (London, 1964), pp. 238–239; P. Ricoeur, "Le symbole donne à penser," pp. 62–3, 66–7, 70–3; *De l'interprétation*, pp. 95–119, 161, 225 (passim).

40. A. Vergote, *loc. cit.*, pp. 204–209, 217–18, 218–24.

41. P. Ricoeur, "Le symbole donne à penser," p. 63; *De l'interprétation*, p. 24.

42. A. Vergote, *Ibid.*, pp. 217–18, 223–24; A. Van Leeuwen, *loc. cit.*, p. 2; P. Ricoeur, *De l'interprétation*, pp.23–4; G. Bachelard, *La poétique de l'espace* (Paris, 1957), p. 7.

43. A. de Saussure, *Traité de linguistique générale* (Paris, 1916), p. 101.

44. A. Lalande, *loc. cit.*, pp. 1079–81.

45. A. Vergote, *loc. cit.*, pp. 201–54; P. Ricoeur, "Le symbole," p. 68.

46. G. Dumas, *Traité de Psychologie*, 14 Vols. (Paris, 1932), Vol. II, pp. 576–87; Vol. IV, pp. 264–338.

47. C. G. Jung, *Psychology of Types,* pp. 601–10.

48. J. Bonsirven, *L'apocalypse de Saint Jean* (Paris, 1951), pp. 24–8.

49. Mircea Eliade, *Images et symboles*, p. 12, 13–4, 33–5.

50. P. Ricoeur, *De l'interprétation*, p. 27.

51. R. Alleau, *op. cit.*, pp. 18–20.

52. P. Ricoeur, "Le symbole donne à penser," p. 62; *De l'interprétation*, pp. 23–25; Carl R. Hausman, "Art and Symbol," pp. 261–70.

53. P. Ricoeur, "Le symbole," pp. 64–6.

54. Cf. for instance: Max Scheler, *Der Formalismus in der Ethik und die materiale Wertethik* (Bern, 1954), pp. 341–56.

55. J. Piaget, *La formation du symbole chez l'enfant; Les relations entre l'affectivité et l'intelligence dans le development mental de l'enfant* (Paris, 1954); J.-P. Sartre, *op. cit.*

56. A. Vergote, *loc. cit.*, pp. 213–18.

57. *Ibid.*, pp. 218–24.

58. *Ibid.*, p. 203.

59. M. Heidegger, *op. cit.*, pp. 32–3.

60. *Ibid.*, pp. 78–86.

61. *Ibid.*, pp. 169–72.

62. *Ibid.*, pp. 172–9.

63. Cf. the works of Cassirer, Eliade, Ricoeur, Piaget, Sartre, Binswanger, etc., quoted in note 3.

64. A. Vergote, *loc. cit.*, pp. 203–4, 217–18, 222–3.

65. P. Ricoeur, "Le symbole," p. 63.

66. *Ibid.*, p. 62 and p. 69.

67. *Ibid.*, pp. 70–3.

68. *Ibid.*, pp. 64–5.

69. *Ibid.*, pp. 66–7.

70. Karl Jaspers, "Myth and Religion," p. 18.

71. P. Ricoeur, *loc. cit.*, p. 74.

72. A. Vergote, *loc. cit.*, pp. 218–20.

73. P. Ricoeur, *loc. cit.*, pp. 67–8, 70–3.

74. M. Heidegger, *op. cit.*, pp 177–9; Rudolf Bultmann, *Glauben und Verstehen*, 3 vols. (Tübingen, 1933–1960), Vol. II, pp. 211–35.

75. Karl Jaspers, *op. cit.*, pp. 15–6.

76. *Ibid.*, pp. 15–21.

77. P. Ricoeur, *loc. cit.*, pp. 65–6.

CARL G. VAUGHT

BEING AND GOD

Wherever he begins, the philosopher must at some point attempt to understand and articulate the nature of what is ultimate and unconditioned. He might thus begin with belief and opinion, but will remain unsatisfied until he transforms them both into genuine wisdom. The philosopher's quest for wisdom has often been interpreted as the attempt to understand the meaning of Being-Itself.

By contrast, an equally ancient approach to wisdom has sought to understand the nature of what is ultimate in somewhat different terms. It has identified what is final and unconditioned with God. The concepts of Being and God thus emerge as alternative notions in terms of which the quest for wisdom may be understood.

Now the emergence of these alternative conceptions confronts us with a fundamental question about their relationship: "Which term is to be regarded as genuinely ultimate?" Alternatively, we may ask whether a choice between them is necessary: "Is it possible to construe both concepts as equally fundamental?"

If we take these questions together, two kinds of relation are suggested between the concepts in question. The first involves the relation of subordination and presupposes that one of the terms must be chosen as more nearly ultimate than the other: thus, *God may be subordinated to Being, or Being may be subordinated to God.* The second presupposes that both concepts may be given equal status, and that a choice between them thus becomes unnecessary: accordingly, *God and Being may be regarded as identical, or they may be thought to be strictly coordinate.* We must now consider briefly the nature of the four alternatives which this initial distinction makes possible.

According to the first, God is subordinated to Being, so that God himself appears to lose his status as ultimate. As a consequence, the question of his reality emerges a meaningful, though problematic issue. Within this context, 'God' is characterized as 'a being'; and a dispute arises about whether he is to be assigned a place within the *whole* of being. Because 'Being-Itself' is said to be the fundamental notion, 'God' is characterized as 'a being who may or may not be,' depending upon a proper evaluation of the arguments for his existence.

Now by contrast, the alternative relation is possible in accord with which 'God,' rather than 'Being,' is said to be the basic concept. The meaningfulness of disputes about the reality of God is thereby called into question. If Being is subordinated to God, it is inappropriate to attempt to assign him a place within the whole of being. It is equally inappropriate to claim that he does not exist. From this perspective, it is also mistaken to claim that the concept of God is to be interpreted in terms of ontological categories. God not only transcends the distinction between something and nothing, but also the ontological framework in terms of which all ordinary things are understood. He thus transcends the concept of Being-Itself—the fundamental notion of traditional ontology.

There remain, however, two further ways in which the concepts in question may be related. On the first of these alternatives, Being and God are thought to be identical. As identical with Being-Itself, God is not to be understood as a being who may or may not be. Consequently, the question about the place to which he is to be assigned within the whole of being fails to arise. On the other hand, though God transcends the distinction between something and nothing, he fails to transcend altogether the classical ontological framework. As identical with Being-Itself, he is to be equated with the most fundamental notion of the traditional philosophical enterprise.

Finally, the notions of Being and God may be related in such a way that each is construed to be coordinate with the other and so that each is thought to be the fundamental notion within its own domain of discourse. This position is committed to the view that ontology and theology are to be radically distinguished and that two ultimate concepts are to be acknowledged as mutually exclusive notions. Accordingly, it is claimed that philosophical criticism is strictly irrelevant to religion and that traditional ontology may be conducted without essential reference to the standpoint of religion.

In this essay, I shall examine the problem of the relation between Being and God from the standpoint of the first and third of the previously mentioned alternatives—namely, the view which claims that God is to be subordinated to Being and the position which holds that Being and God are identical. I shall not consider the other positions in detail, for each is committed to the thesis that philosophical analysis is inappropriate for the proper understanding of the nature and existence of God. For the position which claims that Being is to be subordinated to God, God transcends the categories to be employed in ontological inquiry. On the view that God and Being are to be understood as coordinate, God stands outside the framework of categories which are to be used within the context of philosophy. Since an adequate treatment of these positions presupposes a discussion of the proper relations between philosophy and religion, I shall postpone this second-order inquiry and focus upon the views which are more readily accessible to philosophical examination.

At the outset, I shall assume that these positions are mutually exclusive. On this basis, I shall set forth a brief account of the view which claims that God is to be subordinated to Being and shall examine it critically from the standpoint of the view which holds that Being and God are identical. Having opposed it to the contrasting position, I shall *defend* the view that Being and God are the same. I shall then explore the God-Being identification dialectically in the attempt to give its terms a richer, concrete content. I shall argue that Being and God are to be understood as the unity of logos, mystery, and power and that their unity is to be understood by analogy with the unity appropriate to concrete things. In thus denying the ontological difference, I shall maintain that Being is in fact a special kind of being and that the opposition between the initial alternatives is not so fundamental as it first appeared. In conclusion, I shall raise a question about the proper relation between the concrete view of Being to be developed here and the traditional notion of Geist or Spirit. I shall maintain that Being remains the fundamental name for God, in spite of the Hegelian suggestion that the Absolute must be construed in terms of concrete Spirit.

[215]

I

We must notice from the outset that when God is subordinated to Being, he is usually accorded a special existential status. Thus, he is sometimes said to be a perfect being. In his perfection, he is thought to be supreme among the concrete things which have a place within the cosmos. As supreme, he illustrates a mode of being which is infinite. He is thus to be regarded as the ultimate, concrete being and is to be understood as different in kind from every other entity. As ultimate and concrete, God is sometimes distinguished as sacred. He thus becomes the supreme 'object' of worship. Finite entities stand in contrast with God as final, concrete perfection; and the contrast between these two such different modes of being is to be mediated by man's unreserved respect and devotion.

Now, it must not be forgotten that the foregoing account of the nature of God has received the sanction of a number of strands within the classical tradition.[1] In fact, it might deserve to be regarded as itself the classical account. On the other hand, we must notice that apparently decisive objections may be urged against it from the standpoint of the view which claims that God is to be identified with Being-Itself.

In the first instance, when 'God' is defined as a 'perfect being,' it might be argued that the concept of a being is incompatible with the concepts of ultimacy and absoluteness, and hence incompatible with the concept of perfection itself. Items which have being are to be distinguished from the being which they have. If God were defined as a being, he would then be distinguishable from the being which he might possess. As a being, he would presuppose the being which he had. Being would then become the basic notion rather than God as the being who possessed it. Accordingly, it might be claimed that God in his perfection cannot be defined by the concept of a being. That concept reveals its own imperfection in that it presupposes the notion of Being as more nearly basic than itself.

By contrast, though the concept of Being is presupposed by every kind of being, God as identical with Being-Itself presupposes nothing other than himself. In the language of the tradition, God must be regarded as self-caused. For this reason, and in contrast with the alternative interpretation, the identification of God with Being preserves the concept of God as absolute and ultimate reality.[2]

Now the foregoing conclusion may be elaborated in a different way, in terms of an analysis of the concept of a being. Beings are, in essence, individualized entities; as such, they comprise a framework of actual and possible beings. If God were defined as a perfect being, he would appear as a term within that framework. Yet the restriction of God to a place within this more inclusive scheme is incompatible with the ultimacy of God as the appropriate 'object' of religious concern. Worship requires that its 'object' be infinite. But if God is to be assigned a place within a framework of beings, he is limited by contrast with them, and hence a finite being in a larger whole.

In addition, an individual entity, as individualized, is deficient in the manner in which it participates in the reality of beings other than itself. Beings are entities in which the polarity of individualization and participation is not perfectly balanced; entities in which the primacy of individualization prevents perfect participation. Since what is genuinely ultimate cannot be deficient, the concept of a perfect being is thus doubly inadequate as a concept of God. That concept mistakenly presupposes that an individual entity, really distinct from other beings, can participate with perfect adequacy in the reality of beings other than itself.[3]

Now if the concept of God as a perfect being were rejected, and if by contrast God were identified with Being-Itself, it seems that the foregoing difficulties could be overcome. As Being-Itself, God is not a term within the framework of actual and possible entities. He is rather the presupposition of the framework itself. He thus is not restricted to the domain comprised of all the finite beings. Yet, as identical with Being-Itself, he participates fully in the reality of every being. Wherever beings are to be found, Being-Itself appears as immanent in them. As presupposed by them, God is to be distinguished from the domain of actual and possible entities. Yet, this fact does not entail that he is to be judged deficient in the mode of his participation in them.

In response to this account, a proponent of the opposing view could claim that the foregoing considerations fail to acknowledge a crucial distinction which was implicit in the earlier contrast between the perfect and imperfect modes of being. It might be claimed that this distinction not only represents a difference between two radically different *kinds* of being, but also a difference between two modes of *existential status*. In effect, one might contend that the perfect being exists necessarily, and that it is thus mistaken to attempt to assign him a place within the realm of

[217]

finite things. To make this mistake, it might be claimed, fails to take seriously the earlier distinction between the modes of being mentioned.

This is not the proper context for a detailed examination of the ontological argument. However, it is necessary to indicate that the conclusion of that argument makes no reference to a being who is to be subordinated to the more basic concept of Being-Itself. The proof rests upon the conviction that the essence and existence of God are identical. Thus, within the context of the proof, God is scarcely to be regarded as a perfect being, but rather as the one whose essence is strictly identical with his being. For this reason, the argument fails to support the thesis that a necessary being exists as a special kind of entity within the cosmos taken as a whole. To the contrary, the ontological argument points to the conclusion that God and Being are identical.[4]

Now before we turn to a dialectical examination of this conclusion, we must mention briefly three further considerations which seem to support the view that the identification in question should in fact be effected. These considerations evoke the distinctively religious dimension of the issues before us and pertain to the relation between man as worshiper and God as the proper 'object' of religious concern.

Religion involves the relation of worship between a person and the 'object' toward which that worship is directed. This relation may be either idolatrous or genuine. If it is to be the latter, it must be directed toward an 'object' which is genuinely ultimate. Since Being-Itself is the ultimate notion, Being might then be regarded as the proper 'object' of religious devotion.

In addition, Being-Itself might be said to be the appropriate 'object' of worship, since the concept of Being constitutes the primal mystery. The essence of a being is transparent to reflection, at least in principle. The being of things, however, is the occasion for irreducible wonder. Since awe and wonder are the marks of genuine worship, the concept of Being may be seen to have an irreducibly religious dimension.

Finally, the ultimacy of the religious attitude of worship is incompatible with a stance of detached reflection or speculation. Genuine religious concern demands unreserved existential commitment. Since man as a being participates in Being-Itself, and since he may not be detached from Being which appears as immanent in him, it may be claimed that for this additional reason, Being is the proper 'object' of religious concern. Being-Itself is inescapable. It is ultimate. It produces awe and wonder. Accordingly, the identification of Being and God seems to preserve the meaning of worship as the proper relation between man and the genuinely ultimate 'object' of religion. In the following section, we shall turn to a dialectical examination of this view.

II

In considering the position before us, we must ask an initial question about the meaning of Being and God. The question may be formulated as follows: "If God and Being are to be regarded as identical, what further characterization of these notions can be given, as they appear in contrast with the notion of a being?"

The first alternative which might be considered is the one which identifies both Being and God with the totality of beings, either actual or possible. This totality is presumably infinite, and is not an individual, at least in any ordinary sense. It is to be distinguished from any given being, and to that extent exhibits a kind of transcendence. It also contains all beings as parts of itself, and thus appears as immanent in them. In fact, this view of God and Being represents a form of religious pantheism which has at times been instanced in the concrete context of religion. How are we to appraise this position as an attempt to provide an initial explication of the notions in question?

I believe that we must conclude that the position before us fails to disclose the meaning of Being which it claims to articulate. To see this, we must first distinguish the concept of the whole of being from the notion of being *taken as a whole*. The primary subject-matter for the philosopher is not the totality of beings, but the pervasive structures which transform this totality into a cosmos.

For the position which identifies Being and God with the totality of beings, the categories of individualization and participation are the most significant of these pervasive structures. To be is to participate as an individualized part within an infinite collection. The meaning of being presupposed by this position is thus not Being *as an infinite totality*, but Being *as the categories of individualization and participation* which transform this totality into a cosmic whole. To mention merely the infinite collection of beings is to leave unmentioned the structure of being. It is to leave unmentioned the meaning of Being as presupposed by the totality of beings.

The distinction between the whole of being and Being, taken as a whole, presupposes a contrast between beings and the structure of being. This structure may comprise a plurality of levels and may be described in a variety of ways. We shall not attempt a detailed description here. It is sufficient for our purposes to indicate the existence of a distinction between the structures of being and the totality of beings.

Now if God and Being are to be identified, neither with a being, nor with the totality of beings, and if the structures of being are more nearly basic than the beings structured by them, a problem arises about the proper relation of God and Being to those structures taken in themselves. Indeed, Being-Itself transcends the realm of beings. But what are we to say in this respect about the relation of Being to the structures presupposed by this domain?

On the one hand, the structures of being, like Being-Itself, are not mere beings among others. On the other hand, it follows from this consideration that the original distinction between Being and beings is too simple and undialectical. Since the structures of being are to be distinguished from the beings structured by them, the original contrast is not simply between Being and beings, but between Being, God, and the structures of being—and all the beings, subject to structure, to determination, and to the categories of existence. Since from this perspective, however, both Being and the structures of being are to be distinguished from the realm of beings, the problem of the relation of Being and structures seems to require a different solution from the one provided by the Being-beings contrast.

Two solutions may be given. On the one hand, we might claim that Being and structures are inseparably related. For this reason, we might not only conclude that Being and structures stand in contrast with beings, but that they contrast with them as a structured unity. Being and God would then be structured; they would stand in contrast with beings, which are subject to a structure of their own.

On the other hand, we might claim that beings and the structures of being are not really distinct. Structures might be regarded as abstractable aspects of things. It might still be claimed, however, that Being and the structures of being comprise an indissoluble unity. Accordingly, Being and the structures of being would both be regarded as abstractable aspects of the realm of concrete things.

Now both of these solutions require that a distinction be drawn between the ways in which Being and beings are subject to structure. The structures of being are structures of finitude. Beings which are structured by them are limited and finite things.

We thus must ask, "Regardless of whether Being-Itself is really distinct from beings, how is it, as structured, to be distinguished from beings which, as structured themselves, are thereby merely finite things?"

Perhaps we could provide an answer by claiming that though the structures of being *imply* finitude, this means only that the beings structured by them are finite and limited. We could add that though Being and God are related to that structure, the relation is one of identity rather than subsumption. Since, presumably, the structures themselves need not be finite, we could conclude that Being and God are identical with the structure of being, without implying the finitude of either God or Being.

The plausibility of this position rests upon the familiar distinction between ontic concepts and ontological categories. Ontology is possible, only because there are concepts which are less universal than Being, but more universal than any ontic concept which designates a special realm of beings. These ontological concepts, as contrasted with ontic concepts of a limited range of designation, comprise the structure of being, and thus the structure of everything that is. As universal in their scope and application, it might seem that they are indeed identical with *ipsum esse*.

The religious equivalent of the view that Being is to be identified with the structure of being is to be found in the traditional suggestion that God is to be equated with the logos. When the logos is said to be really distinct from the world, it is usually regarded as a normative structure which receives its concrete expression in the notion of the God of justice. God stands over against the world as judge and is to be identified with the demands of a normative nature which he makes upon the beings which comprise the cosmos. By contrast, when the Logos is regarded as an abstractable aspect of the world as a whole, God is thereby identified with what Spinoza called "the soul or essence of the world." God is not to be equated with the totality of beings, but with the intelligible structure of the cosmos taken as a whole. This position represents a sophisticated version of pantheism, and is one of the forms in which the view that Being is to be identified with structure receives a concrete religious expression.

Now despite the initial plausibility of the suggestion that Being is to be identified with the structure of being, further examination reveals that this position must in fact be rejected. Persuasive and cogent considerations to this effect emerge from careful reflection upon the phrase, "the structure of being."

If the question of the meaning of Being is a question about

what it means for anything definite or determinate to be, it would seem that the structure of being presupposes Being as more nearly basic than itself. Whether or not it is really distinct from beings, the structure of being is determinate, and is to be contrasted with the beings structured by it. But if that structure is itself determinate, it presupposes Being as the fundamental notion. Being must then be distinguished from the structure of being, and the identity of Being and structure must be rejected as an explication of the meaning of that notion. Though ontological concepts are universal in their range of reference, they are still less universal than the concept of Being-Itself.

In addition, it seems that in the case of God, emphasis upon the concepts of transcendence, ultimacy, and unconditionality effectively negates the claim that God possesses a nature which is concretely determinate. To the contrary, it would appear that the mystics are to be taken seriously in their insistence that mystery precedes all structure in the being of God. But if this is true from the side of God as well as from the side of Being, and indeed, from the standpoint of God as identical with Being, Being and God are presupposed by the structure of being considered in itself. Of course, it is not to be suggested that the structures of being are mere beings alongside others. However, it does not follow from this admission that they appear as identical with Being in the contrast with beings. For the purposes of that distinction, they do appear to have a place within the realm of finite things.

Now when this point has been reached, it might appear that the dialectic requires us to return to the original dichotomy between Being and beings. It could be maintained that since the structures of being are determinate, they are either abstract, upper-level beings, or abstractable aspects of concrete beings in the chain of finite things. As abstract or abstractable, they are presupposed by concrete beings. As presupposed by them, they are themselves not merely concrete things. However, as beings or abstractable aspects of beings, they themselves have being. Consequently, the structures of being presuppose the concept of Being as the fundamental notion. The original distinction between Being and beings thus re-emerges as the underlying contrast which must be maintained.

The radical distinction between Being and the structure of being which results from the foregoing contrast yields a set of consequences of genuine significance. First, the distinction in question suggests that there is mystery in Being and God. As contrasted with structure, Being and God are radically indeterminate. As indeterminate, they are essentially mysterious. Second, the search for a notion which is presupposed by the domain of determinate beings finds a terminus in the foregoing contrast. If Being and God are said to be determinate, Being-Itself is presupposed by them. However, as indeterminate themselves, *they* are presupposed by every being. Finally, the distinction between Being and the structure of being provides for the contrast between the notion of Being and the features which may be ascribed to beings. Being is a transcendental notion. It is not an ordinary concept which is predicated of a being. The distinction between Being and the structure of being preserves and underlies this insight. It points to the mystery of Being as contrasted with the intelligiblity of the structures of being.

Now despite the apparent advantages which result from the distinction between Being and structure, and in spite of the mystic's preference for the foregoing view, we must not fail to notice difficulties in the view itself which tend to undermine its value. In fact, critical appraisal of the position in question leads eventually to the view that Being-Itself must be regarded as a special kind of being.

In the first place, once it has been claimed that the structure of being is finite, the seemingly innocent contrast between Being and beings becomes more problematic than it first appeared. It is one thing to say that God transcends all ordinary beings; quite another to maintain that he transcends the structure of being, as well. The identification of God with Being presupposes that we understand the meaning of those notions. But if Being and God transcend all structure, upon what basis can that understanding rest?

Were it to be claimed that the identity in question is mediated by the common mystery of its terms, mystery itself would seem to be a form of determination. But all determinations presuppose the concept of Being. As essentially mysterious, Being and God would then be determinate. As determinate, they would presuppose the concept of Being-Itself.

On the other hand, were it to be maintained that mystery is not a determination, how could it provide the attribute in virtue of which God and Being are to be identified? To the contrary, it seems that reference to the mystery of Being and God would signalize our inability to speak intelligibly of them. If this were the case, the attempt to effect the identity in question would be unsuccessful. The attempt itself intends to provide an intelligible identification between these notions. But if reference to mystery signalizes an inability to speak intelligibly, and if the affirmation of identity purports to be an instance of intelligible speech, reference to the mystery of Being and God does not provide the identification which so clearly was intended. It would indeed appear to be the case that the position in question fails to provide us with a proper view of God.

We must ask, however, whether the foregoing position points us to a view which is more nearly adequate as a way of understanding the issues before us. Does it suggest an alternative which avoids the difficulties mentioned? I believe that an affirmative answer can be given, and that we may label the position to which we are driven, the view of God and Being as dialectically determinate. It arises from reflection upon the inadequacies and insights of the foregoing view.

Reflection upon the mystery of Being and God confronts us with a dilemma. Either mystery is a determination, and Being-Itself is presupposed by the notions of Being and God; or reference to mystery signalizes radical indetermination, and one is unable to effect a meaningful identification between the notions themselves. But both alternatives are unacceptable. To adopt the former is to surrender the ultimacy of Being and God; to affirm the latter is to render speech about them ineffective.

On the other hand, it does not follow that all reference to mystery is to be precluded when one speaks about these notions. Otherwise, the notions in question are given determination, and thus they lose their ultimacy; otherwise, the distinction cannot be maintained between the determination of structure and the transcendental role of Being as a notion which produces awe and wonder. It would seem that inadequacy is balanced by insight and that the demand for a more nearly adequate position is generated.

If God and Being were both determinate and indeterminate, if they were regarded as a special kind of unity in which aspects corresponding to this contrast were distinguished and mediated, a position might emerge which avoids the difficulties mentioned, and incorporates the insights which must be preserved. As determinate, intelligible reference could be made to God and Being. As radically indeterminate, utter mystery possibly could be included. As dialectically determinate, intelligible speech would be permitted, and the mystery of radical indetermination maintained.

In the following section, we shall consider this position as an attempt to combine the logos of structure with the mystery of radical indetermination. I shall suggest that the distinction between logos and mystery is to be mediated through the introduction of the concept of power. I shall then attempt to hold this triad of aspects together in the unity provided by the concept of a special kind of being.

III

The position which we now consider purports to combine the logos of structure with the mystery of radical indetermination; to mediate the distinction between mystery and structure by means of the concept of power; and to unify this triad of aspects in terms of the concept of a special kind of being. From the standpoint of philosophy, this position represents a view of God and Being as dialectically determinate. From the standpoint of religion, it involves the belief that Being and God must be understood as the unity of a trinitarian structure.

Now before we consider the problem of unity as it is provided by the concept of a special kind of being, we must focus initially upon the concept of power as a mediating notion. In this connection, we must ask the following questions: "Why must power be included as an aspect of Being and God, and how does it serve to mediate the distinction between the concepts of mystery and structure?"

Power must be included as an aspect, since structure and mystery presuppose the notion of power as a necessary precondition. Mystery and structure possess the power of self-manifestation. Mystery appears within the human context as that aspect of Being and God to which awe and wonder are the appropriate responses. Structure appears as the aspect of God and Being to which the human being seeks to respond by means of intelligible speech. In both instances, power is presupposed as the ground of Being's self-manifestation.

In addition, mystery and structure presuppose the concept of power in the guise of the power to be. If structure and mystery are to be manifest, they first must *be*; they must possess the power to resist non-being. Power, then, is not to be subordinated to mystery and structure. To the contrary, it is presupposed by them as an irreducible aspect of the meaning of Being and God.

Finally, power may not only be regarded as an aspect of Being and God, but also as a term which mediates the distinction between the notions of mystery and structure. In the first place, power appears as the common ground of the notions in question. In this way, they are bound together by their common reference to a single term. In the second place, it provides a middle term between them, and is thus to be regarded as neither completely intelligible nor totally indeterminate. On the one hand, power is not identical with an intelligible structure. On the other hand, it is not utterly mysterious. It exhibits at least a minimal structure in the guise of duration and intensity. Power thus participates in the nature of both of the terms which are said to stand in need of mediation. It provides them with a common ground, as well as with a common point of intersection.

Now the argument of the previous section has indicated that the determinate aspect of Being and God is the structure of being, even though the simple identification of Being with structure is inadequate, forcing us beyond it to a consideration of radical mystery. Reference to mystery is itself insufficient as an explication of the meaning of Being and God. A dialectical view is demanded in which the notion of power mediates the distinction between the structure of being and the concept of mystery.

Before this position may be adopted, however, it must be developed more fully by a consideration of a number of difficulties which pertain to it. One of these difficulties arises from the fact that the structure of being is determinate. In the previous section, we accepted the identification of determination with finitude. But if determination implies finitude, Being and God in their determinate guise are also finite in an aspect of their being. If this were the case, it would appear that even as dialectically determinate, God and Being cannot be identified with ultimate reality as distinct from merely finite things.

In addition, if the structure of being is finite, it seems to have no privileged place as an aspect of Being and God. At best, it is the highest level of a hierarchy of finite items, all of which are modes of being. Even concrete beings have a place within this finite order. Thus, they also would comprise a part of the aspect of Being and God as determinate. If this were the case, the question would arise even more insistently: "How can Being and God be identified with ultimate reality as distinct from merely finite things?"

If a satisfactory answer is to be given, it is evident that we must examine carefully the identification of determination with finitude. This identification rests upon the conviction that 'determination' must be defined as 'limitation by negation.' Presumably, limitation is taken to imply the finitude of that which is limited. The structure of being as determinate is thus thought to be limited, and as limited, also finite.

A solution for this difficulty may be found, I believe, if we consider carefully the customary meaning of finitude as subjection to change, and ultimate subjection to the loss of being. Ordinary, concrete beings are finite in this sense. On the other hand, it is evident that the structures of being are not finite in this way. Both qualitative change and loss of being presuppose the structure of being. Individualization and participation, essence and existence, characterize both change and diminution. As a consequence, the structure of being must not be regarded as finite in the ordinary sense.

Now the structures of being are determinate. But they differ from concrete beings in being subject, neither to change nor possible loss of being. There is thus no reason to include them, together with concrete beings, in a hierarchy of merely finite items. Though the determinate structures of being are limited, this simply implies that structure does not comprise the totality of Being and God. But this has been acknowledged already in the adoption of the thesis that the structure of being is an aspect of a more inclusive complex. Determination, as limitation by negation, merely reinforces the need for a dialectical view. It does not entail the finitude of Being or God in any customary sense. We may then agree with Plato that the structure of being is both eternal and non-derivative. We are free to incorporate that structure as a non-derivative aspect of Being and God, without the need to include with it all merely concrete beings.

We have now enriched the account of the determinate aspect of Being and God by giving it a content which is both eternal and non-derivative. Yet, if our argument to this effect is granted, further questions arise about the need for a dialectical position. At this stage, it might be claimed that a triad of aspects is unnecessary, and that the meaning of Being may be given by exclusive reference to the logos.

The earlier objection to the simple identification of Being and God with structure rested upon the claim that the structure of being presupposes Being-Itself as the genuinely ultimate notion. That claim was supported by the assumption that the structures of being are finite. However, if those structures are eternal and non-derivative, we might ask whether we are driven any longer to suppose that they presuppose a notion more nearly basic than themselves. As non-dependent and not subject to change, they are included already as an aspect of Being and God. May we not then eliminate all reference to aspects and return to the simple identification of Being with structure?

Were this to be done, it could be claimed that the limitation of the structure of being is present, only when parts of that structure are considered separately. When they are taken together, it could be argued that the structure itself comprises a complex but unlimited totality. In addition, it would seem that the exclusive identification of Being with logos would enable us to lay aside the troublesome reference to radical mystery, and it would no longer be necessary to undertake the even more difficult task of attempting to effect a unification of the aspects of logos, mystery and power. It might then appear that the demand for a dialectical position is vacuous; it might seem that the structure of being comprises the exclusive meaning of Being and God.

However, upon reflection, it becomes evident that the foregoing problems cannot be laid aside and that the demand for a dialectical view must be acknowledged. In the first place, the view that God is identical with the structure of being is itself dialectical. Whether or not the structures of being are really distinct from the world, a distinction can be made between the structures taken in themselves, and structures as they constitute the structure of the finite order. A duality of aspects pertaining to the structure is thereby distinguished, and the demand for an account of their unity is generated.

In addition, we might ask whether the structures of being themselves have being, either as really distinct from the world, or in their dependent role as abstractible aspects of the cosmos taken as a whole. Since at this stage Being is said to be identical with the structure of being, the answer would be that the structures of being presuppose themselves as the meaning of Being. When this answer is given, however, not only does a distinction of aspects emerge in the relation between the structures of being and the concrete beings structured by them, but we must also consider the structure of being as the self-referential structure of itself. Such a consideration leads to further distinctions. Contrasts emerge between: (1) the structure of being taken in itself; (2) the structure of being as itself requiring structure; and (3) the structure of being as presupposed to provide the structure for itself. We would be committed to show that the terms of these distinctions can be unified within a single, concrete notion.

Finally, we are not only confronted at this point with the demand for dialectical unification. The notions of mystery and power also re-emerge as essential components in the discussion of the meaning of Being and God. The need for mystery as an aspect arises in the following way: When the structure of being is said to presuppose itself as the meaning of Being, either the regress of presupposed to presupposing is at some point stopped arbitrarily, and the question of the meaning of the structure of being as presupposed is left unanswered; or the regress is continued indefinitely, so that mystery appears in the guise of the infinite regress itself. In either case, the meaning of Being is not given by exclusive reference to the logos. In the first case, silence indicates the inadequacy of a reference to structure as an answer to the question and points to the mystery of Being. In the second instance, the appearance of an infinite regress shows that reference to logos is not sufficient as an answer. That answer must be given repeatedly. It does not constitute a terminus. This is once again a kind of silence. Repetition itself thus indicates the presence of mystery as a regulative demand. As a consequence, a duality of aspects re-emerges, not only between two sides of the logos, but also between logos and mystery.

Now it might be suggested that the regress in question may be compressed into an internal, circular relationship which requires a perpetual, infinite vacillation from one aspect of the complex to the other.[5] In this case, the regress would not be linear, but circular; and the model of an infinite regressus would be replaced by the occurrence of self-referential circularity. In any case however, the transition from one aspect to the other would be dynamic and unending. It would not terminate in the structure of being as an unambiguous answer to the question about the meaning of Being and God.

It is mistaken, then, to suggest that reference to Being and God as identical with even an eternal logos is exclusively adequate as an account of their nature. The structure of being *does* appear as a permanent and non-derivitive aspect of Being and God. It also provides an intelligible content for the determinate side of those fundamental notions. However, the identification of Being and God with structure leads to the demand for dialectical unification. It issues in the re-emergence of radical mystery. And it reinforces the need to bring about a unity between the aspects of structure and mystery, even where the nature of structure is more complex than it first appeared.

Now we have suggested that even if the logos is regarded as an eternal aspect of Being and God, mystery re-emerges as an irreducible component. Moreover, we must not forget that power is also required as an aspect, since it is presupposed by both structure and mystery, and since it provides a term which mediates between them. In fact, *power is a necessary component, even when mystery and structure are understood as eternal and inescapable.* The relation among these terms is not temporal, but logical. In referring to them, we have reached the standpoint of autonomous, self-referential circularity.

We should observe that just as in the case of the structure of being, power is a dialectical notion. Taken in itself, it may be distinguished from power as shared by every concrete being. Immanent and transcendent modes of power thus emerge. In addition, power is related self-referentially to itself. We may ask whether the power of being itself has being. The answer would involve a reference to the power of being as a self-transcendent ground.

In addition, power bears the following relations to the other concepts of the triad: first, power presupposes mystery in the manner in which the structure of being also presupposed it. As before, mystery appears in the arbitrary refusal to continue to ask the question of the meaning of being with respect of power, or in the need to ask that question repeatedly without a termination. In the second place, power presupposes logos in terms of which its dynamic activity is to be made at least partially intelligible. Thus, for this additional reason, logos is not to be excluded as a necessary aspect of the meaning of Being and God. In the third instance, logos presupposes power, and not simply itself, together with mystery. As the self-referential structure of itself, it must *be*, in order to be structured. The structure of being thus presupposes the power to be.

IV

In the previous section, we have not only attempted to exhibit the relations of mutual presupposition between the notions of mystery, power, and structure; we have also argued that power constitutes a middle term between the other two. It is both common ground and common point of intersection. On this basis, we must ask the following question: "Do the foregoing considerations provide us with a solution for the problem of the unity of Being and God?"

We have claimed that the aspects of Being and God are interrelated as a series of mutual, self-referential presuppositions. It might be suggested that these mutual interrelations provide us with the unity we seek. In addition, we might argue that as a middle term between the others, power binds them together and thus provides an additional dimension of the unity in question.

Before this suggestion can be considered, however, we must observe explicitly an asymmetry which is to be discovered in the mutual relations among the aspects which have been distinguished. We have claimed that power and logos presuppose themselves; that each presupposes the other; and that both presuppose the notion of radical mystery. In addition, we have argued that mystery presupposes power in a dual way. It presupposes the power of self-manifestation, and it presupposes the power to be. On the other hand, we have *not* claimed that mystery presupposes itself, or that it presupposes the structure of being. To the contrary, mystery is not sufficiently determinate to presuppose these notions. It manifests itself as possessing the power of indeterminate existence.

Now if mystery is indeterminate, and if it fails to presuppose either itself or the structure of being, it might seem that the notion in question can scarcely be integrated as an aspect within a larger, complex whole. Mystery is irreducibly transcendent. And though it bears some relations to the complex in question, those relations are inevitably asymmetrical. It would appear that the circularity of the notions of Being and God is thereby called into question.

Now if the notions of mystery, logos, and power fail to form a bounded whole, how can we speak of their unity? It would appear that what unity there is is only partial, and that the concepts of Being and God must thereby be construed as open-ended notions.

The element of truth in this proposed conclusion consists in the fact that the notions in question are not to be regarded as a static, stable complex. The complex is inherently dialectical. Its dialectical structure prevents the unification of its aspects within a bounded whole.

However, the foregoing fact about the nature of that structure does not prevent a certain kind of unity. It does not prevent the kind of unity which can be found by analogy in every concrete being. This fact suggests that the complex in question may itself be regarded as a special kind of being, where a being is to be understood as a structured center of power.

Ordinary beings are unified with respect to their past and present; but the unity in question is dynamic and changing, since these beings face an open-ended future. The unity appropriate to beings is an accomplished fact only with reference to the past. Unity with respect to the future represents a task which must be undertaken anew in every changing situation.

By analogy, I would suggest that God and Being may be understood as a being, the unity of which must be accomplished repeatedly from the standpoint of the Absolute itself. In this case, the relations are logical rather than temporal, and the repeated 'accomplishment' of *de facto* unity is never problematic as in ordinary cases. God and Being always have sufficient power to effect it. However, this fact fails to change the fundamental structure of the situation.

Now the suggestion that Being is to be understood as a special kind of being might be regarded as radically mistaken, especially in the light of our earlier arguments to show that Being and God are to be distinguished from the realm of concrete things. At this stage, however, it should be clear that those earlier considerations depended upon an inadequate understanding of the concept of Being. In those earlier arguments, we simply assumed that the notion of Being is incompatible with the notion of determination as such. It was thus to be contrasted with the concept of a being. In our later discussion, we attempted to show that contrary to this assumption, the determinate structure of being may be incorporated as an aspect of Being and God. *The presence of this structure as an aspect makes possible the truth of the thesis that Being and God may be understood in terms of the concept in question.*

One further condition must be fulfilled, however, before the concept of a being can be used to interpret the meaning of Being and God. It is essential that these notions be construed as a series of mutual, self-referential presuppositions in which the concept of power plays a central role. Unless this form of self-reference and mutual presupposition were present, it would be possible to claim that Being and God are identical with a set of abstractions which lack the concreteness necessary for the application of the concept of a being. Self-reference, presupposition, and determination thus provide a triad of conditions which are necessary for the application of this concept. Their presence undermines the rationale upon which recognition of the ontological difference depends and makes possible the resolution of the problem of the unity of Being and God.

Now even if the foregoing account can be elaborated so that it proves to be finally acceptable, one further problem remains. We must mention it briefly. We have assumed that the concept of Being is the most satisfactory notion in terms of which the concept of God is to be understood. Our inquiry has been conducted in terms of the contrast between the concept of Being and the notion of an ordinary, finite thing. However, could it not be argued that this assumption involves a fundamental mistake? Should we not consider the Hegelian suggestion that the notion of Absolute Spirit is a more acceptable concept in terms of which the concept of God may be explicated?

Now it is not to be denied that the foregoing account owes much to Hegel. However, decisive reasons may be given for our refusal to adopt his suggestion that the Absolute is to be identified with concrete Spirit. In the first place, though Spirit is to be understood as the unity of power and meaning, it makes no place for the concept of mystery as an irreducible component. For Hegel, the Absolute is thought to be completely intelligible. From the perspective of philosophical comprehension, mystery is thought to be utterly transcended. In the second place, Absolute Spirit is understood as the final dialectical stage in which the totality of its aspects are said to be together in a perfect, stable harmony. Spirit is regarded as a bounded whole.[6] I have argued, to the contrary, that the Absolute is open-ended with respect to final integration. For this reason, I have not only claimed that logos, mystery, and power are irreducible dimensions of Being and God. I have also argued that this triadic complex can be unified, only by regarding its unity as a special instance of the unity appropriate to concrete things.

NOTES

1. The most notable instance is the point of view defended by Anselm. Cf. *St. Anselm: Basic Writings*, trans. S. N. Deane with an introduction by Charles Hartshorne (2nd ed.; LaSalle, Illinois, 1962), pp. 1, 7–11, 22–4, 37–41.

2. I rely, at this point, upon the writings of Paul Tillich. Cf. Paul Tillich, *Systematic Theology*, Vol. I (Chicago, 1951), p. 235. The essay as a whole reflects a considerable debt to Tillich. However, I have suppressed a number of expository issues in the attempt to deal more directly with the problems themselves.

3. *Philosophical Interrogations*, ed. with an introduction by Sydney and Beatrice Rome (New York, Chicago, and San Francisco, 1964), pp. 380–81. Cf. also, Paul Tillich, *Biblical Religion and the Search for Ultimate Reality* (Chicago, 1955), pp. 83–4.

4. Cf. Paul Tillich, *Systematic Theology*, Vol. I, pp. 204–8.

5. I owe this point to my colleague, Carl R. Hausman.

6. G. W. F. Hegel, *The Phenomenology of Mind*, trans. with an introduction and notes by J. B. Ballie (2nd ed., revised and corrected; London, 1931), pp. 797–8. For the abstract side of the discussion of Spirit as Absolute Idea, cf. also *The Logic of Hegel*, trans. from the *Encyclopaedia of the Philosophical Sciences* by William Wallace (2nd ed., revised and augmented; Oxford, 1892), pp. 374, 378–9.